Why
Eat Their Own

The Real Deal About
the Joy of Raising Children

LORI LARSEN

LoL Inspirations

Published by:
LoL Inspirations
9703 114A Avenue
Fort St. John, B.C.
Canada V1J 7B9
250-785-6819
www.lolinspirations.com

Library and Archives Canada Cataloguing in Publication

Larsen, Lori, 1960–

Why some pigs eat their own: the real deal about the joy of raising children / Lori Larsen.

ISBN 0-9737567-0-5

1. Child rearing–Humour. 2. Parenting–Humour.
3. Larsen, Lori, 1960– Anecdotes. 4. Child rearing–Anecdotes.
5. Parenting–Anecdotes. I. Title.

HQ769.L28 2005   649'.1'0207   C2005-901274-97

Layout and design by the Vancouver Desktop Publishing Centre
Cover illustration by Cheryl Genge
Printed in Canada by Ray Hignell Services Inc.

Dedication

This book is dedicated to all parents and would-be parents, for it is they who prepare the future for greatness. It is their diligence that gives our world the parents of the future, their love that gives those parents the ability to succeed, and their patience that gives those parents the strength to continue to create the new parents of tomorrow.

I also dedicate this book to my children (Bradley and Krysta), and my hubby (John) without whom I would have been unable to write these words, and would not know the truest joy of my success. Thank you to them for having patience with me as I learned and fumbled my way through, and for giving me the inspiration to charge after a dream that may have otherwise remained on the shelf.

And I dedicate this book to my mom. She not only gave me life, but gave me a solid foundation to build it on. Thank you Mom. I understand now.

To Heidi & Chris ("AKA B's Bro")

Enjoy a Read & One Day this Could Be You.

Ha Ha Ha

Love you

Acknowledgements

Special thanks and much appreciation go out to my editor Linda Field. Her thoroughness, professionalism, and hard work are greatly appreciated.

I would also like to thank the talented Patty Osborne for her remarkable effort in giving the book its wonderful appearance and pizzazz.

As my dedication indicated I owe a tremendous amount of consideration to my children, Brad and Krysta, and my husband John. They have supported me throughout the writing of this book and gave me the love and encouragement required to see the project through.

Brad is my coach. Like me, he has a creative flair that sometimes is misunderstood by the rest of the world and sees us sitting on the outside of the ring. However, he is a strong and caring young man who has never given up on me even when I have given up on myself. His sense of humour is a match for my own, and at times I find myself searching for the older person who speaks with me. I am proud to be his mother.

Krysta is my stabilizer. When my head gets a little too far into the clouds, she gently and in her own sweet way pulls me back toward the earth. She too is creative, but the bulk of her abundant energy is spent flitting around like a beautiful, social butterfly. When I listen to her I am reminded of the man I love and married because she is unwittingly so much like him. Her "take me as I am" attitude has taught me to worry less about what people think and focus more on who I am. I am proud to be her mother.

John is my rock. Like any good rock he holds my world down when it seems to be getting away from me. His emotions are solid and consistent, so I always know where I stand. He may not always give me what I think I want, but most definitely always gives me what I need. Our twenty-two years together have been filled with adventures, disappointments, and frustrations, but mostly with love and wonder. We both decided early in our relationship that life was too short not to enjoy what it has to offer, and have tried the best we can to do just that. I am proud to be his mate.

I want to humbly thank my mother, Bev. She did indeed give me a solid foundation. She has been my constant source of hope, laughter, encouragement, discipline, and love. I often play back my life growing up, and in every frame I see my mother who time and again sacrificed for her children. Whether it was the trip to Ottawa on the bus, the homemade butterscotch candy, or the nights of watching slides on the refrigerator door, the joys we knew as children were always the result of her own selflessness. Now through the miracle of technology I am blessed every day with a much anticipated message from her, always ending with her love. She may never really know how much she means to me, but I will continue in any way I can to try to tell her. I am proud to be her daughter and her friend.

I want to extend my gratitude and love to my mother-in-law, Edith. Without even knowing it, forty-four years ago she blessed my life by having her wonderful son. But unlike many mother/daughter-in-law relationships, I was also blessed with the most wonderful mother-in-law and precious lifelong friend. She has taught me to be patient and to enjoy the gifts I have to offer. Her love has been infallible, honest, and real, but by far the greatest thing she has done for me is to give me her friendship and accept my hugs without hesitation. I am proud to be part of her family.

I thank my sister Cheryl for taking me back into her life, for giving me the reality checks I need, but mostly for being the truest sister a girl could ask for. She too is my dearest friend and without her words of comfort, "If I made it through so can you," I no doubt would still be struggling behind the eight ball. Thank you also for your gift in the creation of the cover. And while I am at it, thank you Ted for loving her the way you do and being there for me. To her children, Jeff and Trish, my wonderful nephew and niece, I will never forget the first time I held you and, despite some absences, you have always been a part of me and will always be. I am proud you are my family.

The love and acceptance I received from the Larsen family right from day one is something I am eternally grateful for. Peder, your laugh comforted me amidst the whole gang when I was first around, and now it comforts me in knowing you still enjoy my company. Annette must have seen some potential in me as a sister-in-law, because she treated me like family from the get-go, even though she may not have known if her brother was at all serious about me. Dana managed to push aside his feelings on girls from the east to welcome me like a true family member and in the true Robinson fashion, jabs and all. Their children, my nephews and niece, grabbed a part of my heart the very first time I laid eyes on their cute little faces, and they have made me feel special every day since. Thank you Brent and Lindy, Mark, Daniel, Adam, and Natalie. I am proud to have been chosen.

To Dad, Roger, and Madeline, and brothers Dan and David, thank you for never forgetting me and all the special occasions in my life. I know we have been distant at times, but we are never more than a heartbeat away.

Family aside, thank you Cody for saying, "I know you can, Lor."

The list of family and friends is endless and I am beginning to sound a bit like the latest Grammy winner, so forgive me if I did not mention your name specifically.

Thank you from the bottom of my heart everyone who believed in me, inspired me, and kept my fingers typing.

A special thank you to the life models who grace these pages with their beauty and poise: Daryl, Lisa, Charlotte, Barb, Krysta, Bradley, Erika, Les, Caylie, Cody, and Courtney.

It Goes Like This

*My beautiful charges:
Krysta (1 year) and Brad (2 years)*

Introduction

This book is a collection of thoughts — some humorous, some heart-felt, but all true and all providing the same message. When you sign up as a parent you sign up for life. But this book is not just for parents, it is also for children of parents. The content is not referenced by years of Post Secondary schooling, nor is there a PhD after my name. The content is just honest. In no way is this book intended to point fingers or diminish the importance of parenthood. It is more like a form of cathar-sis needed by any parent at some or many points in their lives.

I began writing this book on July 7th, 1999, two days into taking care of an eight-year-old nephew for nine days. I found myself standing on the back deck, tears streaming down my face; I had seven days to go. My husband had assured me it wouldn't be that bad. His reference of mind: "I will be working nine hour days until the nine days are up, then we're on holidays." But I leave this thought for Chapter Five. Alas I regress, which I find I do more and more these days. This particular day I suffered from P.M.S., Parental Mental Syndrome (Chapter Six). I was at my wits' end when oddly enough I began to think of my mother. My tears turned to chuckles and soon after, snorting with laughter, those words my mom used to say were now frightening truths haunting me, "I can hardly wait until you're a parent, then maybe you'll understand."

Oh yes, Mom, I do understand. I am a thirty-nine-year-old mother, I work part time at my own business, and full time as a parent. I have a husband who I love, but who finds retreat in his work, tearing the car apart on the driveway, or building an outhouse in the front yard. I have great expectations that the hard work raising our children will pay off in the form of well-adjusted, reasonably happy adults. I am not holding out for surgeons or famous artists, I simply ask for satisfaction. So if you wonder why my tears turned quickly to laughter, it's because my one salvation on this seemingly dark day was the thought in the back of my mind: "You guys just wait until you have children of your own."

No one told me it would be easy, in fact many of my predecessors told me just the opposite. It is hard, damn hard, and it gets harder before it gets easier. This sounds like the actual birth itself. I recall that when people told my husband and I that our lives would never be the same, I laughed. I don't laugh at that thought anymore. But parenting does have its great moments, some of which I will share with you, lest you not be too discouraged if you have yet to partake of the wonderful world of parenting.

Doc Spock I'm not, in fact I don't have my degree in child psychology or child and youth care or anything remotely close. I am one of the millions who claim the title of Parenting Student, a lifetime learning discipline whose only form of evaluation are the children and how adjusted they are for the path that lies ahead of them. The letters behind your name do not read out PhD or M.D., instead they read MOM or DAD. That's all you get, folks — no recognized professional status, no large sums of money, no fancy banquets on your behalf. When you graduate, if you graduate, from this process — your ultimate accomplishment is a child who doesn't hate society because they eat red meat, likes themselves enough but not too much, doesn't think some cartoon character is the next coming of Christ, and has a strong desire to be on their own before the age of thirty. It doesn't seem like a lot and at times you will think it isn't — so hold fast, there really is a light at the end of the tunnel. This bright light shines on those wonderful first words, first steps, independent washroom breaks, ballet recitals, gym meets, hockey games, award ceremonies, graduations, weddings, and the eventual gift of grandchildren. This light will outshine even the darkest of moments.

I once read that a baby humpback whale depends on its mother for survival for the first two years of its life, during which time the baby gains up to one thousand pounds every ten minutes. The mother, however, will fast for three months during her journey to warmer waters, resulting in a loss of 27,000 pounds. This is a sacrifice she endures in order to give birth and ultimately nurse and protect her baby.

On the other hand, I also read that if a mother pig has too many piglets to tend to, she will actually throw them out of the pen, or in more severe cases . . . well you get my drift. As despicable as that may sound, it is nature's way, because let's face it, no one really wants to have to deal with a stressed-out 250-pound sow.

Nature's way is reflected extraordinarily in every species, and when it comes to parenting most days are whale days . . . but every once in a while there's a pig day. As a new parent you will learn to understand and appreciate whale days and pig days. There are moments of pure joy and some of frustration, moments of success along with the failures, moments of trial and many of error — the secret is striking that balance.

CHAPTER ONE

Honey, I'm Un-expecting

The Joy of Pregnancy

I debated about beginning at the beginning, conception that is, but decided that was a topic best left to romance novelists. My theory is if you don't know how you got pregnant in the first place, then this book will no doubt miss its mark. So I will begin instead at the moment of truth, "Honey, guess what. We're expecting a baby."

Whoever coined the phrase "expecting a baby" had no idea what they were talking about, because as parents are destined to find out, most of what raising children is all about is, quite frankly, unexpected.

Symptoms Galore

Warning: pregnancy can be accompanied by many side effects.

The marvelous event begins at the point of conception and the rest will become your own page of history. After the blessed announcement, the mom-to-be is about to weigh anchor on nine-ten months of pregnancy, a period filled with endless possibilities, all of which have been endured by countless generations before us. It begins with morning sickness, which should be more appropriately named "all day sickness," an interesting biological wonder that comes about with little to no warning, and despite some well-intended advice is not lessened by a plain soda cracker, but is in fact induced by the smell of toothpaste.

For those lucky enough not to encounter projectile vomiting which can be brought on by the sound of the can opener, there are a myriad of other side effects which are rarely discussed on the education channel. For example, water retention. Somehow the Joy of Pregnancy chronicles forgot to mention the small fact that your body suddenly turns into Hoover Dam, storing water behind all your extremities. This is the real reason for the sudden increase in unwed mothers-to-be. When your hands and feet make the Michelin man look anorexic by ballooning to five times their recognizable size, wedding rings are no longer a viable option.

Heartburn and indigestion are two more side effects of pregnancy. I never knew what heartburn was until I became pregnant. Suddenly my stepfather's poignant description made perfect sense. First comes the burning sensation in the pit of your stomach, then by some freak of biological nature the sensation begins moving up your chest and lodges itself into the base of your throat like a gob of unspeakable substance stuck between your esophagus and your larynx. And there it remains, and try as you may you can't cough it out or shove it down with a piece of white bread, because what feels like a good-sized cotton swab is later explained by your OB to be trapped gas. Now you're Mount St. Helen. Forget buying single rolls of antacids, splurge and go for the 5000 Value pack, believe me it is money well spent. You will actually grow accustomed to the chalky after-taste, but skip the fruit-flavoured because they taste nothing like any fruit I ever bought at the produce counter. Heartburn, aptly named, seems to strike most frequently at night, a half hour after you have settled in for a reasonably fair night's sleep. The sudden fire in your stomach disturbs your feeble attempt to get at least one night of decent slumber which, thanks to the rapid increase in the need to relieve your bladder, is next to impossible.

Which brings me to the next side effect. Doctors eloquently refer to it as the desire to urinate more frequently. That's putting it mildly. The truth is it feels similar to what I refer to as swimming bladder, that feeling a female gets when she has been swimming and she has an unexplainable urge to urinate, and yet once positioned over the bowl she is sadly disappointed when she can only manage to squeeze out three drops. The big difference being that this happens to a pregnant woman no less than fifteen times a day. This side effect will subside somewhat midway through the second trimester, but will return with a vengeance in the third trimester as the baby's weight increases and it uses your bladder as a trampoline.

And if that isn't bad enough, many pregnant women suffer from bouts of constipation resulting in the uncontrollable need to push so hard their eyes develop broken blood vessels, as does the opposite end of the spectrum, which become the dreadfully known hemorrhoids. Until pregnancy most women have had no experience with these fascinating little medical aberrations, but after weeks of walking with what feels like a bunch of grapes rubbing between their cheeks, they give in to the embarrassing chore of having them examined by their doctor. More than likely your doctor will snidely inform you they are hemorrhoids, as if to imply you should have known all along and never bothered him with the gruesome task of inspection. How's a girl to know. The remedy involves the application of a cream whose scent is similar to a sore muscle ointment as well as a diet that is intended to lighten the load, so to speak. What the doctor fails to tell you is that as the baby's weight increases so does the pressure on your lower area, and consequently you will be subjected to a "Return of the Killer Hemorrhoids." If they persist you may be faced with the option of having them removed, either surgically or by a procedure best described as tying the knot. When you come to learn that this involves tying a material similar to dental floss around the offending swellings until they suffocate and shrivel, you will suddenly have nightmares about precisely when and where one may decide to drop off.

During pregnancy the body begins preparing itself for the soon-to-be-nurturing of offspring by supplying the mammary glands with a more than sufficient amount of milk. The end result is enlarged breasts. One of the true signs of nature's sometimes satirical sense of humour has to be the fact that a woman's breasts take on mammoth proportions during pregnancy. Suddenly a woman becomes unbelievably well-endowed, all to the extreme gratification of her mate. Ironically, the woman becomes the epitome of sexuality. I say ironically because to a woman who is vomiting and urinating at the stroke of every hour, has bouts of indigestion and heartburn that could bring down a healthy bull elephant, and can perform a one-woman show of Dr. Jekyll and Mr. Hyde, sexuality is the last thing on her mind. But it doesn't seem to matter to a "breastmerized" mate that she is leaning over a toilet; his eyes never seem to get past her amazing mammary glands. To add insult to injury, the sudden onset of swollen breasts is accompanied by a tissue tenderness that brings about new challenges to strapping on a bra. And it is never enough for a man to admire from a distance; he has this uncontrollable urge to touch, a touch that could be fatal.

No thesis on pregnancy would be complete without mentioning the two most common side effects which often have the longest-lasting consequences: unusual food passions and food rejections, and of course, the infamous mood oscillations.

Pickles, ice cream, coffee straight from the bag, cheezies, oysters on graham crackers — the list is as varied as the women who compose it, but the principle is universal — pregnancy brings about some of the most unusual food cravings. Speaking from my own experience as a normally devoted tea granny, I suddenly couldn't get enough coffee, and the stronger the better. I woke up craving coffee and lay down craving coffee. After about a month of as close to intravenous coffee as I could get, I realized that my restlessness may be caused by something other than my new physiological condition. I had become a coffee addict. On the wise advice of my doctor, I cut back to coffee twice a day at work only. To this day I am amazed at the absolute precision with which my passion for coffee stopped the day my son was born, and then began again days before I discovered I was pregnant with my daughter. I drink very little coffee now, but by some strange coincidence my son and daughter have enjoyed a good cup of java since they were about three years old. Along with the sudden inexplicable food passions comes an equally forceful abhorrence for certain foods which can be triggered by the smell alone. Some women have told tales of becoming violently ill at the mere presence of raw meat, or the taunting odour of vanilla, or the sight of "yack" on undercooked eggs, but whatever the cause of food abhorrences, they can have cataclysmic results and have been known to remain with the mother throughout the remainder of her life. My own account involved vegetable soup, a product I otherwise loved, but unfortunately cannot even open a can of to this day. Worst case scenario, your food abhorrence could be chocolate.

Imagine yourself sitting watching Wheel of Fortune and the contestant spins a bankruptcy. With that and that alone you burst into tears, sobbing so hard your shoulders shake. All your spouse can do is stare in disbelief and try to comfort you with words of encouragement, "It's only a show," and that's all you needed to hear to put you into a complete 360 emotional spin. The tears dry instantly, your eyes transfix, your teeth clench, your blood boils, and you explode in a fit of rage.

"What do you mean by that, you think I'm a basket case, you sit there all smug thinking it's easy living inside a body that has taken on a personality of its own, you think this is just put on, that I can control my emotions or my bladder. Well I can't and I hate being fat, and you think I'm fat, don't you, I've seen the way you look at other women. Well just you don't forget who got me in this predicament in the first place, Mr. Man."

With that you get up and walk to the kitchen because it's time for a cheezie fix, but to your anguish you discover they are all gone. With empty bag in hand you storm back to the family room and shake the bag in the face of your "unexpectant" spouse, all the while making unfounded accusations that he plotted to eat the last cheezie just so he could save you from putting on more weight. All at once reality sets in and you remember that in fact you ate the last cheezie last night while watching Letterman. You respond the only way you know how, "Honey, I love you so much, would you run over to the store and pick up some more cheezies?"

It takes a while for most spouses to catch on to the games of mood oscillation. The safest bet is for him to never, never respond immediately, because chances are her mood is going to take another 180-360 rotation within seconds.

Tip:

On a very serious note: "Baby Blues," also known as post-natal depression, can have terrifying effects on women and their families and can happen instantaneously after the birth or take up to a year to appear. Nonetheless, any and every woman who feels she is suffering from post-natal depression should seek medical attention immediately. The birth of a child is a wondrous yet traumatic occasion that has a great impact on the parent's lifestyle, which now focuses all attention on the care of that child. For this reason we all need to be more supportive and attentive to the needs of the parents and offer them a sympathetic shoulder to lean on, a non-judgmental ear to talk to, and a much needed break for themselves.

The only logical explanation researchers have derived for mood swings is the raging war of hormones going on inside of the woman during pregnancy, the same hormones that wreak havoc during a woman's menstrual cycle, only on a 24-7, 30 x 9 basis. At this point I would love to tell all the expecting and wanna-be mothers that the mood swings will disappear the day of the blessed event, but unfortunately there is still the possibility of the non-scientifically phrased "Baby Blues."

During this entire period of symptomonious suffering, the mom-to-be is subjected to at least fourteen visits to the doctor's office. These not-so-appreciated intrusions to her privacy afford her the opportunity to inquire about the many symptoms she endures as well as to purge her feelings about her changing physiological being. However, these are the only two bonuses of having to assume the horizontal squat position while doctors and their assisting nurses poke, prod, and peek into places otherwise totally unknown to sunshine. After which the mom-to-be's dignity and any hope of reticence has been shredded and she is left feeling more vulnerable than a thirty-pound turkey on December 24 at a farm auction. As the months go on a sense of apathy takes over, and moms-to-be face the fact that these physical and emotional trespasses play a vital role in the well-being of her and her baby. Rest assured her dignity will return shortly after the birth when she must undergo her last exam for at least a year, barring any unforeseen birthing difficulties.

As a result of a somewhat painful experience of my own, I feel it imperative to mention some do's and dont's that would be wisely noted by all physicians and nurses attending to moms-to-be.

DO   Warm all examination tools and your hands prior to the exam.

DO   Offer to have a female nurse in the exam room.

DO   Give the mom-to-be sufficient time to dress and undress — embarrassing doesn't begin to cover having a doctor walk in on you while you are not so gracefully trying to slip out of your oversized panties.

DO   Listen with sincerity; even though this may be your hundredth pregnant patient and you may have heard it all and treated it all, it is more than likely the most important concern in the mom-to-be's life right now.

DO   Weigh mom-to-be in in a private location.

DO   Reply with more than grunts while the mom-to-be is talking and you are examining.

DO   Offer a sani-wipe after an ultrasound examination. Having petroleum jelly seep through a silk maternity blouse can be frustrating, costly, and of course, humiliating.

DON'T   Ever refer to a pregnant woman as fat, no matter how much weight she has gained.

DON'T   Automatically assume the mom-to-be knows what you are talking about.

DON'T   Use words like "Uh-oh," "Oh my," "Goodness," "Wow," "Yikes," "Oops," "Holy man, what the heck is that," when conducting pelvic exams, ultra sounds, or monitoring vital signs.

DON'T   Ever dismiss the mom-to-be's feelings, aches, pains, uncertainties.

DON'T   Stand at the foot of the exam table when you inform mom-to-be she is having twins, gaining too much weight, you were wrong about the due date.

DON'T   If a male doctor, remark "I know how you are feeling." Until you grow giant-sized breasts and can't pee comfortably standing up, you have no idea.

Many women suffer an array of other side effects, some of which can be a medical threat to the mother-to-be, all of which makes us realize that what is happening inside the host body is nothing short of a miracle.

Psychobabble and Hard Cover Education

One of my first thoughts when I found out I was pregnant was that I had to buy the book. You see, I am a "by the book" type of person, so I was convinced one or perhaps all of the multitude of books that were and still are on the market would tell me everything I needed to know. So began my library of "How to Parent" literature, ranging from the most sophisticated textbooks to any magazine article I read the headline for while standing in the line at the grocery store. Most of what I have read over the past ten years has been helpful, at least in making me realize there is no easy solution. But the helpful hints didn't stop at the book-shelves; it seemed that everyone had something to offer. Talk shows, which I once watched to see how they could miraculously transform "too sexy" of a gramma into a stylish second-generation parent, were now crowding the airwaves with advice on how to be a perfect parent. The local college advertised courses on parenting for the future; even the health centre had seminars available to point parents in the right direction. Suddenly I felt like it was a huge conspiracy — the minute I gave birth the only information that would be available to me would be Parenting 101. Even my horoscopes appeared somewhat suggestive. "You are about to embark on a long journey. Make sure you are well prepared." "New joys will enter your life; care must be used in dealing with them."

Well maybe this was a little paranoid, but one thing was sure: there was and still is information everywhere on the subject.

What I have come to realize is that most of the information is nearly always psychologically based. There are references to proper parenting, which I have translated to mean "maintaining the child's self-esteem while sacrificing your own sanity." Don't get me wrong, I am an advocate of positive child-rearing, but the books seem to leave out the parts about the difficulty with which this is performed. I have spent some time doing my own analysis on some of the more popular concepts that have been suggested for successfully raising children.

Corporal Punishment is Taboo

The experts and not-so-experts tend to believe that corporal punishment is not only harmful to children, but it teaches them to use it on each other, defending this finding with the fact that everything we do as adults children will mimic in their own lives. Instead, the suggested form of discipline is perhaps a "time out," or an even more recent discovery, "time in." If you have no idea what I am referring to, let me provide an over-simplified explanation of these concepts.

Time out means removing the child from the situation to a quiet place where he can think about his behaviour and why it has made you upset. At first I was delighted. This was a positive way of dealing with unacceptable behaviour, and I would get time to do some things that needed to be done while my child sat quietly thinking about what he had done wrong. Of course the experts suggest that you tell the child

> **Tip:**
>
> *I found that misbehaviour started around the age of eighteen months, as soon as the child could crawl to things he knew were out of bounds. How did he know they were out or bounds? Because he was told no less that sixty-three times.*

why he is getting a time out. When what time out really meant was listening to a child scream and cry at the top of his lungs, one has to wonder how much thinking was going on. As my children got older, I discovered that when the crying stopped, it was an equally bad sign. The time they should have spent thinking about what they did wrong they now spent re-arranging their room in a not-so-appropriate manner. Time out at school is an automatic labeller, because the child who has been sent into the hall is now seen by any passers-by, including their friends, siblings, and sometimes parents, teachers, and of course on occasion the principal. The child in the hall is bad! And let me warn you that there are parents out there who really have nothing better to do than to wander the halls of the school searching out the "hall kids." This way they can get on their cell phone and call you at home to let you know your kid has been bad. Thank you Detective Gettalife, you can chalk one up for your perfect kid now. There again, when the child gets a little wiser, this provides an opportune moment to sneak to the bathroom to do who knows what. But the thinking went right out the door with the child. I am not saying this isn't a viable solution, I am simply saying that it isn't all it is cracked up to be, although it is very useful in removing yourself from the situation. A little trick I found even more successful was granting myself the time out. Bathrooms work wonders for providing refuge in tense parenting moments.

Time in is a fairly new concept which means you send the child to his room and you go with him. In essence it is a time out with you, which is supposed to make the child feel loved even though his behaviour is unacceptable. When I first tried this with my eight-year-old, his response was, "How come you're staying in here?" I must say the question concerned me somewhat, because his tone didn't sound like that of a loving child — it was a tad bit more suspicious. But I bit the bullet and lay down beside him, wrapped my arms around him and cuddled. The next thing I knew it was twenty-five minutes later, he was gone, supper was not ready yet, and there was a dreadful sound of silence in the house. I guess the neighbour's trampoline was more compelling than a mother who had drifted off and was now drooling on his pillow. Well, the theory is good, but the practice is not always as easy as they make it sound.

I sometimes find that behaviour simply warrants a spanking (not a line I would use on my husband). When did a spanking turn into child abuse? I seem to recall getting a few good lashings when I was a child and I have no deep-rooted psychological problems, at least none that I can blame on my parents. A spanking usually means that the behaviour was the last straw, and let's face it, if the child has pushed you to that point, then he is most likely aware of the consequences. I am not suggesting it fits for everyone, and I am certainly not suggesting it is the only way to deal with behaviour problems, but I am sick and tired of beating myself up over the fact that once in a while my child may just get a rap on the backside. As for it teaching them to go to school and spank other kids, I haven't heard any feedback from the school yet. It saddens me to think our society has got to the point where if you spank your child for good reason, you could be looking at hard time.

Let's Talk

Another popular cure for disciplinary problems is to talk it out. The experts say that sitting the child down and explaining the situation and telling her why you are upset gives the child a better understanding. They also suggest you let them tell their point of view. I agree. After all, children are just smaller people. However, we forget that they have smaller experiences as well and sometimes the only points of reference they have are the ones that come with their invisible friend that lives in the closet.

If you will indulge me for a few moments I would like to relate an incident where I found myself yelling instead of talking. At three years old, my daughter had a fascination with talcum powder. Then again, that was not unique to my daughter. Her fascination led to a discovery as she dumped the better half of a container of talcum powder on the floor in the bathroom. To this day I am convinced she knew this would not go over well with her mother, so she fled the scene of the crime. Normally such an act of mischief would have been dealt with by having a heart-to-heart, but in my haste to answer the call of nature I found myself hydroplaning across the bathroom floor, landing flat on my back covered in the essence of fine fragrance. I must admit my first reaction did not pass the "Parenting for Better Children" test. All I recall were some nasty words in a pitch that would bring down jetliners. My husband arrived home to his daughter crying and me looking like Casper, that not so friendly ghost.

I tried to imagine myself using the "Let's Talk" approach. "Why did you feel you had to dump mommy's talcum powder all over the bathroom floor?"

"Cause it smells pretty." You just cannot argue the mentality of a three-year-old; on the other hand, you can't ignore it either. In all fairness maybe that would have been a better solution, and as I look back on many of the situations where I instantly flew off the handle, most of them I can chuckle at now. I do find that I use the "Let's Talk" strategy more now, but it's definitely a challenge. "Hi, my name is Lori, and I'm a yellaholic."

It's Only Ever an Idle Threat

Once again the experts feel this will create negative connotations. The child will eventually see the threats for exactly what they are and ignore the true meaning behind them, a way for the parent to express her disapproval of the child's behaviour. In fact the experts are so adamant about this theory that they discourage the over-use of the word "No," claiming it becomes so ritual to children that they simply ignore it. My dad would have said we were just being belligerent. I have an exceptionally hard time with this one.

"Oh, sweety, mommy wishes you wouldn't play with her really breakable snow globe that daddy gave her for her birthday." You see, the way I figure it, by the time I have spoken these gentle words of warning, my child has thrown all caution to the wind along with the snow globe. A simple "No" is so much faster, and given the right tone, usually gets results. Let's face it, looking for just the right words at a time of high intensity is not the easiest task. "No," in my opinion, is a good word, and is after all universal. "Oh, no, no, honey, I have had this old thing forever."

The experts maintain threats such as, "If you don't stop that I am going to get really angry," lose their validity unless you carry them out, but by the same token getting really angry isn't healthy either. You just can't win for losing. Once again I question the words of the experts, knowing that if my mom and dad had legitimately carried out their threats, my siblings and I would be trying to find our way back from the moon, still walking home from my grandparent's place, still grounded (life is a long time), still living with the gypsies, and in therapy for constant silliness as a result of all the slaps. None of these are true, although the jury is still out on my brother Danny.

I must admit, idle threats can come back to haunt you. My children have become engrossed with the latest craze of cartoon trading cards about a group of kids that spend the better parts of their days trying to capture characters. Like most adolescent marketing ploys, this phenomenon comes equipped with trading cards, plastic toy characters, and a slew of other over-priced gadgets. Thanks to the world of multi-media our kids can be bombarded daily with the latest, greatest gimmicks. Despite gallant efforts on my part, I fell into the trap of believing my kids would be not only austere-sized, but even more devastating, they ran the risk of becoming permanent hall kids because of their inability to socialize with the other kids if they didn't conform and be part of the "card trading" in-crowd. Oh what tangled webs seven- and eight-year-old children weave. However, now I had leverage. When things were not getting done or I wasn't being listened to, I would threaten to cut off their lifeline — I was going to cancel cable. At first the tears flowed and the begs for mercy were non-stop, but after a month of non-compliance, then two months, and the cable man was still gainfully employed, the leverage began to slip as did any interest in meeting my demands. But my constitution was also weak — what would my life be without my favourite sitcom making me laugh, and my favourite talk show hostess filling me in on the latest great books. Most importantly, I would have never known the meaning behind, "Is that your final answer?" I too feared being austere-sized by the rest of the world.

Let them Fail

This interesting piece of advice is a hard pill to swallow for most of today's fast-paced, highly competitive, thrill-seeking, ladder-climbing adults who are otherwise parents. What the experts are trying to say is that allowing children to fail lets them know that it is okay not to be perfect. While this is supportive in theory, it doesn't blend well with the demands of our society. The pictures in magazines show beautiful people with perfect physiques. The world is going so techno any child that cannot surf the Net, install programs, or play in the world of virtual reality is going to fall way behind, and that is never good for self-esteem. Teachers are burdened with class sizes of thirty or greater, leaving little room to work with the strugglers. Competition has replaced good old-fashioned fun, and if you need verification of this fact, go watch a minor league hockey game. Watch the game for the first period, then watch the fans (better known as parents) for the rest of the game.

Olympic athletes are getting younger and younger every year and the benefits they reap are ten-fold. They get sponsorships and promotional considerations that pay in the millions, instant fame, and the admiration of loving fans who otherwise would never know they exist. When surrounded by all of these temptations, it is very hard to tell a child it's okay to fail. Heck, as parents we're afraid to let them fail; it may mean significant bruising to our own self worth. In some ways I too feel the tinge of, "I want my kid to be the best," and when good grades come home, I hang them on my fridge. Fortunately my children are very conscientious about our family finances, and so far I haven't had to run out and purchase one of those big double-sided refrigerators.

One of my biggest bones of contention with myself regarding child rearing is the fact that I don't brag enough about my children. It's not that I don't think they are terrific kids, and it is most certainly not because I am not proud of them, I just find it redundant. I tell my children how great they are and how successful they are, but I don't see the need to compare notes with other parents. This all came to light one day at my child's school. I was playing helping mom in my son's classroom. It happened to be the day report cards were going home and the teacher asked me and the other helping mom if we wouldn't mind putting a newsletter in each of the childrens' report card envelopes. We graciously accepted. Now it didn't take a rocket scientist to figure out you could simply slip the newsletter in without fully opening the envelope, and so I did. I was disturbed to see the other mother removing the report cards and taking quick glances at them. Not being an overly shy person, I asked her what she was doing. Her reply disturbed me.

"I just want to see how my little Ricky is doing compared to the rest of the kids."

I couldn't believe my ears. What possible business was it of hers, and why should she care? If little Ricky was as exceptional as she had been known to say he was, then the only possible reason she would check other report cards was to stroke her own ego. I gave one of my famous looks of disapproval and then quickly sorted through the remaining envelopes until I found my son's. I wasn't going to give her the satisfaction.

Sure it is healthy to allow children to try and subsequently fail, but first and foremost we have to convince society it's okay.

The list of "nine out of ten psychologists recommend" advice is endless, and as parents I am sure you have your own topics of researched information that have blessed your life and boggled your mind. The parents of tomorrow will have their share as well, with more and more information readily available at their fingertips — a quick surf of the Net will provide them with information overload. But the simplest piece of advice will nearly always suffice: Lead with your heart, your head will follow.

You Know, Dear . . . In My Opinion

When you grow weary of all the reading involved with "The Psychological Approach to Child Rearing" you will be delighted to know there are over two billion people, otherwise not bestowed with letters after their names, who are more than happy to give you advice. Of course they begin with the ones closest to home. Your own parents suddenly become the experts, and in spite of your vague recollections of blindness caused by sitting too close to the television, left and right brightly displayed on the bottom of your school runners, your initials brightly displayed on the inside of your underwear, fears of gum trees growing in your stomach, and worries of getting pregnant if you kissed someone before you were married, they can hardly wait to enlighten you with their version of perfect child rearing. I'm not suggesting that parents of past generations didn't possess good parenting skills, but now as an adult it is a little clearer that some of their mind sets made very little sense. (I am sure that twenty-five years from now I will eat these words.) From conception to graduation, as parents you are subjected to a variety of innuendos that take the form of "Well when I was . . .""In our day . . ." and so on. Your parents will also take every opportunity to remind you of all the ways you misbehaved and caused them grief. Your mom will give you a blow-by-blow account of the pain and suffering she went through in order to give birth to you, including a slight on how lucky you have it today with all the new medical procedures and the wonderful hospitals. At which point you begin to imagine you must have been born in a stable. And like a good fishing story, the labour gets longer and longer every time you hear the tale. You will find yourself feeling extremely grateful these "how-to" tales were reserved for pregnancy and raising children and not conception. Your dad will refrain from a lot of advice, because for the most part fathers of the '50s and '60s were able to escape the entire birthing experience sitting in waiting rooms with good magazines and cheap cigars. They do, however, manage to slip in the odd reference to how easy fathers have it today: "At least you have colour television."

But parenting advice doesn't stop at just family. The minute the joyous news is announced it becomes open season for Dr. Spock wannabes. A pregnant mother will endure countless stories of other women's pregnancies, including but not limited to detailed accounts of morning sickness, how to have sex when you feel like a minivan, the truth behind Kegel exercises, and many more you are never really prepared to hear. As the baby grows you will find yourself being stopped on the street by complete strangers asking if they can rub your tummy. Whoever came up with the unwritten rule that a pregnant woman's stomach becomes public domain for pleasurable petting should be institutionalized.

Normally some stranger requesting to rub a person's stomach would be a call for 911, but it seems the stomach that carries life takes on a whole new identity; it is now the magic lantern of life.

There are also the wise ones who come out of the woodwork, as you discover your family tree includes great-great-great-Auntie Augustine who has a home remedy for indigestion involving pine needles, white vinegar, and sitting in the lotus position for three hours. Great Auntie will also guess the sex of your child by swinging a string with an assortment of small objects attached over your exposed stomach, all of which is done to the delight of your relatives and the humiliation of the mother-to-be, but does come with a fifty percent accuracy rate.

Doctor's waiting rooms also provide an excellent source of free advice. Despite the twenty-five other empty chairs, people somehow feel a magnetic pull towards a pregnant woman. A ten minute wait at the doctor's office can turn into a forum for open discussion about every possible delivery disaster that has ever occurred, and I can assure you the last thing a nine-month pregnant woman needs to hear about is the size of forceps, or that it's possible to receive fifty stitches in a place that otherwise covers approximately one and half inches. The stories are enough to weaken even the strongest constitution, the most amazing of which is usually told in painstaking detail by some overly zealous husband. The mom-to-be can rely on at the very least ten horror stories about delivery, including one breech birth, one C-section after forty hours of labour, and one student doctor's observation requirements. But the final word is always the same — your delivery will be unique to you and will someday be the topic of conversation at a family Thanksgiving. And it can be used as leverage when you want to lay a lot of guilt on your children: "I endured twenty-five hours of hard labour (like there is any other kind) and ten stitches so you could be part of this world, so don't tell me about what's fair and what's not."

Unfortunately the barrage of advice does not end once the child is born, and in fact it takes on a whole new dimension. Anything you know is really nothing you know, which is partly the truth, but constantly being reminded of your ineptness at raising children can and does wear on a person. Ironically, the first piece of advice regarding parenting skills comes from your often male doctor and is verified by an endless number of earth parents — the debate over feeding preferences. The breast is best is a personal belief that many shamelessly try to push on the new mother. Their logic stems from the natural goodness that breast milk holds over that of the other kind. My theory is that if breast milk is that wonderful and can create a bond like no other, than we should find a way to commercially produce it and put it in the coffee cups of our not-so-attentive spouses. Imagine the connections we could make by milking this one simple idea (pun intended of course). I had some problems with people telling me I wouldn't be as close to my children if I didn't breast feed, and I had even bigger problems with men telling me that breast feeding was a wonderful and sensual experience. This topic is so close to my heart (no pun intended), I spend a little more time on it later in this chapter.

The advice moves on to "let 'em cry." The jury remains split on whether you should let the baby cry until she eventually passes out from pure exhaustion (or you do), or attend her every attempt to make noise. No matter what you decide, there will inevitably be someone who disagrees with your choice. Advocates of 'town criers' are determined to tell you that you will spoil the child by picking her up so much, convinced that an eleven-pound three-month-old baby is devious enough to have you wrapped around her three-millimetre finger. And, sadly, you believe it must be true, so you suffer the pangs of guilt as you let the little ones cry themselves to sleep. Still others are adamant that every tiny whimper is a call for immediate alarm, and the best solution is to strap the child to your chest in a babypack, a contraption which was modified from its distant cousin the straight-jacket. This way the child is always near you and can constantly hear your heartbeat, the music of choice for infants. Eventually you will establish your own set of rules regarding your child's calls of the wild, rules that are necessary to soothe your own nerves and best fit your lifestyle.

As the baby grows, so too does the amount of advice. There is free advice on how to dress babies in order to establish early on their genetic place in life. Dressing a boy in pink can send shock waves through the older generation, resulting in a generous bestowment of train and cowboy overalls and t-shirts. Likewise, cladding little girls in less than lace can devastate the apparel police. There are helpful hints on potty training, including placing pieces of paper in the toilet bowl so little boys can practice hitting them with their fountain-like spray. Not only does this teach the little tike that the stream needs to go directly into the bowl, but it gives him his first all important view of the man's role as a hunter by starting target practice early. (This is explained in detail in Chapter Three.) I'm convinced this method was invented by the same group who firmly believe in the harmful effects of cross-gender colour dressing.

All that advice and the reasoning accompanying it could provide enough material for a whole other book, but is more often than not given out of love and concern for the new "unexpecting" parents.

The best way to raise a child remains a mystery, or better yet, a myth, because there really is no true blue right way. There is, however, the way you as a parent come to know, a way befitting both you and your child's life.

On What's to Come . . . Much a Due about Something

From the very minute the pending news is announced the infamous inquiry is on everyone's lips, "So when are you due?" At first the question is somewhat exciting for new parents and until moms-to-be actually begin showing, is only addressed by family and friends who have been made privy to the good news. On the other hand, once moms-to-be begin to show signs of motherhood, the inquiry is made by every person they come in contact with. Often the inquiry is also accompanied by some physical gesture towards the growing tummy. While once cute, now it is annoying as it occurs sometimes two to three times daily from the fifth month to the ninth month. Personally, I considered designing a t-shirt bearing a small rip-away calendar with a message above in bold print: **I am due in** . . . and then the days could be ripped away as the due date approached. Of course, a few concerns stopped me from approaching the fashion industry, such as having to wear the same t-shirt day in and day out for some 150 days, and the fact that many people couldn't do the math and would still ask, "And exactly when is it you are due?" Perhaps a better idea may be designing a large button that simply states the mom-to-be's due date, similar to the buttons worn later in a mom's life . . . *I'm a hockey/soccer mom*. Due dates tend not to be very reliable and are quite simply an educated guess by the doctor. After all, unless you are making a concentrated effort to become pregnant, more often than not pin-pointing the exact day where the practise paid off is next to impossible. So the doctor gives you his best guess and that day becomes the target day. Rarely the blessed event arrives as scheduled, and for some moms it occurs days, weeks, even months early, the latter being a health risk for mom and baby. For other moms it can occur days and sometimes unimpressively weeks late. Despite any effort to assist the baby along with bumpy car rides, standing on your head, or drinking cod liver oil, the fact remains the same: baby will come when baby is ready to and not a minute before. Well-informed or experienced moms-to-be may recognize some warning signs of the soon-to-be event. Nesting, a term used to describe the sensation moms-to-be get just before delivery, involves the need to prepare the home for the new arrival. Some moms-to-be experi-ence this sensation with such intensity they will actually mega-clean the entire house just before they go into labour. Others will get the sudden, uncontrollable urge to paint the baby's room some pastel colour and adorn it with cutesy little ornaments and accessories.

> **Tip:**
> *If you feel the need to paint the baby's room, always use a latex paint, free of any toxic fumes.*

While mom prepares the nest, her body and mind prepare themselves. There are some physical signs that accompany the event, such as:

- a small discharge of blood and mucus. No matter when this occurs it should always be taken seriously and checked by your physician,
- cramping in the lower stomach or upper leg region, which are not necessarily labour pains,
- extreme lower back-ache,
- increased urinating (as if it were possible to pee more frequently than you already do),
- restless leg syndrome,
- extreme discomfort when trying to sit or lie down,
- increased anxiousness,
- dizziness or light-headedness,

• the most obvious, the "water breaking," when the embryonic sac breaks and the fluids contained within are released. This is most often your last warning.

These particular signs are the most common, but I am sure there are numerous others which I will leave to the medical journals to document. On a very serious note, any dramatic changes in blood pressure, heart palpitations, or breathing should always be checked by your physician.

As the body prepares itself, so does the mind, heart, and soul, and moms-to-be may find themselves peaking out at emotional overload. Tears could be flowing at the same time you are laughing or screaming. The roller coaster ride you have been experiencing for the last nine to ten months has hit the highest hill, and the last part of the ride can have you soaring from extreme highs to extreme lows. The only advice I can offer during this ride is to hang on, it is about to come to an abrupt stop.

Some less fortunate moms-to-be may experience no warnings for what is about to happen, other than counting days around the target date. There have been cases of moms-to-be delivering in their own bathrooms, or on their own fine bed linen, or more devastatingly, in the back of their brand new SUV, a taxi, or an ambulance. Emergency 911 calls have documented and ultimately been the lifeline to frantic husbands, children, neighbours, and of course cab drivers who have been suddenly caught off guard and chosen as midwives to these poor, unfortunate, but highly volatile soon to give birth moms-to-be. As mentioned earlier, when the baby is ready, baby will strike no matter who the catcher may be and the play is about to be delivered.

UPS vs DOWNS (Delivery Options with No Satisfaction): The Other Delivery Service
No we don't guarantee overnight delivery

Internet delivery has taken on a whole new meaning these days. I am fascinated by the fact that there are women out there who have no qualms about delivering their baby on the WorldWideWeb for any and every curious, slightly demented adult or haphazard web-surfing child to watch. This sort of liberal behaviour makes those of us who request a sheet draped over our knees and hung like a one-man tent down past the birthing bed seem like a bunch of apprehensive jam tarts. But let's face it folks, childbirth may be miraculous, but given a choice over watching ER, where we know the blood and afterbirth are simply the product of a special effects guy's overactive imagination versus the real McCoy, the majority of us opt for the Grammy winner. After all, this is the moment of truth. Do you really want all those four letter words heard on the public electronic waves?

Those Precious Last Minutes . . . All Forty-five of Them

In the beginning the mom-to-be may be a bit intimidated by the mere idea of delivery. Terms like stirrups, forceps, episiotomy, Sitz baths, injections, epidural, and contractions are all cause for a pregnant woman to become disenchanted with the whole delivery concept. Not to mention the fact that the woman finds herself in an extremely compromising position flat on her back with her feet placed firmly in stirrups and her knees pointing directly east-west, where she has no control and is at the mercy of a steady parade of medical spectators. Who wouldn't be somewhat unnerved — it's enough to daunt even the most liberated of women. But all that early anxiety over the delivery and the horrific attack on a woman's pride is in vain, because in actuality there's not much left of a woman's pride after enduring up to twenty pre-delivery pelvic examinations. Truth is, when you are laying in a hospital bed, if you are lucky enough to make it to a hospital and you are about to perform the medical miracle of what could otherwise be described as pushing a bowling ball out through a nostril, all you really care about is getting the darn thing out. But alas, moms should be forewarned that this event is not likely to happen in a split second. In fact, those precious last minutes are more likely going to last any where from twenty minutes to nineteen hours. If you are lucky, only the last forty-five minutes will consist of what they rightfully refer to as Hard Labour, not unlike Hard Time.

Those precious last minutes may begin with the flood waters of the onset of labour, which for many women usually occurs in the comfort of their own freshly laundered sheets. The medical term for this unsettling phenomenon is Water Breaking, but should more appropriately be called Gushing Body Fluids. The reason why it often occurs at home while resting is because when the expectant mom is standing, the baby's head acts as a plug, so when mom lays down for some much needed time off her grossly swollen feet, the plug loosens and the bathtub drains right out all over anything and anyone within five metres of it. Your mate, who may be wakened by the sudden sensation that he is four years old again, will likely not need to be told, "Honey, my water just broke." Cleaning up before heading to the hospital may or may not be an option. Some fortunate women have delivered within half an hour of their water breaking, while others have been sent home, giving them time to not only change the now soaked sheets and return to a very rest-less slumber, but also to clean the house the next day and return to the hospital perhaps twelve hours later. My own experience with the floods of labour occurred on a wheelchair in the hospital elevator with a hor-rified eighteen-year-old security guard who, unfortunately for him, was the only available hospital personnel at 1:20 a.m. I did, however, thank my lucky stars he wasn't some over-zealous, under-trained, security-emergency-technician wannabe who may have crouched down at my feet and started yelling, "Push Hupp 2 — Push Hupp 44 — Push Hupp 57." The elevator doors barely opened as he four-wheeled me over the three inch gap between the elevator floor and the maternity ward floor and sped down the halls to the nurses' station, then disappeared as fast as his 210 pound body could move him. And there I sat bewildered and somewhat wet when the nurse looked over the counter and wisely exclaimed, "Oh, my, I think someone's water broke." I remember think-ing to myself, What was your first clue, the puddle below my wheelchair, or the terrified security guard bolting down the hallway? Her wisdom only got better, "Are we about to have a baby?" I didn't know about her, but it was either that or I was going for the award for best place to hide ammunition during a water balloon fight. Could we please get on with this?

After enduring witty repartee from a nurse who had worked far too long in the maternity ward, I was wheeled off to a birthing room, changed into a designer hospital gown (note: if you think those gowns don't cover up well in the back normally, try carrying an extra eight inches out front, and suddenly you're lucky if they even reach the front of your hips, overexposure to say the least), then assisted up onto a birthing table to await what I was hoping would be my last examination for a while. This exam is usually done by the attending nurse, and unless a baby's head is sticking out between your legs, the chance of your physician being in attendance is fairly slim. The nurse will measure to determine how dilated you are, and I am not referring to your pupils, and from there decide if you are ready for delivery or just practising.

More so today then in the past, if mom is not dilated very far, they may send her home and advise her to wait for more meaningful contractions. A cruel twist of fate causes some women to experience what is referred to as false labour, meaning they are not ready to deliver. For experienced moms, it means some extra time at home before her life is thrown into a frenzy with the induction of a new life, but to a first-time mom this can be a devastating blow to her stress level. Unsure when the event is about to take place, first-time moms can do anything but relax, anticipating that the next set of contractions may come fast and furious, bringing with them the real thing. However, if this is the real thing and you are dilated enough to prepare for the oncoming of what you hope to be a head, then you are about to experience those precious last minutes, and as I said before, they could vary vastly. Some moms have been wheeled into the birthing rooms as the head crowns, while others have endured contractions and pushing for up to thirty-six hours. Every woman's dream is to experience enough time to get horizontal on the birthing table, but not so much time that she actually witnesses three hospital shift changes before the event.

It's Called Labour for a Reason

There's a myth that has lived over many centuries, which claims there is no pain like that of childbirth, but that the woman will forget it all soon after the miracle has occurred. I reiterate it is a myth, or at least the part about forgetting. There really is no pain like childbirth. The contractions feel like the worst menstrual pains known to womankind, and as the cramps bear down on the entire lower section of your body, they are accompanied by a pain in your back which you can only imagine feels like being tightened in a vice grip. All of this takes place in a matter of ten to twelve seconds, but occurs anywhere from three minutes to twenty seconds apart and is coached by a nurse and doctor demanding you push when you don't want to and stop when you can't.

My own experience was enhanced with the induction of forceps as my son changed his mind mid-birthing canal and turned his head. In anticipation of my discomfort, the nurse proceeded to jab a needle into my inner left thigh with the brute force of a pro boxer. With the innocence of a hurt child, I questioned her motives. She informed me it was a muscle relaxant which would stop the trembling that had overtaken my lower extremities. The drug held fast to its promise and my legs suddenly fell wide open with gymnastic ease. The doctor was now able to insert the forceps, much to the concern of my husband who I recall exclaiming, "You're putting those where?"

The drug had such powerful relaxing effects that before I knew what was happening the forceps were in place and apparently had a solid grip on my baby's head. The doctor calmly requested just one more push and I willingly complied. The final push brought my son into the world, his tiny head clamped between the metal spoons of what I now saw as darn big salad tongs. It wasn't until then that I realized my husband's earlier cause for concern.

The contractions continued for a short while after the birth, ensuring all of the other baby-producing by-products were completely expelled. I held up my end of the bargain while the doctor cleaned and checked my much paid off efforts. Then my long awaited baby was placed on my stomach as the clean-up and repairs began. The doctor gently informed me that the baby had torn me a little on exit and it would require a few stitches, all the while threading what appeared to look like the needle my husband used to stitch up his deer hides. My only hope was that the relaxation drugs were still working, and they were, but it still didn't stop me from counting the number of times the doctor's arm swung up in a weaving motion. As I recall, it was at least five until the tying of the bow. Once things were settled down below, the doctor handed my husband a pair of scissors, and a wave of horror flooded my mind. Surely he didn't want him to cut the thread? My fears subsided as the doctor bequeathed my husband with the honour of cutting the umbilical cord. One small snip for boykind. Baby Brad was swathed in a turquoise hospital blanket and handed to my extremely elated husband who beamed in pride and paled in exhaustion. After what seemed like hours, my husband somewhat reluctantly handed the baby over to me. This was my first chance to hold this baby even closer to my heart than the previous nine-and-a-half months.

Labour, defined in the dictionary as physical or mental exertion, includes these synonyms: work, toil, travail, sweat, effort, and strain, which is a word, I am convinced, derived from childbirth. There really is no job like it, despite its seemingly short length. Labour for childbirth is usually defined as the period between the first excruciating contraction and the last impossible squeeze and can include a genre of not so pleasant and in some cases harrowing experiences, beginning with the contractions themselves. Every woman will have her own way of describing a contraction, but for those women who have not yet experienced them, or for people who will never experience them, this is the best I can do. You are getting over the worst bout of influenza you have ever had. Your stomach is completely empty from vomiting and diarrhea, both occurring at the same time, and you decide to try to nourish your body with one small soda cracker. Suddenly a cramp so bad it causes your legs to voluntarily cross and twist takes over your stomach, turning its lining inside out, accompanied by a pain so horrific you rush for the toilet. But you are afraid if you sit down the crouching motion will cause your stomach to fall out and you will be forced to shove it back up where it belongs. Finally your body self-erupts in a gaseous explosion and it is all over in ten seconds or less. The main difference being, contractions occur much more frequently and can continue for up to thirty-six hours. Along with contractions, some women experience back pain that feels as though a monster truck is slowly driving down the lower part of your back onto your hips, then finally changing gears on your pelvis. The urge to urinate and worse yet defecate is undeniable, but a rush of fear comes over you. What if the baby should decide this is the time to make it's entrance? What if my baby is born in a toilet bowl — imagine the therapy costs. So out of fear, most women hold the urge with the unfortunate result of releasing during the actual delivery, much to the embarrassment of the mom and the dismay of the attending medical staff.

The term "push" is one of the four-letter-words commonly used throughout the entire labour process; others I cannot repeat here. Early on the nurse tells you that you may feel like pushing, but don't. By pushing I refer to a sensation not much different than constipation, the feeling of getting rid of whatever it is that is blocking the way. Heeding the nurse's advice is easier said than done. Imagine feeling a pressing urge to relieve yourself, but you are in a twenty-person line-up to the only available restroom at your office. Your body says go while your mind says no.

Then at long last the moment comes where you are not only told but commanded to push, and low and behold you have virtually no energy to do so. You lay there after an exhausting time of not pushing, breathing like an obscene phone caller, moving up and down like an Olympic sit-up contestant, and enduring gut-wrenching contractions, all the while fending off your overly-anxious-to-please mate. All you really want to do is sleep and let the doctor go about getting it out of you anyway he deems possible — get a winch for all you care. But that plan is not on the agenda, and when you momentarily lay your head back on the pillow, the nurse gets nastier and begins yelling at you, "PUSH, PUSH." I believe birthing room nurses are mean for a reason. The mom-to-be gets so annoyed with them that she sits up ready for a fight and in preparation for shooting back some blustery retorts. She takes a deep breath and pushes out, all the while thinking, "Push this, sweetheart."

The first time I heard the term episiotomy, I thought it was the procedure they show on television when a person can't breathe normally and some medical wizard cuts a hole in their throat and inserts a straw. I was young and obviously uninformed. How was I to know that was a tracheotomy, and despite the similarity of cutting, there was virtually no other resemblance between the two procedures. An episiotomy is the truth behind the fact that a six- to ten-inch spherical object is not physically capable of squeezing through the open end of a balloon without some assistance from a sharp pair of scissors and an expert craftsperson. Of course sometimes the babies just can't wait for the doctor to open up his pencil case and take out his scissors, so they push through anyway, even though the physiological challenge still exists, the result being "Natural Tearing." What the heck is natural about that? Either way, this experience presents yet another problem — mending the damage, and reveals your doctor's skills in needlepoint. They say if the doctor is good everything will go back into its normal place and no one will ever be able to tell. I say, who the heck is going to be looking there anyway? If your mate has a sense of humour, now is not the appropriate time for him to wittily remark, "Make sure you stitch up all the right parts, Doc." While his humour may be appreciated by the hospital staff, it is not at all funny for the mom who is not only unable to view the procedure, but may be experiencing some anxiety about how and when the stitches will be removed. These experiences occur during a fairly normal, trouble-free birth. However, unfortunately problems can and do happen during birth.

In some cases, such as the birth of my first baby, the baby isn't coming out exactly how he is intended to, head first. If the doctor is able to catch this early enough he can rectify the situation with a little assistance from either suction or forceps. Both devices are used by attaching them to the baby's head, maneuvering the position of the head, then aiding in the pull-out. Usually the moms-to-be have little awareness of what is going on in this situation, and by either luck or well-thought-out planning, don't get an opportunity to see the tools of the trade and where they are inserted. However, eager dads-to-be can get a much regretted glimpse of the procedure, and will stand in awe as the tools are no sooner inserted than they are removed, clamped firmly on their intended target, a head. Oddly, most men cross their legs during the whole procedure and make dreadful grunting noises. Sometimes the doctor is unable to catch the baby before it turns completely, with the formidable result being a breech birth. Once again, my ignorance was bliss, and my only experiences of breech birth were the stories and pictures I had seen of calves breeching during birth. Imagine the horror. In fact, breech birth means the baby turns around just before delivery and decides to come out feet first. The greatest concern stems from the fear the baby will change his mind about coming out, opting to remain in the warmth and security of mom's tummy and defiantly stomping his feet down on either side of mom's pelvis just before exit. In some rare instances when the baby is not going to budge and mom is totally drained, there may be no choice but to perform a caesarean section, commonly abbreviated to C-section. This procedure requires the mom-to-be to endure surgery and consequently have the baby removed through an incision in the stomach. It may seem like a better alternative to the natural method of pushing, ripping, and stitching. However, that is simply not the case. Surgery is never a good option — the recovery period after this very invasive procedure is much longer and entails a great deal of healing and bed rest.

After all is said and done and the final push or pull takes place, the result of all that labour enters the picture in the form of a slimy, wrinkly, often purplish in colour human life form. The doctor may place the mass of flesh on mom's stomach and wisely exclaim, "It's a girl/boy." At first glance mom may think, *It's not very pretty, put it back,* then the overwhelming emotions of tenderness and love take over and suddenly the wrinkly little creature is the most beautiful child in the world. The cord will be cut by doctor or dad if he tends not to be squeamish and has a fairly steady hand, and I am talking about the doctor. Babe is then swathed in a warm blanket and handed over to mom. And this, folks, is life's imitation of the Cracker Jack surprise.

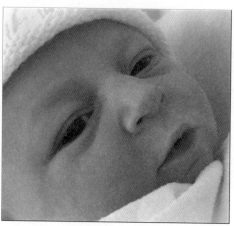

So much to be thankful for.
Welcome to the family, Charlotte.

Baby Care 101

Child birth, inclusive of the hours of labour, is mind blowing and body breaking, and although the mother's spirits are lifted high, her energy level takes a dive. All of the excitement, anticipation, frustration, and final relief take its toll and what the new mom really wants to do now is sleep for the next week. Nursing moms envision the use of duct tape to strap the feeding infant to the breast, therefore allowing it to nurse whenever it desires and likewise allowing her to sleep. Those who choose to bottle feed take the first few shifts, then hope for an overwhelming amount of baby cooers to willingly hold the bundle of joy for the feeding period, thus allowing the new mom some much deserved sleep. But alas, the world doesn't work that way. Nurses bestow upon the new mom a jam-packed curriculum of Baby Care 101. First time nursing moms are treated to an intrusive demonstration on how to milk the cow. A nurse takes the mom's unsuspecting breast into her hands, like clay to a potter, and applies a not so gentle massage in hopes of encouraging the flow of milk. The baby is then placed on the breast while mom awaits the natural occurrence of suckling to take place. All of which transpires on a very sore, very swollen, very tender breast.

Bottle feeders are handed a small bottle containing an ounce or two of formula and are instructed on how to feed the baby, including angle of projection, proper holding and handling, and when too much is too much and not enough is not enough.

After a short period of successful feeding, the next instruction involves the proper method of burping. The nurses are quick to point out that supporting the infant's head is the most important detail. Passing the lesson on burping is a hard task. Just the right amount of pressure has to be applied to the baby's back, usually in the form of rubbing or light patting, which must be continued non-stop until the babe finally releases a tiny almost imperceptible sound which resembles that of a distant frog croak. The key is to stay awake for the monumental event; fervent nurses can be very nasty when they wake you up. After the babe is fed and burped, he can be carefully swathed in a baby blanket and placed in the hospital bassinet. Swathing, however, is not limited to carelessly wrapping the blanket around the child. Instead the nurse will provide you with a blow by blow account of how to properly wrap the baby up. If you failed map folding in social studies class, you could be in for a long haul. After twenty minutes of neatly gathering, precisely folding, and carefully tucking, you are ready to place the cocoon into the bassinet, and maybe settle down for a nap.

But class isn't over yet. The nurse informs you it is time for your Sitz bath lesson, a word unfamiliar and not overly charming. A quick tour of the washroom reveals a style of basin you have never seen before. Low to the ground and fairly large, it resembles something between a very large urinal and an overgrown toilet bowl, but it's in the shower area. When the nurse turns on the water you are astounded to see a swirling tidal pool that is intended for you to sit in. If you are unlucky and have Nurse Ratchet, she may want you to try your hand, not literally speaking, at it so she can ensure you are using it correctly. Fortunately I had a nurse with plenty of discretion and she opted for me to experience the delight on my own.

> **CAUTION**
>
> When you do finally take the plunge and use the Sitz bath, the sucking noise may cause you some concern. But rest assured, once you get over your fear of having your derriere sucked into the drain and being stuck there until you are rescued by some twenty-year-old good-looking, hard-bodied intern, you will actually enjoy your time in the Sitz bath, and may even consider having your husband install one in your own home.

After your facility tour, you will finally get some rest, only to be awakened in what seems like five minutes, by a nurse requesting you to void. If the term is unfamiliar, you are not alone. I was introduced to the term at 2:30 in the morning after about one hour of deep slumber when a nurse, who failed bedside manner training, burst into my room, turned on the light, and told me I had to void. Unsure of what she was referring to, I politely declined, indicating I didn't need any drugs and was sleeping fine. The response was none too sympathetic as I was abruptly told I needed to get up and go the bathroom. I tried to convince her that I didn't, but she was not about to take no for an answer. She with her 110 pound frame came over and began hoisting me out of bed, half dragging me towards the bathroom. She plopped me down on the toilet and told me to try to void. There was that word again, and if it was urinating she wanted, I was never one to pee on demand. Despite my every effort, I just couldn't muster up any fluids, and before I knew what was happening, I began to pass out. My last recollection of the evening was me thrusting my head backwards, hitting the wall behind the toilet and subsequently knocking myself out cold. I came to in the arms of one of those twenty-year-old, good-looking, hard-bodied aides as he placed me back into my bed. I was told the next morning by my favourite nurse that I had lost too much blood and actually had a seizure.

The second day of your hospital stay involves a lesson on baby bathing, and is usually attended by both parents. You are put through a detailed course on how to properly and carefully bathe your newborn, after which you will no doubt feel like the most ignorant parent on earth. Under tight supervision, you will be requested to bathe your baby in the same step by step manner that was just demonstrated on a plastic, rather pathetic looking, but extremely sanitized doll. The entire procedure takes well over an hour, and at this point you begin to feel a bit overwhelmed at the amount of time every little bit of care is going to take, and anxiously wonder if you will be able to do everything you need to do in twenty-four hours of a day.

If you bring a baby boy into the world, you may be faced with another life-altering decision — whether to circumcise or not. Both factions are more than adequately represented by coalitions whose top priority is to convince the new parents of the benefits of their view and the horrifying disadvantages of the other side's view. Either way, the parent is left feeling like a wrong choice could be the deciding factor in the mental and physical well-being of this boy for the rest of his life. If we circumcise now, he will undergo excruciating pain for a total of thirty-five seconds, but has less chance of infection at a later age. If we do not circumcise now, he is spared a painful experience now, but may suffer at the cruel teasing of other boys later. The decision should be agreed upon by both parents and should reflect the best interests of the child, no one else.

If childbirth was natural and the mother was spared the atrocities of having her stomach cut wide open, having the baby plucked from her now exposed belly and then being stitched from one end of her to the other, otherwise known as a C-Section, fondly named a "never-come-near-me-again" section, then her hospital stay could be as short as one day. C-section moms are admitted for a longer stay to promote healing and because lifting anything heavier than a John Grisham novel could rip her stitches and result in an ugly infection.

Thanks in part to the rising cost of health care, healthy moms and babes are whisked off home with a box filled with flower arrangements and cards, an uneasy sensation in the pit of mom's stomach, and a suitcase full of reading material and videotapes on subjects ranging from post-natal depression to sex after childbirth. (Note: the latter is not recommended for at least six weeks, but is the only date your husband has no problem remembering.)

Other reading material titles may resemble the following:
Nursing like a Pro for Mommies on the Go,
First There Were Two, Now There is Me,
Introducing Rover to the New Addition,
The Gentle Art of Burping, Music to My Ears,
Daddies are Important Too,
Au Naturale is Best, How to Make Your Own Baby Food,
Baby's First Everything, (because let's face it, once they have done it, it's no longer the first) and much more interesting yet oddly confusing information on rearing a child.

Babes in Blankets and Little Knitted Toques
Welcome home baby, now meet the rest of your family

Arriving home can bring about an array of mixed emotions. If the joyful event is celebrated with a houseful of warm well-wishers it can be

Blanketed bliss.

bewildering for the mom who walks like she is balancing a fifteen pound frozen turkey between her legs. While the thoughtfulness is appreciated, the exertion of child-birth leaves a woman feeling ex-hausted and somewhat emotionally drained. All she really wants is the comfort of her own bed with the warmth of her newborn's head nes-tled into her neck, a cup of soothing tea, and maybe even some aromatic candles strategically placed around her room. However, she is more likely going to be greeted by a gauntlet of hugs, sounds of baby cooing and clinking dishes, the smell of casseroles, desserts, an urn of coffee, and a bed that is cluttered with pastel-coloured home knit sweaters, packages of diapers, and an array of velveteen sleepers. Then after what seems like hours the well-wishers will head home taking one final gaze and gently placing a kiss on baby and mom alike. Despite the relief the peace and quiet brings, the house will seem different. The realization sets in that you are no longer alone yet oddly quite lonely, and for brand new parents the feeling can be overwhelming. This is the beginning of a new life, and its success is all up to you.

The days to follow will be filled with ogling family and friends, their kindness and well wishes accompanied by a slew of warm, cozy, cutesy little outfits; soft, cuddly, adorable little toys; and knitted, crocheted, hand-sewn little collectibles. At this point the baby is introduced to the rest of her heritage, family members who move in for such a tight close-up the baby begins to think she is related to the likes of the fun house mirror people. The same people that sit around the Christmas dinner table debating the capabilities or lack of them of the government sud-denly turn into baby-talking buffoons leaning over the unsuspecting, tiny newborn, making noises otherwise considered as reason for committal. The baby's first impression of her extended family consists of creatures with giant cheeks, blown-out eyeballs, and fish lips moving in and out towards her with a limited vocabulary of "googoo gaagaa, youuuu cutesy wittle booboo, sooooo tweet and poopoo, yumyum, yumyumyum, tootsie tootsie a boobooboobooboo, we wuv oo yes we doo we just wuv oo to det." Unfortunately, as the child grows she comes to learn these seemingly unintelligent, rather frightening looking ogres are actually her relatives. And so begins the expensive therapy.

With the sincere congratulations comes another bout of "in my opinions." Parents, especially new ones, should be prepared to endure an all new "how to, when I was, we did it, you should" campaign. If you thought everyone had an opinion on pregnancy, just wait, because the advice on baby care and subsequent child rearing is endless. Suddenly your thirty-eight-year-old single brother, who can't even commit to a brand of shampoo, is now the expert on raising children. He will offer bizarre rituals for discipline including some time in the military, "Something every kid could use so they learn to respect their elders," to advice on how to succeed, a topic a single, thirty-eight-year-old who still lives in the basement suite of your parent's house is likely to have no experience with. Eventually he will boil it down to one hardened tip: "Don't ever take the kid to a public place, 'cause they'll just disturb all the people who don't have kids, and that's just plain rude."

Once Auntie Augustine is finished kissing cheeks, cooing, rocking the babe back and forth on her hip, humming German lullabies, and making chirping noises with her tongue, she will no doubt begin offering a novel of advice she assures you will guarantee lifelong health, happiness, and of course a well behaved baby, concluding with an astonishing axiom: "Babies will take advantage of you if you let them so let them cry, don't always pick them up, and whatever you do use a stern voice when you talk to them . . . . Ithn't tat wight o wittle cutesy baboosky."

Of course, your own mother will offer many hints at caring for and raising this child despite her promise to let you do it your way and learn for yourself. The urge is just too tempting.

She might say something like: If I was you, but of course I'm not . . .

1. **Always dress the baby gender appropriate** or later in life she will be confused. Do babies really know the difference between pink, blue, yellow, and green? Why not dress them in black and white — that way they are not only gender friendly, but politically correct as well.

2. **Hold the head, hold the head.** I realize this is well-intended advice, but frankly, as new parents you aren't allowed to even handle the baby until you have had Baby Care 101 at the hospital, which makes no less than 635 references to the importance of supporting the head. I have yet to see a parent

pick a baby up by the feet and carry him around like some gorilla.

3. **Don't take the baby out in public** for at least three months; you don't want him to get sick. I can't imagine any proud new parents not wanting to show off the results of their hard work in the first week, let alone the first three months. Besides, mom really needs to get out of the house. Fresh air is not only healthy but recommended, and for the most part the baby has better immunities than the majority of the family that smothers him with germ-infested kisses.

4. **Put honey or corn syrup on baby's soother** to help lull him to sleep. Actually, this practice is not recommended due to the high content of sugar. There are wonderful products on the market such as gripe water which contains a harmless amount of alcohol and helps to sooth the baby's stomach. And if all else fails and the baby won't settle, mom and dad could mix a couple ounces of gripe water with some soda and lull themselves to sleep.

5. **Breast is best:** the baby will bond better with mom and the natural milk is so much healthier for him. Some mothers are so adamant about this issue that they will try to assist the new mom. Get your hands off my boob, this is definitely a personal choice. Bonding does not mean bound to, babies will bond with either parent if given nurturing, care, and most importantly, love. In my opinion the breast is not a symbol of ultimate motherhood. If that were the case then there would be giant breast statues, monuments, even floats in the Macey's Parade.

Oh What Lovely Breasts You Have

Prior to my days of motherhood, I can remember sitting beside mothers who joyously nursed their babies in less than private places. It was these experiences that formed my earlier opinion that breast feeding just wasn't my cup of tea. In fact, the following story is what made my decision to keep my mammary glands tucked safely inside final.

In one of my fortunate occasions to witness the natural phenomena of a nursing mother, I found myself awkwardly unsure of where I should look. There were twenty-seven empty chairs in the dentist's waiting room, and she sat right beside me. I mean here we were sitting in a public waiting room: me, earth mother, and a receptionist who had the good fortune to be behind a Plexi-glass enclosure. The room was unbearably silent, except, of course, for the unnerving sucking noises accompanied by the occasional sigh, which came from mother and child alike. I happily found escape in the magazine I picked up from the table. I was actually reading an article on Canadian legislation when the slurping rhythm was broken by a voice. "Sure is unusual to be this slow in here."

Suddenly I was thrust into a whirlwind of anxiety, the same anxiety I face when approached by a naked woman in the change room who wants to strike up a meaningful conversation. Renowned for my belief in full eye contact when speaking to another person, I was faced with a choice to just rudely nod and continue reading or politely turn and reply. I turned my head slightly and looked at the youthful face of the mother, then strained my eyes to maintain visual contact above the shoulders. "Yes, it must be a bad day for . . ." Before I could finish my reply the mother winced and yelled out in pain.

"Ow, you little monkey, you aren't supposed to bite mommy."

It was at that point that I quickly glanced down and was aghast at the site before my eyes. This was no one-month-old suckling from the breast of its mother, this child appeared to be at the very least twenty months old. Then it dawned on me, they have teeth at that age. This was no longer a case of a toothless baby calf, this woman had a human piranha hanging off her chest, and she had the teeth marks to prove it. She yanked the child's head away from her now tender breast and began massaging herself. I became transfixed in disbelief and suddenly heard what I thought was my voice but hoped wasn't: "Boy, that's gotta hurt."

Boy, that's gotta hurt. What kind of comment was that. After all, we weren't talking about someone hitting themselves on the thumb with a hammer, this woman's child just bit her breast. The very sensation had me putting my own arms across my chest for fear the hungry little barbarian might think he was in a buffet line. The mother looked at me and snorted a laugh. Obviously aware of my discomfort, she made a statement that has stayed with me forever: "Oh, it's really not that bad. Aside from the odd biting it is quite an arousing sensation."

Eating chocolate is arousing, watching the pro rodeo is arousing, bubble baths are arousing, but having some sharp-toothed twenty-five pound child gnawing on the tender skin of your normally unexposed nipple, in my mind was far from arousing. The dental hygienist finally appeared and called my name. I couldn't get into the dentist's chair fast enough. Besides, you never know, according to some people's standards, a drilling might be arousing.

Despite some stinging comments from "anti-bottleists," I made my declaration and stuck to my guns. I just could never be comfortable with a small human being attached to my chest like a suction cup, making the same slurping noises that had come to irritate me at the breakfast table. It was bad enough standing in front of a mirror each month and squeezing my breasts, but the thought of the same sensation happening ten times daily for the next few years was enough for me to invest in case lots of Playtex plastic bottle liners. My husband didn't show signs of disapproval, but I knew he had read and heard a multitude of stories about the sexual appeal of a nursing mother, so I promised to take him to the local sidewalk cafe where he could view a variety of earth mothers in their prime of sensuality. Through two births I have steadfastly maintained my grounds; if squeezing into a fitness bra causes me grief, then enduring six pounds of vacuum pressure on my breast was liable to put me into therapy.

Twenty-four Bottles and a Dozen Diapers

The memories are still vivid — a counter top covered with upside-down plastic bottles, freshly sterilized and waiting to be filled with formula. I was not the breast-feeding type, as you may have gathered already — the very thought of an infant dangling from my chest left me feeling queasy at best. Not to mention, I never could envision myself sitting in a shoe store with a flannel blanket draped over my shoulder and suckling noises coming from beneath. I do profess to be a woman of the '90s, but even I have my limits. Ah, but this was quality time for John and myself. The little one was tucked into his crib snoring off his last feeding, so we could talk about our day while bent over a sink of numbing hot water diligently scrubbing little nipples. No, it wasn't foreplay either; we surely had learned our lesson. The washing was the easy part; the difficult part which I cleverly appointed to my dearly beloved was stuffing the plastic bags into the bottles. Manufacturers of baby supplies really do need to spend more time with their products. You see, the art of stuffing the bottles was somewhat similar to stuffing Kleenex back into the box; it just never fits the right way. Similar experiences are encountered when trying to dress an infant child, but that will be covered later. Now for those of you foolish enough to have your family close together in age, you may find yourself in a similar predicament as my husband and I. About four months and a day after my son's birth, we were lucky enough to steal another magical moment of bliss. Did I say lucky? Did I say bliss? At any rate thirteen months and one day after our son was born, our angelic daughter was born. This created quite a whole new situation. Now instead of being faced with twelve bottles to wash and sterilize, we doubled our capacity. Suffice it to say that we spent the better part of our evenings at the kitchen sink, and our weekly grocery bill now included two cases or formula, four bags of disposable diapers, and oh yes, the odd box of prophylactics.

We began our quest with good intentions of saving the environment by using cloth diapers. The thought was wonderful, the reality a whole different ball game. Washing twenty-eight to thirty cloth diapers a week was slightly bearable, but facing forty-eight to sixty urine and now poop-stained cotton diapers was mind numbing. So we caved and began purchasing disposable diapers, basing our decision on the product packaging promises of being able to hold up to thirty pounds — it was a lot of poop — but it would save on waste. Of course, as reformed disposable diaper users we soon discovered the reality behind the product packaging promises; after all, thirty pounds of poop was a lot of weight to carry. Changing diapers was never really going to be my forte, even despite the already experienced mom's assurance that when it was your own child's, it didn't bother you as much. (Another useless piece of advice.) The beginning was doable — I mean, after all, how much can a little baby's urine really smell? Well, as long as they fed on formula for the duration of diaper town it wouldn't be so bad, but at some point, usually around four months, their little bellies crave more and pabulum is introduced.

You are now in for a not-so-pleasant surprise at the far end, because what somewhat resembles weak cream of wheat going in looks more like a bad can of pumpkin pie mix coming out. Then as solids are introduced to the diet, a whole new collection of undesirable food by-products begin presenting themselves in the diapers. The makers of baby food must test their products on rats and monkeys, because what person in their right mind would not be able to anticipate that the by-product of mashed peas would be even less visually appealing. But the visual aspect was only the tip of the iceberg — the odour; well, let's just say our house was rid of any pest problems. To this day it amazes me how one grunt from a ten-month-old baby can clear a room of people and animals alike. Even the dog knows enough to make headway; after all, he could be blamed for this onset of unwelcome fragrance. All that is left are the parents, the only people in the world who still love the baby even after the release of mount effluvium. Small grunts are usually accompanied by a sound similar to wet porridge squeezing between toes, while larger and longer grunts are usually accompanied by a sound similar to a rock hitting a plastic bag filled with cotton batting. The wiser parent will quickly volunteer for the latter of the two, thus fulfilling their appointed rotation — after all, lumps are much easier to clean up than puddles. Handy wipes are named so for a reason. They are cleverly made with a baby powder fragrance which if used rapidly can help to override the other less fragrant smells now wafting from your angel's backside. They contain just enough alcohol to leave the surface squeaky clean, and just enough moisture to impede the onset of diaper rash, and after they have completed their duty, they can be easily disposed of inside the offending diaper. This makes them the second best invention of the century. The first place winner goes to disposable diapers.

Hats off to the ingenious mind that developed the now ninety percent environmentally friendly disposable diaper.

Rising to the Occasion

Whoever coined another not so useful phrase, "planned parenting," did so from the isolation of an institution. There is very little planned about parenting. Like the 'un-expectance' of expecting, the only planned part of parenting is the Friday night you penciled in on your calendar approximately ten months before the blessed event. Life is now different, changed, not usual. The new existence that is hanging out in the now yellow-painted, once an office area has brought whole new meaning to your life/lives. Those words fondly told to you by all of your parental friends will now hit home, and hit home hard, "Your life will never be the same, and you are kidding yourself if you think it will." You can remember laughing at their words of wisdom and brushing them off with the now unspeakable reprisal, "Nah, it won't. We will simply go on as we always have and enjoy everything we always did; we'll just have someone else to enjoy it with." The latter part of which is true, but enjoying all of those simple freedoms you had before the introduction of the new existence is simply not simple any more. Sleeping in until noon on your days off, rolling over, fooling around, then going back to sleep are things of the past; rising at all hours of the night for feedings, crying, and checking on breathing are now a part of the future. Partying into oblivion on a Saturday night and waking with a killer hangover on Sunday is no longer an option when you realize you're responsible for another's tiny yet even more meaningful existence. Staying up all night and dancing to the rhythms of jazz is replaced with sitting up all night and rocking to the rhythms of tiny breaths. Worrying about which is more important — a leather interior or an awesome sound system — is fruitless when charged with worrying about Sudden Infant Death Syndrome and providing for someone else for the next twenty-odd years. And as this new existence grows, so too will you, and you will realize that life is not usual, it is different, it has changed. But that's okay, because there is no challenge in standing still. Plenty of rewards can be discovered when moving ahead.

CHAPTER TWO

Maybe the Dingo Ate Your Baby

One Small Step for Babykind: Grab the Video Camera, the Baby Just Smiled . . .

By some mysterious and frustrating coincidence, the video camera is never where is should be when it should be, and when you do finally find it and start to record, that irritating little icon of a battery begins to flash. So you frantically find and untangle all the cords and plug in the machine and once again begin recording only to discover there is either no tape in the machine or only twelve and a half seconds left. The result is that that precious first moment which comes only once just passed without being recorded for posterity, or grandparents, or blackmail later when the child is much older and experiencing another milestone, such as a wedding. Even more sadly, the parents often miss the momentous first occasion as they busily try to prepare an array of recording devices. Firsts are named so appropriately; they only happen once, unless you are an otherwise sneaky or should I say industrious parent who records the event the second or third or fourth time, but passes it off as the first.

Some not so grand scale firsts include: burping, grunting, and some may say smiling which is often mistaken for gas. All are fair game, however, for eager parents and a video camera. Unfortunately, not all relatives and friends share the same exuberance for these minor events. So a word of advice — save the viewing debuts for the more momentous occasions.

The first major first is usually crawling. The ages will differ, but babies begin to see the world as a big playground just waiting to be discovered and learn quickly that waiting for some tall person to move them around like a chess piece is not only time-consuming but restricting. So they roll onto their chubby little bellies and take their first movement towards independence. Some babies prefer a method referred to as combat crawling, which entails dragging their overextended bellies along the floor using their forearms and shins, similar to a soldier skulking through enemy grounds. Other babies choose the inch-worm method, a painstaking procedure involving pushing their butt into the air causing a natural arch in the stomach, then dragging their knees up to their elbows and ultimately inching their way across the floor. Still others resort to imitation and manage to get onto all fours, just like Rover, then gallop madly across the floor. The latter is the speediest, but the hardest on the knees of all those adorable toddler outfits, and if parents insist on dressing little gals in cutesy dresses, it can be the cause of some disastrous collisions of floor meets nose. Crawling brings with it a new-found sense of freedom for baby, but also carries with it a whole gamut of hazards for baby and parent alike. Suddenly that shiny glass bowl filled with smelly flowers and stuff is on the hit list of things baby must consume. Once seemingly harmless electrical outlets become like a baby's nostril, somewhere to stick a finger.

The commencement of crawling can also be a frightening experience for the family's beloved, once King of the Carpet, pet. With little to no warning, Junior invades Rover's territory and relentlessly follows the poor creature everywhere, including the bizarre ritual of eating out of Rover's dish. Before the imitation extends to the cat's litter box, parents wisely assign the pet a new and private eating and hiding place, thus saving themselves the agony of listening to that one friend everyone has who is a self-proclaimed animal activist and suggests that the assistance of an animal therapist may be necessary. Crawling, otherwise referred to as Rug Rage, signifies a whole new dimension in the parenting process. At first parents welcome the new-found skill, thankful that baby is progressing and showing signs of increased motor skills and to some degree critical thinking skills. But after rearranging the entire decor of the house, tending to the psychological needs of the pet, mending torn clothes, and building elaborate mazes within the confines of the house, the novelty soon wears off and parents find themselves daydreaming about the days of carrying a cuddly baby around snuggled safely to their neck.

The theory of natural procession would suggest walking would be the next big "first." However, most babies stay carpet bound for a few months, affording them time to discover other skills such as talking. Baby's first words are a huge event which turns reasonable parents into unbelievable lunatics. No matter what the word is, the parents will argue white is black that it was Mama or Dada. The first word could be "voracious," but to every parent it sounds like Dada or Mama. So once again mad dashes are made for the video camera; this moment must be recorded and therefore provide the necessary proof required to win the case of "Which word was it?" While mom and dad push playback over and over, baby is forming full sentences trying to explain to Rover the physical components of a doggy doody. Baby's vocabulary will likely extend beyond the confines of "mine," "no," "up," "down," and other one syllable commands to some more unfortunate imitations.

Walking is likely to be the next big first as babies learn that the real use for all that fancy furniture is to haul their little butts up off the floor onto their not-so-sturdy feet. Like Bambi on ice, these moments are prize-winning and should be shot on video. Several attempts will be made to get baby mobile on two feet, some of which may result in scrapes, bruises, cuts, and other undesirable sufferings of pending success, but success almost always follows determination, and soon baby will be vertical and ready to take on the world or anything in his path. It is likely the cat will stay in hiding for yet another eighteen months or so.

Other firsts are not as suited for video due to the sensitive and possibly offensive nature of the subject matter: baby's first poop, baby's first needle, baby's first hair cut, baby's first tooth, baby's first cold, and so on. As babies grow into toddlers, there will be plenty more opportunities for video moments, as referred to in Chapter Three.

Toddlerhood

On your mark, get set . . .

The sleepless nights have subsided and none too soon, because the next phase of child rearing, which I like to refer to as Toddlerhood, is about to bring a whole new meaning to the hours between 7 a.m. and 7:30 p.m., give or take half an hour. You see, once the child is about twenty-four months old, he grows out of that cute baby stage and zeros in on the terrible twos, the stage of discovery. Now that he is capable of upright travel, there is a whole new dimension to access. Tiny fingers find their way to all sorts of trouble.

He awakes with a vengeance, totally rested and ready to roar. First comes the foreboding sound of thirty-five pounds of flesh jumping up and down on a crib mattress, which is quickly followed by the chanting of "up, up, up." Yes, mommy's up now and she is coming, just let her zone back into reality. A smell inspection indicates that the child has more reasons than just playing to want to get out of the crib. A quick change of diaper and then it is off to the kitchen for another round of cheerio checkers. Few two-year-olds are content with simply eating the cheerios; it is far more interesting to move them around the table. It is now plain to see why manufacturers put holes in cheerios; they are, after all, just the right size for the index finger of a two year old. Feeding time leads to dressing time; smart mothers catch on quick and realize that reversing the two phases is fruitless. The dresser and closet reveal a wardrobe designed by the creator of the mini-me concept. There are a variety of miniature t-shirts with matching tear-away pants, all purchased by overzealous grandparents who have nothing better to do with fifty dollars than to dress their cherished grandchild in the latest fashions. If you are lucky enough to have a girl child, you're likely facing a closet full of the pinkest, frilliest, most exquisite replicas of doll dresses you can possibly imagine, once again the generous gifts of proud grandparents. But junior isn't about to embark on a night at the opera, he is simply getting dressed for a normal day, most of which will be filled with a mess of trouble. On goes the well-worn teddy bear t-shirt, a pair of runt size blue jeans, and white socks.

Much to be Discussed or Discussed too Much

I need to digress here on a very important issue. Why is it that the most frequently manufactured colour of socks for children is white? Are the sock companies in cahoots with the bleach manufacturers? Do sock companies test their products on fish? I have yet to get any reasonable answers to these questions; I think there is some deep spiritual meaning to white socks. I have learned, however, that soaking and scrubbing socks is more than just a waste of time, it's pointless. So instead, let the toddler wear the socks out into the muddiest place you can find, and instantly you have blackish, brown socks.

Oddly enough, yet not without merit, many toddler outfits come adorned with stripes running down the seams, and if you are not sure why, the answer will come to light as soon as the little one is dressed for the day and the race is on. Lift him from the dressing table or bed and note that his little feet are already in a scurry of motion. It's as though someone wound him up and now he is ready for action. Suddenly your house turns into a two-and-a-half-foot-high danger zone. Anything within that reach is considered fair play; take note that the purchase of certain child-proofing gadgets is a must. Electrical outlets can be adorned with an array of colourful plug covers. However, the experts suggest sticking to plain white or a colour that will blend with your walls, reasoning that anything too colourful will simply attract the little one's attention. Suddenly the beautiful becomes the breakable, and all of those cherished knick-knacks get stored away or relocated to higher elevations. Toddlers, like pack rats, will seek out bright shiny objects; however, unlike the furry long-tailed rodents who simply steal and hide the objects, toddlers are on a "seek and destroy" mission. I am convinced that toddlers are programmed by the producers of Mission Impossible.

"Your mission today, Bradley, is to retrieve that pretty crystal bowl handed down for three generations. You will begin the mission by locating it when no one is looking then twirl it around the table several times, grab it, and run like the dickens. If you make it to safety, you should test the authenticity of the bowl by clanging on it with your toy drumsticks. If the bowl holds up, then it is the object of the enemy and ultimately must be destroyed. Remember, Bradley, your mission is top secret; if at any time your identity is discovered, you are instructed to put on the cutest, sweetest, most innocent face you can. At no costs should you allow the enemy (mom and dad) to know your true intentions with the bowl. Good luck. (This message will self destruct so mom and dad can never decipher the code.)"

Busted.

Inspector Gadget, Eat your Heart Out

Like disappearing socks, the fascination with bright bobbles is a mystery to be sure.

You have graduated into parenthood when your closets, cupboards, family room, kitchen, and other highly visible areas are lined with an array of plastic storage containers, toys, neon-coloured fake fur, and pint-size chairs bearing life-size pictures of carton characters. The beautiful and likewise expensive oriental area rugs have been rolled up and placed away in storage awaiting the day when grape juice stains are no longer a possibility. Glamorous glass top coffee tables become a dream and are more than likely substituted with soft cornered, inexpensive alternatives. Valuable, irreplaceable heirlooms are tucked away in a safe place not only out of reach, but unfortunately also out of sight. Pristine painted walls become the casualty of Handprint Shadowing, a new yet not so desirable decorating technique. Oak, cherry, maple, pine, the trim adorning your beautiful home, will now be subjected to chipping, painting, carving, and other tests to the strength of their natural endurance.

Your once stylish home, which could have been page forty-seven of Your Stylish Home Magazine, has suddenly taken on a remarkable resemblance to page twenty-eight of the Plasticworld home party order book. Plastic storage containers can be seen in almost every corner of your home. I must admit though, the manufacturers of these handy units are becoming more creative and are making them in a variety of neon colours and sizes. Unfortunately they still clash with Early Americana or Contemporary Sleek.

If you live in a house with more than one storey, then the purchase of a gate of some sort is necessary to avoid the tragedy of falling down flights of stairs. I am in no way poking fun at the seriousness this particular danger can inflict, but these gates, as wonderful an invention as they are, do cause some grief to the parents. To begin with, affixing them in the proper manner between the supporting structures at either side of a staircase can be somewhat challenging, especially if one of the sides happens to be a railing. That's when dad gets excited. The very thought of being able to use any type of high-powered electrical tool will send him into a state of delirium. (For more on this topic see Chapter Five.) Suddenly the once beautiful oak railing is trimmed with an assortment of screws, bolts, chains, and metal objects. All of this to ensure the gate is securely in place. However, the misery does not end there, because more often than not moms and dads forget they have secured the staircase with the gate and in a fit of hurry will go tumbling over the gate, bounce down the stairs, land ass-over-teakettle at the bottom, to find themselves staring up at the gate that remains firmly in place, attached by an amass of hardware capable of warding off even the most persistent burglar.

Hints from the Pen

I am convinced playpens were invented by a frustrated parent who, despite her most concentrated effort, was unable to complete a task that prior to the child took only five minutes. Playpens, or "Mini-Penitentiaries," are a household must when there are small, curious people around. When the telephone rings send them to the Pen, when supper needs to be made send them to the Pen, when the house needs cleaning send them to the Pen, when you want to steal a few minutes to yourself send them to the Pen. The Pen is useful in other surroundings besides the home, and now they are constructed so they can be folded into small, light packages and easily transported in the trunk of a vehicle. However, they do require a map-folding course in order to successfully fit them into the tote bags that accompany them, and although the manufacturers ensured that the construction was extremely child safe, unfortunately there was little consideration for adult putting up and taking down. The labels should read: *Caution, some pinching may occur during take-down.*

For starters, make sure the Pen is an approved apparatus free of loose screws or slivered wood, with rungs close enough to prevent a small head squeezing between them, and that are not loose or wobbly. Place only soft toys inside the Pen, which will guarantee the avoidance of marks on walls, furniture, and foreheads when the toys get tossed by the inmate. If placing more than one inmate in the Pen, remove all objects that can be used as weapons. Never leave an inmate unattended for any length of time.

Along with this marvelous invention came some other very useful inventions. Strollers or carriages have been around for ages. However, in recent years we have seen the introduction of the newly approved, smaller, safer, cleaner, and more convenient prototype. After all, strapping one of those carriages with thirty-inch tires to the top of your two-door sports car was never an appealing concept. Similar to the Pen, the new strollers are designed to fold up in one easy step and be placed in the back of any size economy car. They no longer weigh more than a small horse and are constructed of sturdy, easily cleaned plastic. Almost every part of them can be taken off and put into the washing machine, which considering the amount of food consumed inside of a stroller, is a godsend. They come in a variety of colours and patterns and are available in compact, mid-sized, family, and multi-passenger. All come with the standard package, which includes cloth seats, seat belts, four tires, and brakes. However, the luxury units come equipped with anti-lock braking systems, safety belts that include shoulder, waist, arm and hip straps, reversible plush seating, leather interior, convenient parcel storage, side console for bottles, rattles, toys, blankets, etc., advanced suspension, extra wide all-weather tires, onboard stereo, four-flap air conditioning, sunroof, and of course, five position reclining driver's seat. These, however, may cost more than your economy car. Any stroller is only as good as the seat belts, and unless adjusted as per the ten page instruction sheet, can be easily defeated by an ingenious little tot when the stroller is in a stationary position. It may require two days of reading and several dry runs with a lifelike doll, but it is well worth the effort to know how to properly strap the tot into the stroller.

Car seats are the wisest and most imperative gadget when a new baby comes on board, the importance of which is so vital that several Federal governments felt it necessary to make their (proper) use mandatory by law. And as a parent, I could not agree more. Unfortunately, it doesn't negate the fact that car seat usage and installation is, to say the least, challenging. In our country the car seat must be available at the hospital the day the baby is due to go home, otherwise discharge may be postponed. As a result, parents are faced with the puzzling task of putting an average eight pound, wiggly, limp-headed baby into a contraption which resembles an inverted forty-pound turkey roaster. Stuffing the seat with sheep-skinned, fleece-lined, thick blankets does help to buffer a fraction of the unused area, but if the baby is born in mid-August, excessive sweating could result in the loss of a much required extra ounce or two. Tipping the car seat backwards while placing the infant in and subsequently strapping him to the contraption is also a viable option, but be prepared to have the tiny package scrunch down into a wrinkly ball of flesh with a bobbing head attached, resembling those odd-looking toy dogs people place in the back windows of their vehicles. As you strap baby into the car seat you need to be aware of the placement of all limbs, including your own. Many a new parent has somehow managed to strap her own arm into the car seat. Until one becomes proficient with strapping in the babe, it may be necessary to use a "two person tag team" method. Once baby is snugly in place, the next challenge begins, installation into the vehicle itself. In theory, that is with reference to the ten page manual parents are instructed to read before departure from the hospital, installation is simple and limited to the right way according to the age and weight of the child, type of seat, and location in the vehicle. Infants and light-weights face the rear, toddlers face the front, anyone under the age of twelve takes a back seat, and if the vehicle is equipped with an air bag, and I am not referring to a meddling relative, than children always ride in the back. The latter becomes a handy excuse for settling the "I get the front seat" battle which inevitably occurs between children at a later age. (See Sibling Warfare in Chapter Three for further details.) All that theory will mean nothing once you actually try to put the car seat into the vehicle. Suddenly you will find straps you never knew existed in your vehicle and the slots that allegedly correspond to these straps are never where the diagram indicates. After a frustrating twenty minutes or so, you stand back and gaze at the finished product — a baby strapped to a plastic roaster which in turn is strapped into the back seat of your leather interior luxury vehicle like a pack strapped to a mule headed down a mountain trail. There are so many straps weaving in and out it looks like an army SEALS parachute. But rest assured junior is going nowhere. The designated hospital official will likely give a final inspection, and if you are lucky and pass, you will be on your way. Despite hard-working efforts and the final inspection to ensure the car seat is secure, both parents will still glance back at the baby no less than forty-eight times each during the trip home. In some instances (most commonly the first baby) there may even be up to six unscheduled stops in a four kilometre radius to check on the tightly-strapped baby.

> **Tip:**
> While it may appear unsightly in your once hip-looking vehicle, the best piece of advice I can offer is to leave the car seat in place during the entire growing process and simply unstrap the child. The small indentations left in your vehicle's upholstery are nothing compared to the saving of time, backache, and frustration.

Baby Beware

Household cleaners, medicines, and other toxic chemicals have been huge concerns for parents for years, once again a matter not to be taken lightly. Parents will be amazed at how many of these items are actually stored in their house of which they are totally unaware until charged with the duty of finding them and rerouting them to a safer location. For example, an SOS pad looks like a huge blue marshmallow to a three year old, and cough drops take on an uncanny resemblance to candy. The tops of dish soap bottles look somewhat like nipples to the baby and the unfortunate result of suckling on them can cause bubbles to appear in the strangest of places. There are other hidden dangers that rear their ugly heads, such as the high alcohol content of mouthwash or pure vanilla, the sweet odour of windshield wiper fluid which is deadly when ingested, the extremely high potency of vitamin pills, and the frightening results of combining what may otherwise be harmless substances such as ammonia and other household cleaners, all of which are deadly. Products have been invented in order to assist parents in assuring a safe living environment for children, such as cupboard locking mechanisms, child-proof caps, spill-resistant bottles, and many others.

I would like to offer some advice when using cupboard locking mechanisms. To begin with, you may wish to store personal necessities in a place other than these cupboards; nothing spoils the moment more than trying to yank off a plastic locking device while standing naked in a dark bathroom during a rare heat of the moment. And as children grow, don't rely entirely on locking mechanisms; while they may be remarkably efficient at baffling an impatient adult, they somehow can be easily defeated by a curious toddler. I am not sure if it is the food they eat, the air they breathe, or the coded information available to them on Sesame Street, but toddlers these days have much more advanced problem-solving skills than what I remember as a child. We were delighted if we could successfully hammer the round peg through the round hole, or place all the colourful plastic rings on their holder, while the toddlers of today aren't content until they can re-program the DVD player.

Besides these dangers, there are the other household items that can and have caused parents the despair of injury and worse, the pain of death. I feel it my duty as a concerned parent to provide you with a list of some of these cleverly disguised monsters.

Hidden Hazards of the Home
1. **Strings from window blinds** can cause death by strangulation.
   Solution: Tie the strings into knots and shorten their length so they can't wrap around a little person's neck.
2. **Cupboard doors** not only open to some deadly items, but can also cause painful finger slamming.
   Solution: Purchase plastic sliding locks which attach to the pulls on the cupboard and render them inoperable by little people.
3. **Tipping stoves and other furniture.** Standing on the

open door of an oven, the open drawer of a chest of drawers, or the shelves of a bookshelf can cause a child to tip over and trap her underneath, resulting in crushing. As well, heavier items such as televisions placed high on stands can be pulled off or tipped over to fall on the child.

Solution: Purchase a mechanical device (angle braces or anchors) which, when affixed to the bottom of the piece, prevents it from tipping. Place heavier items on the floor.

4. **Unused refrigerators** or other large appliances such as dryers and freezers. Toddlers may climb inside and suffocate.
   Solution: Dispose of these items at the local dumping area, but remove all doors from hinges first.

5. **Electrical cords** from lamps, televisions, VCRs, etc., can get accidentally wrapped around a crawling toddler's neck and result in strangulation.
   Solution: Wrap the extra cord around the leg of a table or tie it up with an elastic band.

6. **Water** holds a certain fascination, yet drowning is the number one cause of accidental death among children. Water in a pail, bathtub, sink, toilet, etc., can be an open invitation for the child to fall in and drown. Face-down, a person can drown in as little as one inch of water. Pools and hot tubs can be extremely dangerous to children.
   Solution: Never leave water in a pail or tub unattended; put locks and latches on doors, toilets, etc. Take every precaution with pools and hot tubs, including locking caps, approved pool covers, locking gates, and even purchasing alarms that can be placed in a pool which will signal if something goes in the pool unattended.

7. **Uncleaned counters or cutting boards** can harbour deadly bacteria such as e-coli.
   Solution: Use a mild combination of bleach and dish soap to clean counters; always wash cutting boards in dishwasher or boiling water.

8. **Pots and pans.** When cooking on the stove, pots and pans can be accidentally tipped or pulled off and cause serious burns, scalding, and fire.
   Solution: Turn pot and pan handles in towards the centre or

back of the stove. Never allow them to face out away from the stove or leave them unattended.

9. **Cribs and child restraints.** Some of these items have been proven to be deadly. Cribs with the rails too wide can cause suffocation when a little person's head gets stuck between them, and cribs whose mattresses do not fit snugly likewise can cause suffocation when the child's head gets stuck down between. As well, children can suffocate on large fluffy blankets and stuffed toys. Child restraints not government approved and not properly placed are lethal weapons.

   Solution: Purchase only approved equipment, read the instructions on proper building and installation, and always check the news or health clinics for recalls or updates. Remove any loose blankets or toys from the child's crib, bed, or playpen.

10. **Clothing hazards.** Nylons and synthetics are not recommended as nightwear for children because they are highly flammable. Loose clothing such as scarves, pant legs, long toques, shoe and boot laces, strings from hoods, etc., have been known to get caught in places such as playground slides, escalators, moving parts on rides or machines, and can cause strangulation.

    Solution: Use cottons or natural materials. Where practical, remove loose strings, tie strings and laces into double knots, cut laces short, wrap scarves and toques inside of the coat, tuck pants into boots or purchase pant-leg clamps.

11. **Sharp items.** In the wrong hands these can cause severe injuries and death.

    Solution: Simply put them out of reach, remove fancy knife racks from counters, and lock up jackknives or hunting knives. Purchase drawer locks for cutlery drawers. Never under any circumstances allow children or yourself (be a good role model) to run with sharp items.

12. **Matches, lighters, flammable material.** Again, in the wrong hands can prove deadly.

    Solution: Always store out of children's reach; in fact, where possible, lock them away. Some parents believe in the theory of letting the child touch the burning candle to experience the pain and thus avoid it. I, however, believe that prevention is the best medicine, and when children are old enough to comprehend the power of fire they can be taught valid lessons through local fire departments or educational films. I never relished the idea of sticking my children's fingers in an open flame.

13. **Fireplaces**, if not properly secured and attended, are not only extreme fire hazards, but open invitations to curious young minds. Like water, fire is fascinating to children.
    Solution: Always be present when a fireplace is going; never leave a child alone in the room with a lit fireplace. Install a proper front door on the fireplace; screens allow hot cinders to escape. Teach children at the earliest age possible the dangers of a fireplace.

14. **All household taps.** Scalding hot water can come out of every tap. Once again, children are fascinated with water and will at some point experiment with the magic of Tap Niagara. However, in their innocence they are unaware of the dangers that linger in a fully turned on hot water tap. Burning and scalding is inevitable.
    Solution: Before the baby arrives home turn the hot water temperature down to a comfortable 120° F. Warm showers are better for your skin, and this way there is no chance of you running a bath that is too hot for baby. As well, toddlers will only be able to run warm water from Tap Niagara.

15. **Pets** are wonderful additions to the family, but can bring about a myriad of danger issues. If the pet was present before the child, there is always the possibility of jealousy. A jealous animal can be very dangerous. Biting and scratching may occur as a result of a pet's feelings of desertion. Unfortunately, there are recorded cases of family pets seriously injuring and ultimately killing a newborn or small child. Some other dangers include allergies, and in some cases of exotic pets such as snakes, skunks, etc., there is a chance of bacterial infection.
    Solution: If the pet is a long time member of the family, adopting out may not be an option. However, you can ensure you still give the pet as much attention as possible, including play time and walks, and showing the pet the importance of children. When dealing with the child, talk to the pet. Don't allow

the pet to sleep in the same room with the children, and make every effort not to leave the pet alone with the children. If the situation is handled with continual love and care for the pet, it will most likely readily adapt to and even become protective of the children. If at any point the pet shows overt aggression to a child, your first priority should always be the safety of your children. It is not recommended that a new pet be introduced at the same time as a baby; this can prove to be too much for new parents and the pet may end up being sent away or worse.

NOTE: As children grow, so does their curiosity regarding the family pet, and in some cases their idea of playtime can border on cruelty to animals. Animals' tails quickly become objects by which to grab, fling, drag, and swing them. Cats tend to hide for the first six to seven years of the child's life, hoping the child loses interest. Dogs, however, are willing participants and will often endure such atrocities as being painted, pulled, ridden, chased, jumped on, wrestled with, soaped up, sprayed down, and in some cases, dressed. Goldfish have a tendency to be over-fed and can take on a striking resemblance to Koi. Birds are often set free so they can be viewed flying around the house into walls and mirrors, or more devastatingly, out an open door or window to fend for themselves with the crows or magpies. You will rarely see a purple budgie make it in the great outdoors. Hamsters and guinea pigs have short life spans for a reason — no creature that small can possibly survive long when they are constantly squeezed, hugged, dropped, fondled, chased, and made to perform in spinning balls and mazes. Part of being a parent includes warding off exhausting pleas from children for pets. Children will use any and every excuse as to why they should have a pet, the most common of which is everybody else has one. They will appeal to your senses by stopping at every pet store and making you view all the cute, cuddly creatures they claim are kept inhumanely behind glass windows. They will make promises of responsibility for feeding, walking, cleaning up after, and of course loving. They will even go so far as to claim, "Mom/Dad you always said you wanted a pet." But alas, be prepared, because the average time it takes a child to lose interest in the newly purchased family pet is about three and a half weeks, then the nightly pee breaks, daily walks, and of course the clean up, is entirely left up to you. Think it over and be sure you make the wisest decision for all involved, including the precious pet.

16. **Home and garden**. Many plants either in the home or around the yard are known to be not only toxic but deadly poisonous if ingested. Some of these plants include: buttercups, milkweed, lupines, wisteria, rhubarb/tomato leaves, potato plants, Birds of Paradise, Algerian ivy, aloes, dieffenbachia, English holly, tulips, daffodils, and spider plants — the list is endless, but there are numerous resources available. If you are like me and have black thumbs, you may opt for artificial plants. Usually these pose no real threats; however, if the leaves are ingested they could cause choking. But more importantly, the decorative moss used to line the planters can be toxic.
   Solution: Remove the moss and relocate smaller leafed plants. Remove all plants where possible or place in a higher location, educate children, fence off the garden, never leave toddlers in yards alone — place them in a playpen if necessary. Have the number for your local poison centre at hand.

17. **Food.** In the case of food allergies, the effects will present themselves on an individual basis. Unfortunately, there is no sure-fire way of pre-detecting food allergies. Some of the most common and deadly are nuts (particularly peanuts), milk and by-products (lactose intolerance), seafood, tomatoes, and flour. On the other hand, food additives and pesticides can also pose a real danger. Additives can result in some very serious allergic reactions, and pesticides have been known to cause death. Children can be exposed to lead in paint, pipes, and even their diet. Foods cooked or heated in the microwave can be very dangerous. There is a hidden heat factor that may not be noticeable to the touch, but when swallowed can cause serious burning. Improper handling of raw meat can and has led to serious cases of e-coli poisoning. Choking on food is also a leading cause of infant and child mortality. The common culprits of food choking are hotdogs, peanuts, candies (soft and hard),

celery strings, carrots, cheese, ice cubes, marshmallows, peas, and virtually anything too large or hard for tiny mouths.
Solution: If there is any concern over a reaction to a particular food, have the child tested immediately. Send notes to the child's day care and/or school indicating allergies. Carefully check labels for food additives. Thoroughly clean all fruits and vegetables. When handling raw meat, ensure there are no traces left on the counter or on any of the utensils and always make sure meat is cooked to at least 140° F. Never let a child with open cuts on his hands handle raw meat. Where possible remove anything containing high levels of lead. Avoid the use of pesticides in or around your home. Make note of parks and other areas that are sprayed with pesticides. When cooking or heating foods in the microwave, allow for a few minutes of cool down before giving them to the child. Stir or mix the food often to avoid hot spots. To avoid choking, cut food into small pieces or cook the food until it is soft and can easily dissolve.

NOTE: Other items such as balloons, small pieces of toys, puzzles, tree tinsel, etc., can also be choking hazards.

18. **Other Hazards: Plastic bags** can cause suffocation. Make sure they are out of reach. **Dark hallways** can cause nasty falls or bumping into items. Use a low wattage nightlight. **Sharp corners** can cause painful cuts and scrapes. If possible tape the corners with masking tape. Some models of heavy overhead **garage doors** have trapped small children underneath and crushed them. Devices can be purchased to stop the garage door from lowering when an object is detected underneath. **Small electrical appliances** such as curling irons, irons, or space heaters can cause serious burns to children, as well as fires. Always unplug these items when not in use, and make sure space heaters are not in the path of flammable material such as bedding, clothes, and curtains. **Electric fans** can be mesmerizing to small children, but tiny fingers will easily fit through the grates. Place fans out of harm's reach. **Firearms** in the hands of the inexperienced can cause serious injury and death. Always store firearms properly and in accordance with the

law. Keep keys for locking cabinets on your person at all times. Do not clean or handle firearms around small children. Educate children on the danger of firearms and show older children the proper methods of handling and storing.

IMPORTANT NOTE: Have proper CO_2 and smoke detectors installed in your home. Check and maintain them regularly. Your children are the most precious commodity you will ever know — treat them as such.

The Many Wonders of Their Worlds

Other items in your house will suddenly take on new identities, as toddlers tend to wreak havoc with everything from make-up to technology. Having watched the magic of a VCR, toddlers imagine if you can stick a videotape into the little window and it will disappear, then so should a sandwich or pen or dinky toy. Alarm clocks mysteriously come on at 2:38 a.m. at full volume, television remote controls become gummed with jam, peanut butter, and other unidentifiable substances, even computer keyboards look very similar to those made for action toddler computer toys. The buttons on touch tone telephones lure a toddler, and with little ease they can dial up such places as Bangladesh, Hawaii, and Newfoundland, and of course thanks to the wonders of educational television, there are always a few unfounded 911 calls. Experience has it, if you leave your toddler for even a few seconds alone in the bedroom and your telephone rings an unusual three quick rings, someone has just dialed for help. When you answer those odd rings, you are more than likely going to be confronted by a somewhat irritated emergency operator who will in no uncertain terms suggest that you keep a more vigilant eye on your little ones, and that when they are using the 911 line to play, they are taking away from a real emergency. Ouch.

> **Tip:**
> *Unplug any phones not in constant use, and remove all portable phones and place them so children cannot reach out and touch someone.*

Toddlers who are given an opportunity to watch mommy put on make-up are usually fascinated by the magic with which those pretty powders and even prettier gooey sticks put colour on mommy's face. If they work that well on mommy, they must work great on walls, colouring books, mirrors, their own faces, and oh yes, of course, the family pet. Sometimes the toddler's fascination is limited to twisting the gooey sticks up and down and up and down, then shoving the lid back on them while the pretty coloured gooey stick is still in the up position. The pending result is the shocked look on mommy's face when she opens her favourite ten-dollar tube of lipstick only to discover the lipstick itself is stuck to the top of the lid, and no matter how hard one tries, one can never stick the stick back onto it's base. Sooner or later a certain degree of humour can be found in a four-year-old boy descending from the bathroom with blue and green eyeshadow covering the majority of his lids to the base of his forehead, huge pink gooey circles adorning his cheeks, and bright red lips from the base of his nose to the tip of his chin. The only decision the parent should have to make is whether to grab the camera and ensure there is blackmail bait for when he is older, or call the rodeo.

Daddy's tools are another source of intrigue. Hammers, screwdrivers, pliers, wrenches, and such cannot only be used to put things up and nail things together, they work equally well at taking things down and pounding things apart. After all, daddy seems to have a blast when he uses these gadgets. He's always yelling with delight, or so it would seem to the toddler who is not yet familiar with the meaning of all those words daddy blurts when he uses his tools. Besides the usual, some households come complete with an assortment of other alluring tools such as those handy gadgets used to create chalk lines when measuring a straight line over a long distance. This is just too cool for a toddler who is restricted to using a big fat piece of chalk on the chalkboard in her room or on the driveway. With this handy-dandy "toyol," the toddler can make a beautiful pattern of spider webs all over the hardwood floors. Measuring tapes also provide toddlers with minutes of unsupervised fun, and everything is fine until the snake-like "toyol" decides to make a quick recoil to it's house, taking with it the skin off of tiny fingers.

NOTE: It goes without saying that power tools should be stored far away out of the reach of unsuspecting hands. These potentially dangerous objects can mean nothing but tragedy to young children and should only be used when toddlers (especially) are a safe distance from the site. Locking storage cabinets is highly recommended.

After children enter the picture it seems as though tools, like socks, take on lives of their own and escape via some black hole looming somewhere in the house, often referred to as the "Idunno Triangle."

Considering their short experience with life, almost everything is a wonder to toddlers, worthy of inspection and ultimately trial, which too often includes taste-testing. For this very reason many manufacturers have found it necessary to label products with "Possible Choking Hazard," for anything containing parts smaller than a bread box and therefore fair game for analysis in a toddler's mouth. Once they get bored with the not so pleasant taste of their own fingers, toes, hair, and some unmentionable body exclusions, they curiously move on to other tempting morsels, including but never limited to: snow, icicles, toys, clothing, electrical cords, rabbit droppings, the cat's tail, rocks, dirt, and — well you get the picture. So all parents would be advised to closely monitor what goes into junior's mouth, obviously for the sake of safety, but also as a warning for what may astonishingly appear coming out the other end.

Remember, what seems ordinary to us is often a wonder to someone who is just beginning to experience the world.

The Day Goes On

As a day in the life of a toddler continues, you are bound to be imparted with moments of sitting cross-legged on the kitchen floor while you roll a ball back and forth, crouching on your knees in front of a pint sized-table creating works of crafty art, chasing miniature thieves around the kitchen table after they sneaked the last piece of bologna, and even playing the odd game of tag or hide-and-go-seek. All of this endows you with the majestic privilege of being a three-year-old again. If only your day

Tip:

One of the most worthwhile pieces of advice I can offer a new parent is, during your little one's nap, take a much needed break for yourself. Whether it is to have your own fifteen minute nap, or sit with a cup of tea or other refreshment and read a book, or just sit and relax, the break will allow you to rejuvenate. I realize that there are more than a dozen things you could be doing during this time, and I am not suggesting you need to use the entire nap time, but a fifteen to twenty minute break is well worth it. In a day already filled with plenty of tasks, chasing a toddler around can be very wearisome.

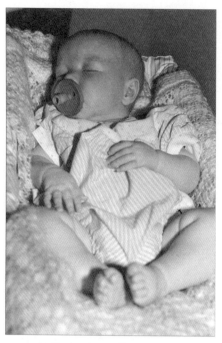

Isn't she lovely?

were that simple. Unfortunately, parents are also charged with cleaning the house, balancing the books, making the meals, doing the laundry and ironing, and boundless other responsibilities, so alternate forms of entertainment must be utilized. In addition to the vast variety of entertainment offered by television, it is also a highly effective and extremely convenient fill-in for an otherwise chore-loaded parent. I am not in any way suggesting nor do I condone using the television as a replacement for responsible parenting. However, there are certain television shows that will literally mesmerize your toddler, affording you the opportunity to get caught up on other duties. If you can stand the repetitive and often nerve-grating songs, along with the mind-numbing voices of the hosts of these television shows, you will be treated to anywhere from a half hour to one and a half hours of toddler down time. For some toddlers, this time also includes their midday nap.

Nap time will end far too quickly, and usually toddlers awake with a renewed vengeance. After all cartoons have taken them away from the real action, and so they are off. Little feet will reach sonic speeds to find the next adventure and no doubt the next challenge for the parent. A snack may be in order and is best served in the confines of a highchair. Snacks are limited only to the parent's imagination and of course the "chokeability." Crackers are always a good choice, popsicles in warmer weather, dry cereal — the choices are endless. Once the snack is consumed and the energy level resumed, the squalling for freedom will ensue. "Down, down, down." The afternoons are very much like the mornings, filled with antics and adventures, devilment and delight. As the afternoon winds down, the duty of preparing dinner fast approaches and the parent finds herself scurrying around picking up mini-messes, finishing undone chores, and frantically pulling something edible together for dinner. As if all this weren't madness enough, suddenly the toddler becomes a whirlwind of activity. Chalk it up to imitation. After all, junior is watching you hurry about so this must be the thing to do. Out come the pots and pans in preparation for their big debut with the newest pop band. If they don't have those tiny sticks that accompany toddler xylophones, then almost any other long, hard stick-like item will get the job done, such as wooden spoons, paint stir sticks, etc., and a star is born again. While you try to accomplish the equivalent to building the pyramids, you are serenaded by something that hardly sounds like music to your ears, but at least you know where the toddler is and for the time being the cat, dog, ornaments, floors, walls, toilets, furniture, and anything else in the rest of the house is safe.

Some days may include errands outside of the home and therefore require the parent to take the toddler on mini-tours. These mini-tours may be fun for the little ones, but are more often than not a grueling task for the parent. Even a quick trip to the grocery store can involve loads of preparation and likewise loads of take down, resulting in an extra twenty minutes tacked on to the actual time allotted for the specific errand. Shopping takes on a whole new dimension when it involves a toddler. What used to be considered enjoyable by most women becomes survival of the fittest for moms with toddlers, and considering their abundance of energy, apple juice snacks, and the nap they managed to get in, toddlers are likely to be the fitter. Have stroller will travel; all excursions should be accompanied by the stroller, thus saving on the wear and tear of a parent's hip and back. I won't bother to again detail the ins and outs of stroller use. Suffice it to say that you should not attempt to shop without one despite the challenge it poses putting up and taking down. If your errand involves shopping, the quicker and less distracting route should be chosen, saving you the frustration of replacing unwanted items back on the shelf and having to ward off pleas for everything from rubber plumbing gadgets to the newest and best toy which is advertised no less than sixty-five times on television during the hours of 8:30 a.m. to 4:30 p.m. Once you are ready to check out, quickly scan the cash registers to find the "child friendly" one. Some retail industries have recognized the aggravation endured by parents shopping with children and provide checkouts free of any desirable items. *Hats off to industries for employing parents as product placement consultants.*

As you check through, you are at the mercy of the cashier, and if you are lucky your toddler will begin wailing in the line-up, a sure remedy for a slow-moving, eighteen-year-old, baby-faced store employee who obviously has no children of her own. If you are forced to stand in a line-up, be prepared to ward off the possibility of dirty looks and perhaps snide remarks by other customers around you. I offer you a retort I have found to be useful: "Never use condoms that are more than one week old."

If your errands involve visits to a doctor, dentist, lawyer, or banker, be sure to take some small, quiet toy or book to keep the little one busy. However, be aware of the possibility of such items being used as projectiles if the visit should last over twenty minutes. Another tip worth mentioning: while it may be convenient to provide the toddler with instant amusement by offering your car keys as a distraction, it is not always wise. Keys are not only sharp metal objects that can inflict a nasty wound on some unwitting person in the line behind you, they are also a necessary tool for getting home again, and when tossed into a sewer drain can put a very inconvenient glitch in your plans. As a courtesy to the person you are meeting with, leave the toddler safely and securely strapped into the stroller during the visit. He may beg for freedom, but turning a toddler loose after being pent up in a stroller for a while is simply asking for trouble, and to say the least unfair to the person and his office surroundings.

Sometimes a stay-at-home parent is given a rare invitation to join a friend or spouse for a luncheon or coffee date. I say rare, especially if the friend works outside of the home. Taking the toddler along is not only not recommended, but can

> **Tip:**
>
> *Many doctors' offices provide an array of toys for the little ones to play with while awaiting a visit. However, consider for a moment that the majority of the children playing with these toys are visiting the doctor as a result of some highly contagious, snot-infested, cough-inducing bug they have contracted, so if your toddler wasn't sick before the visit but played happily with the toys during the visit — just wait. In a few days you're bound to be making another visit.*

put a great deal of strain on already fading relationships. My advice is to book the luncheon date when your spouse can relieve you in care-giving duties, trade babysitting services with another parent by returning the favour, call upon eager grandparents, or as a last resort offer to make your luncheon partner an awesome home-cooked lunch that can be enjoyed during the toddler's nap.

In the eyes of toddlers, their days are comparable to the years of a dog: twelve or so hours feel like they lost seven days. However, in the eyes of the parent a twelve-hour-day tending to a tenacious toddler can feel like it took seven days. Luckily and by some god-blessed rule, by about 7:30 p.m. a toddler starts to run out of fuel, and none too soon because by this point moms and dads are also tapped out.

So begins the bedtime battles. After a warm bath and a delightful bedtime story, one of two things may occur. If mom or dad lay down with the little one while they read the story, it is entirely possible that mom or dad is now sound asleep on the bottom of a bunk bed befitting the length of a three-year-old. The three-year-old, on the other hand, has wandered off the bed and is probably in the bathroom re-arranging the neatly folded towels or redecorating with shaving cream and baby pow-der. By some unexplained miracle, though, moms are equipped with an uncanny sense, even when they are asleep, to detect trouble. Dads for the most part can sleep through armed vehicles moving through the house. Before too much damage develops, mom is on the case and begins the battle to get the little one tucked in for a good night's sleep. It is a battle to be sure, because unlike when they were babies and they nodded off to sleep with a full belly and a sound burping, toddlers have had a taste of the good life, playing and running and just having fun. So they struggle to keep their eyes open, and pull at your shirt to raise them-selves in their crib or bed. They may stand and stomp their feet on the mattress as a show of defiance, or cry large alligator tears begging you to take them out and stay up with you, worried they may miss something important. If you have an older child who is granted a later bedtime, the fight for freedom intensifies. None-the-less at some point all good little girls and boys need to go to sleep and the best thing to do is to give them a stern warning and walk away. Be prepared, despite your stern warning, to endure at least three attempts to re-join the ranks by using such excuses as, "I need a drink of water . . . I have to go pee . . . There's a monster in my closet." While they sit on the toilet with a small glass of water, you can go in and perform an exorcism in their room, warding off all monsters and other undesirables for good. After all is said and done the once 7:30 p.m. bedtime has now rounded the corner of 8 and your patience has run thin, you flick on the Flipper night light, partly close the door, and let them cry themselves to sleep. Unlike your tenacious three-year-old, you can't wait to get more sleep, so after a half hour of dozing off on the couch, mom heads to bed. It would seem as though the minute mom rises from the couch she unwittingly emits a signal to her mate that she is in heat, and before she can even get her slippers off, her mate is already laying in bed staring at her with the same begging eyes she just witnessed in her three-year-old over an hour ago. It is going to take some special kind of romancing to make this already long and tiresome day last for another eight minutes.

Pixie Dust and Fairy Wings . . . and all those other Magical Things

The creators of those wondrous children's stories, novels, and movies could learn a thing or two from the likes of a child, because true greatness really does live in their imaginations. After all, when a so-called grown up person closes her eyes at night she is not likely going to dream of brilliantly-coloured unicorns flying around the earth delivering happiness and well-being to the world. As a parent, you will come to appreciate the power of imagination. Your once adult world of fantasy will come to an end, and you will be plunged into a new world of fairy tales and make believe. Your mind will flash back to all of the fabrications for imagination your parents told in order to create a childhood filled with mystery and wonder. You'll smile when you remember being so excited over the prospect of Christmas that you actually threw up. In many ways, times have not changed very much; the only difference is that now you feel a tremendous amount of empathy for your parents. You are totally attuned to the anxiety they must have experienced over making magic and keeping secrets.

In the beginning, when your children are still babes in blankets, their interest in majestic events such as Christmas is pretty much limited to staring at all the shiny decorations, but as they grow so too does their ability to understand or believe. Now it is your turn to continue the fabrications for imagination, and if you are so inclined, you will find yourself in an elaborate web of make believe.

The magic usually begins with a child's first Christmas and the sto-ries of a jolly fat man in a red velvet suit flying a sleigh capable of carry-ing toys for every child in the world. But the wonder doesn't end there — the sleigh is powered by eight or nine reindeer, the journey is com-pleted in one night, and this 220-pound man defies all the laws of physics by stuffing his jolly frame down four-feet-by-four-feet chimneys. Of course, his journey is not in vain — the purpose is to leave a pres-ent under your ornately decorated tree, preferably the present secretly told to him in a letter, email, or to one of his many assistants found in any mall six to eight weeks prior to Christmas itself. All of this affords him the title of most recognized hero to children world-wide. If they only knew. Christmas for believers from age two to eight, sometimes earlier, sometimes later, is far more involved than just Santa. Thanks to the influence of media, the hype usually begins around the third week of November, which for Canadians comes two weeks after Thanksgiving and for Americans comes two weeks before Thanksgiving. I'm con-vinced the reasoning for this is to aid children in plying moms and dads with a shower of "and I am thankful for my wonderful parents" pre-and-post Christmas pleas. Parents not only have to contend with toy com-mercials every five minutes of programming, they must also put up with and consequently try to hide enough advertisement flyers to choke a fair sized elephant, the most sought-after of which is the WISH catalogue. It is a very strategic publication which comes out only once a year, yet is the cause of hair pulling, shoulder shoving, all-out battles to be the first child who gets to sift through all the pages of toys. I appreciate the need for retailers to grab their share of the market in any way feasible, how-ever, the unfortunate result of the media blitz on Christmas are children who are literally crawling up walls by the time Christmas actually arrives. The effect is so noticeable that school teachers have had to forego any serious learning from about the first of December to the Christmas holidays. All of this focus has managed to take some of the wonder out of a magical time of year and turn it into a marketing frenzy. The stress is felt by child and parent alike and takes its toll on everyone. But keeping the arrival of Christmas low key is very difficult and even more demanding once children are able to read calendars, which now happens at an earlier age thanks to chocolate-clad advent calendars. As if the children need the sugar rush.

The presence of Santa Claus is everywhere — from cereal boxes to underwear commercials, his eminence is greater than the Pope, his power over children as unbelievable as his alleged achievements. The very mention of his name and his renowned list of naughty and nice can produce miraculous behaviour in some otherwise unruly children. Parents usually get wise to this early and start using the "watchful eye of Santa" blackmail as early as August, which is about when all of the pre-Christmas celebratory activities begin. Whoever said the holidays were simple? Depending on which part of the country you live in and what the weather holds in store, Christmas preparations may begin in the later part of the summer or early fall prior to any heavy snowfall — an excellent time to put up Christmas lights. Parents of babes may be lucky enough to get away with little to no outdoor decorations, relying solely on the somewhat competitive nature of over-zealous neighbours deter-mined to outshine the North Star and lead the shepherds to their own version of the manger. But as children grow, some parents develop an uncontrollable desire to have their own overdone, often gaudy, display of bright lights and plastic life-sized figures, including the jolly fat man and his eight reindeer. Each year will bring about another string of lights until things are finally subdued by a call from the local power company threatening brown-outs for the entire neighbourhood. While outdoor decorations may go up early, indoor decorating can usually be held off until at least the beginning of December.

Personally, I love the whole concept of the season and can hardly wait to dig out the boxes marked XMAS. At the determined request of my husband, I do manage to hold off until the end of the first week of December, but as soon as the sixth rolls around I anxiously descend to the basement and begin dragging the boxes upstairs, and before John gets home from work I have at least two rooms entirely decorated. Once the house starts resembling a mini-Vegas, other pre-season cele-bratory activities also take shape. Prior to this season, eleven months goes by and the only invitations for outings are likely to be adorned with puppies and balloons, rarely bearing the name of a parent. Suddenly the once otherwise socially inept parents are invited to no less than ten parties or events in a period of about three weeks. Some of these events you may even be hosting yourself, which gives rise to more off-the-meter excitement for the children. Mom spends days frantically clean-ing and preparing goodies, while dad stocks the liquor cabinet with enough spirits to host a small wedding. All this rubs off on the children, and by the time the evening arrives they are usually wired for sound. They greet your party guests by bouncing off the couch onto the floor, break-falling over the area carpet, cart-wheeling towards the table of carefully prepared hors d'oeuvres, and completing this spectacle by decorating themselves with the meticulously placed tinsel from the tree. Your party-goers, most likely parents themselves, will probably find this amusing, while you on the other hand find yourself repeating between gritted teeth, "Tis the season to be jolly, Haha ha haha, haha, ha ha." Christmas parties are not exclusive to adults and most organizations offer some sort of children's Christmas party for their employees.

A child's first Christmas party is really nothing more than an excuse for parents or grandparents to go out and purchase the cutest thematic outfit they can find, thus elaborately adorning junior/ette in anticipation of Ooo's and Ahhh's and for their inevitable photograph with Santa. Unfortunately, Christmas parties are not planned around the well-being of these outfits. Parents will stand mortified as junior/ette crawls around on the community centre floor, spills orange pop down her front, manages to stick a half-licked candy cane in her hair, and almost completely tires herself out with two hours of running around like a yard ape, all prior to Santa's arrival and those wishful, perfect photo opportunities. In a futile attempt to clean them up and get them presentable, moms resort to spit baths, turning turtlenecks inside out, restyling hair, and removing once-white stockings, opting for bare legs. All this in preparation for the first ever "sit on Santa's knee." Despite all hopes that your child will be the subject of a picture perfect party portrait by the time you place her on the lap of this overweight dude with the big scary beard, all hell will break loose and she will no doubt scream bloody murder. As you run up to assure her that this time it is okay to sit on a complete stranger's lap and beg for toys, you realize that this experience is likely going to be one of the most traumatic in their young lives, not to mention yours.

The schools have also managed to get into the holiday spirit, and the last few days prior to Christmas break are often reserved for class Christmas parties. Once again parents will be called upon to supply something for this festive event. Depending on the teachers and their definitions of treats, the list of possible contributions could range from neatly cut carrot sticks (just handing in a bag of bulk carrots from the grocer won't suffice) and dip to potato chips and dip. You may also be seconded to assist in the classroom for the party itself, subjecting you to twenty-five or so pre-seasoned, over-excited, emotionally amplified children who by this point are quite literally bouncing off walls. You need only bear witness to this fiasco once to develop yet a deeper appreciation for the work of teachers, and if you are so inclined to give them a small gift at this time of year, some suggestions include a pedicure, a gel eye mask and some bath salts, or four or five of those miniature airplane bottles of liquor.

Christmas, of course, wouldn't be Christmas without some unique traditions involving parental creativity, time, and patience. To begin with, many parents feel the time-tested desire to make an event out of going for and selecting the perfect, natural Christmas tree. If you are lucky enough to have access to a nearby forest, this may involve a day trip, packed lunch, thermos of hot chocolate, buck saw, rope, cutting permit, and a strong belief that despite the fifty-seven trees you already looked at, the next one will be the perfect one. There really is no replacement for walking through knee-deep snow on a freezing cold day to find the one tree which stands out amidst a forest of hundreds. If you are unable to see the forest for the buildings, you may be left to select your tree from one of the many lots that take up root, no pun intended, all around town three or four weeks prior to Christmas. Once again this is an area where experienced parents have the upper hand and quickly learn the benefits of selective shopping. Tree lots serve a wonderful purpose, affording anyone the opportunity to walk around on a chilly December evening trying to pick out the perfect tree; however, the perfect tree may very well require you to take out a second mortgage on the house. Like anything else, convenience has its price. The first few years of our children's lives, we opted for the day out to the forest, but weather and work has since played a role in us taking advantage of the service of tree lots. We soon discovered that having the six foot, precisely manicured evergreen as our tree was not financially sound, and convinced our children it was better to pay twenty-five dollars as opposed to eighty, therefore spending the left-over money on Christmas gifts instead. It wasn't a hard sell.

If natural is not feasible or desirable, parents may resort to purchasing an artificial tree, the initial cost of which may seem a little high, but considering its longevity, can be a wise investment. Either way, the tree will be selected and then put up in preparation for decoration, yet another holiday tradition defined by uniqueness. In many instances, tree decorating becomes a family event, beginning with dad untangling a mess of lights then testing them, only to discover at least thirty-eight of them are blown. After replacing the burned out lights with appropriately colour-coded ones, the lights are ready to be strung around the tree. Then, after a moment of awe as the tree is lit up, there comes an eternity of ornament decorating. Usually the children are eager to help, and to the dismay of mom tear into the box of carefully packed, extremely breakable bobbles, frantically looking for the plastic Rudolph wearing a striped toque. Three broken ornaments, five packages of static tinsel, one argument over whose turn it is to put on the topper, and three hours later the tree is likely to be glamorously decorated and ready for review. With all other lights out in the house the extension cord is plugged in and a truly magical moment occurs. The bright coloured lights and the shiny precious ornaments reflect with a twinkle in the eyes of the young observers, and for a fleeting moment during an otherwise hectic time of the year, the world is wondrously still.

Christmas is by far no exception — in fact, one might say it's the forerunner of traditional holiday food. The entire month is a feast of culinary delights, including fancy sculpted hors d'oeuvres, boxed chocolates, homemade fudge, rum-laced, calorie-filled eggnog, warmed apple cider, the Christmas feast itself which is described a little further on, and of course, the parental favourite — homemade, hand-decorated sugar cookies. Yet another night can be set aside for this holiday event. The children will delight in the thought of decorating cookies with an assortment of dye-laden icing and hard decorative candies inedible to anyone over the age of ten. Parents, however, become less enchanted with the whole event after removing the sixth dozen of cookies from the oven, preparing eight bowls of dyed icing only to discover they all get mixed together to become a horrid shade of brown, stepping on and then cleaning up little silver candy balls, colourful candy sprinkles and sticky ju-jubes, and of course, getting stuck with completing the decorating challenge by themselves as the little ones move onto something more exciting. Several hours after the little ones are tucked soundly into their beds, parents will wash the baking dishes, tidy up the kitchen, then be left staring at approximately sixty-seven star, Christmas tree, reindeer, Santa Claus, and snowmen-shaped cookies now spread all over the kitchen table. A sudden rush of panic comes over them — what are we going to do with all these cookies? And that, folks, explains all the cookies kids get at their classroom parties.

Getting rid of the Christmas cookies is a minor issue in the quest for happy holidays; hiding the Christmas gifts is a huge issue. When the children are very young, too young to actually conduct any type of serious hunt, hiding the gifts, especially Santa's, is fairly easy. Anywhere above four feet will work. However, as their limbs grow and become capable of extending further, so too does their curiosity. Whether they suspect something fishy about the whole Santa concept or whether they know you are hiding other gifts, either way they can somehow easily find hidden presents despite being unable to find their school backpacks or other misplaced items. Over the years I was wise enough to out-detect them, but the past few years have been far more challenging. I have used the trunk of my vehicle, our camper, tops of closets, under beds, bathroom linen closets, empty suitcases, and I have even gone so far as to keep them at Gramma's house. After eleven years of being sneaky, I have run out of hiding places and patience, so now that my children are living in the land of reality, I simply wrap them up and put them under the tree. I am speaking about the presents, of course. I do, however, still have some deviance in my blood and get a little creative with my choices of containers. Whoever said good things only come in small packages never opened one of my ingeniously wrapped gifts.

Some tips for those passionate parents of magic and wonderment

- Wrap Santa presents in wrapping paper used specifically for those presents, otherwise the doubters may notice that the same wrapping paper was used for gifts given by parents. As well, put the tags on the night before and use funny handwriting. While this may seem a bit over the top, you will be surprised at how a child who whines about figuring out simple math can remarkably figure out your handwriting. Use the same funny handwriting to reply to the note left for Santa.

- Put some baking soda on the floor around the fireplace or front door to create the illusion of snow left behind by Santa. I suggest baking soda for two reasons — it helps deodorize the carpet, and pets don't like its taste.

- After the children are sound asleep, go up on the roof and make noises to imitate reindeer.
- Take a few bites out of the cookies left out for Santa, and put the carrots for the reindeer away in the fridge.
- If there is any snow outside, make fake reindeer and Santa footprints on the front lawn.
- Don't wrap large gifts. If they require assembly do so late Christmas Eve and leave them under the tree.

Of course, if you are so inclined to go the extra mile and do some of these magical things, you are also bound to have a very late Christmas Eve night and will probably find yourself crawling into bed around 1:30 a.m., which, I might add, is officially Christmas day. As if by some freak of fortuity, children have a built-in sense of the dawn of Christmas and can wake out of a deep sleep in order to get in on the bounty. When they are able to get out of their beds by themselves, they rise around 4 a.m. and quickly check out the Christmas tree. Once they discover that Santa did make it and there are some new gifts under the tree, they make a bee-line for their parents' bedrooms, all the way announcing the news. Mom and Dad are about to be woken by the children bouncing on them, screaming at the top of their lungs that their extra goodness paid off and Santa came. Before you can barely open an eye, they retreat back to the room with the Christmas tree in order to check the stockings they hung out the night before. The next onslaught will involve a running jump onto the bed, this time toting a stocking filled with whatever goodies you stuffed in them a matter of three short hours earlier. Once again you are privy to a loud announcement about the contents of the stocking, all the while being covered with little oranges, candy canes, toothbrushes, dinky toys, crayons, doll shoes, and whatever other little prizes they find in those socks. But before they can make the final descent back to the tree, you are likely a little more alert, and when they pull frantically on your arm begging you to come see the mother-lode, you will no doubt make some pleas of your own. "How about we all go back to sleep for a couple more hours, then we won't be so tired when we go over to Gramma's house for dinner." Dinner and Gramma are the last things on their little minds. All those brightly wrapped presents are way too tempting and thus the power of parental privilege must prevail as you squeeze the excited bundles of pent up energy between you and nod off for a couple more hours of restless sleep.

With the precision of a Swiss alarm clock, the children will wake again at 6 a.m. This time their persistence will prevail and you will find yourself sauntering off to the Christmas tree and flopping down in the most comfortable chair. In a flurry of wrapping paper, fancy bows, cardboard boxes, flailing arms, and hoots and hollers, the children will look like hungry hyenas on a lion carcass. The once neatly wrapped and beautifully decorated gifts are now scattered over the entire floor. What took you three hours to accomplish will take them thirty-four seconds to devour. And if all that weren't enough, they are likely to add insult to injury by turning to you with dopey looks on their faces and with no regard to your effort, enquire, "Is that all there is?"

Despite your urge to scream and lecture them on how lucky they are to have gotten anything — after all there are children around the world who do without water, food, shelter, and clothing, let alone toys — you refrain and sigh and remember it is Christmas and they are just kids. With the clock rounding 6:30 a.m., your thoughts are to go back to bed and try and get a few more minutes of shut-eye. However, the children have different aspirations. Most of the contents of the once finely-wrapped boxes will no doubt require a certain degree of assembly, and like everything else with children, there is no time like the present. This process may require dad to open one of his gifts and be delighted at the site of a brand new cordless drill, or he may have to go to the garage and collect an assortment of tools, because heaven forbid toy manufacturers get together and use all the same size screws and nuts and bolts, etc. With dad crossed-legged in the middle of the mess, mom can now make some much needed coffee, and if Christmas dinner is planned for their house, begin stuffing a thirty-seven-pound turkey and preparing all the other fixings.

Christmas dinner is likely to be another family tradition. If you are lucky enough as parents to have your own parents still vying for the honour of preparing and having the family Christmas dinner, then the only problems you may be faced with are deciding exactly which set of parents win out and get to be the host, and getting the now overtired, overexcited, children cleaned up and dressed. An easy solution to the hosting issue would be to opt for the every-other-year concept, however, the cleaning up and dressing issue is far more involved and complex.

Usually the children are content to stay in their pajamas all day and play with their new cache, and the thought of catching a snooze on the couch while they do so is appealing to you as well. However, Gramma waits with a kitchen full of food and a table set with all the fine china. So around 2 p.m. the battle begins, with requests to get into the tub and clean up all the candy cane residue. After several minutes of fruitless pleas, the battle turns nasty as you resort to threatening to take away their new toys. This usually gets them mobile. After a quick bath, the time comes to clothe the unhappy participants in their new and often fussy outfits purchased exclusively for this special event. Getting the whiney five-year-old into the frilly, velvet dress isn't half the challenge of trying to put on the matching white leotards. With feet and legs going in every direction, it's at least a fifteen minute venture, after which you discover they are on backwards and juniorette ends up walking like she has a frozen turkey between her knees. If you have a boy, the challenge lies in the process of putting on that adorable three piece suit made especially for the likes of a three-foot-tall entrepreneur. After hiking the pants up nearly to his armpits and tucking in the miniature-cuffed dress shirt, the suit jacket will seem like a breeze, that is until junior starts complaining about how hot it is, how itchy the pants are, and how the cute little bow tie is cutting off his air.

No beautiful babes would be complete without painstakingly primping their otherwise unruly hair. Junior-ettes will endure at least a half an hour of curling, crimping, pinning, and spraying, complete with a matching bow for the top or side, while junior will get his twice a year blob of gel (the first comes at school picture day) in order to make the perfect little swirl just at the crown of the forehead. After some agonizing hours of preparation you may be afforded a few minutes to actually prepare yourself, if you didn't already do so ahead of time. The car will get packed with gifts for exchanging at the grandparents', and the little ones will be carefully set into the car seats with a final warning, "Sit perfectly still or you'll mess up your outfit." If there is even the slightest hint of a possible hair-pulling, bowtie-snapping feud, parents would be wise to give up the front seat for the sake of separation.

Arrival at the grandparents' house will come none too soon as the little ones are unlatched and swiftly escorted into the house, sat on a chair, and once again lectured not to move. All this fuss is usually for one reason and one reason only — family photos. Christmas has unanimously been selected as the one occasion where family photos can be taken; after all, few family members are going to miss the opportunity for a huge, delicious, free meal prepared by the experts. So children will be instructed over and over again to sit nice and not eat any of the tempting goodies set out by Gramma while awaiting the arrival of the final family member, usually the single brother who had to get in the last few minutes of some rerun hockey game on the sports channel.

Once everyone has arrived and the niceties are over, the family photo frenzy will begin with Gramma strategically placing people in their not-so-rightful positions against the only wall in the house large enough to accommodate a background for some twenty people. After fifteen minutes of removing all distractions, shuffling around, trading places, chasing children, sitting on stools, kneeling on knees, rearranging and fussing, one camera will click. Then the portrait pomposity will start all over again as people move in and out of the picture in order to click off their versions of this photographic facsimile of family history. The frustration of sitting posed for nearly forty minutes will eventually wear on children and adults alike, the result being some not-so-pleasant surprises when the film is developed. Gramma is bound to sprout rabbit ears at some point.

Depending on tradition, the next item on the agenda may be gift exchange, but more than likely it will be dinner. When Gramma says 5 p.m. for dinner, that is exactly when it will be served. All the family members will be herded into the dining room where two banquet tables have been set up to cross over into the living room. The tables will be finely dressed with perfectly pressed linen table cloths, real china plates, terribly tempting, tall glassware (also the real thing), and four or five pieces of silverware polished for hours by Grampa the night before. Parents with small children would be advised to take their hands and skillfully lead them to the seat designated to them by Gramma. Years of Christmas dinners have taught me one very valid lesson — never sit all the children side by side, you are simply asking for disaster. As everyone shuffles behind the already-seated family members to get to their chair everything will be almost ready until someone realizes that the very end seat is still unoccupied. With the precision of movie theatre scrambling, everyone will stand until that same single uncle makes his way to his chair and as if by some sick twist of irony, Gramma always manages to place him smack dab in the middle of all the little kids.

Now it would appear that everyone is ready to eat, especially the children who have been sitting for ten minutes, but alas Gramma desires one more photo, this time incorporating the beautifully set table. Several moans later dinner is served. As large heirloom serving platters filled to the brim with lovingly prepared food are sent around the table, a sudden panic goes over parents. Single Uncle Dan has no children and likewise no concept of the fact that these little people can't even lift these platters, let alone take a portion and pass it on to the next person. With you seated seven seats away, you suddenly feel a cold sweat as you watch in horror when Uncle Dan, continuing to converse with other adult men around the table, haphazardly hands off the platter of turkey to your five-year-old daughter. Without hesitation and as if by experience, she reaches for the platter, but her little elbows buckle under the immense weight and unfortunately the inevitable occurs — a lap full of turkey. Wide-eyed in terror, she instinctively looks over at you, unsure of whether she is about to be banished to the spare room or if she will be swept away into your loving arms. Then comes the squeal, then the tears, then the deafening silence. Everyone stops their conversation, that is, everyone except Uncle Dan, who remains oblivious to the situation for which he is in part responsible. Gramma comes to the rescue and somehow manages to get herself to the end of the table, clean up the spilled turkey, replace the serving platter with a fresh load of bird, sponge off juniorette's velvet dress leaving no stain, and scold Uncle Dan for being so careless, all while you sit dumbfounded with your mouth hanging open. No harm done, one more lesson learned; next year Uncle Dan sits by himself at the little card table off to the side.

Dinner cannot end too soon for anxious, now overtired children who really only wanted to unwrap the rest of the gifts under Gramma and Grampa's tree. As dessert gets passed around, the entire table of guests will be subjected to little noses brushing up against their legs as the children try to make an escape under the table. They will use the excuse of having to go to the washroom, but after six minutes of absenteeism, the plot is clear — they have headed for the stash in the other room.

The overstuffed adults eventually make their way to the Christmas tree and the unwrapping tizzy begins again. This time, however, it is a true test of your child's ability to react appropriately under pressure. Unfortunately, at younger ages children are not graced with a lot of savvy, and when they unwrap the big box from Gramma and Grampa only to discover a pair of purple pants, a yellow plaid shirt, four pairs of underwear, and two pairs of socks, they too quickly put the box to the side and look around in desperation for another one to open. When they discover the booty is all tapped out, without hesitation or thought they blurt out, "Is that all we get is clothes?" For grandparents the hurt is real, for children the innocence is real, for parents the truth is real — more time is needed on teaching manners, gratitude, and the value of diplomacy.

As children grow, so too do grandparents, and their will and desire to host the Christmas dinner may wane after several successful years. This is a huge turning point in young mothers' lives as they decide to take over the tradition. In the instances where dinner is hosted at your home, the entire day becomes a blur of cooking, cleaning, hosting, cleaning, serving, pleasing, cleaning, and so forth. Of course there are bonuses to this option — the children get to enjoy their new toys and the worry about the result of the excitement, candy, and rich food being thrown up all over Gramma's new Persian carpet is eliminated.

Christmas day is one of the longest days of a parents' year, and the drive home from the grandparents' house or when the final guest leaves your house is a true blessing. The children will probably doze off in the car on the way home so you can gently carry them into their beds, remove their now soiled *special* outfits, and tuck their nearly naked, little bodies into a warm throw of comforters. In spite of your own fight with exhaustion you and your spouse manage to find the will to sit with a warm cup of tea in a darkened living room lit only by the twinkling of lights on the tree. No words need to be spoken. The day has been filled with conversation. No gifts need to be exchanged. The gifts lay sleeping in purity only steps away. You know that in less than twenty-four hours you will endure the frustration of broken toys and boredom, but this one hour of peace and joy truly makes it all worthwhile. Christmas comes but once a year, and despite the insurmountable stress it brings with it, we still find great pleasure in watching it unfold all over again on video only a short month after it is all done. It is a wondrous time of year and should be spent enjoying the gifts of family and friends. Eventually children will grow out of the phase of make-believe and come to understand a truer meaning: while that day is glorious, it is, ironically, sad. They will likely stop spilling on their new outfits, but then again, they will likely not even want to wear one. They will likely be appreciative of the gift of new clothes, but then again, you'll miss playing with the toys. They will likely sleep in until 10 a.m., but you'll get very lonely sitting by the tree waiting for them. Enjoy the magic while you can.

Children are the masters of ploys for toys, as every significant event and holiday becomes a major fund raiser. Once again commercialization plays havoc, with the will of the parent versus the want of the child. The once religious holiday of Easter has become a banquet of delectable delights ranging from chocolate in the shape of anything includ-

And to think we spent all that money on the presents.

ing race cars, every popular movie character, chickens, ducks, and of course rabbits, to a variety of egg-shaped purely sugar candies available to the Easter Bunny for hiding. As if all the hypertension from the candy weren't enough, the holiday is advertised as yet another reason for children to beg their parents for a toy. I admit I caved once again, and as the years have passed, the fun of just hunting for Easter eggs has turned into another flyer-inspecting fury with the sole purpose of selecting the ideal Easter gift for the bunny to strategically place at the end of the sugar egg trail.

Unfortunately once you begin a tradition it takes lengthy, well-timed explanation along with some fancy footwork to try and change, and sometimes it's easier to just leave well enough alone, biding time until the magic wears off. Easter, like other magical events, does bring about challenges, and once again parents find themselves fighting off the need to sleep so they can go undetected as they skillfully hide the goodies throughout the house. I must admit, however, as the years have passed, my skills at hiding the Easter goodies have gone from spending up to an hour carefully placing each goody in great little hiding spots to taking ten minutes to toss a few on the floor and leave a trail to them from their bedrooms. As for those wonderful outdoor Easter egg hunts, let's just say it loses its fascination after a late snowfall.

Like Christmas, Easter is also accompanied by a few pre-celebratory traditions, none of which is more involved than the painting of the Easter eggs. At the merciless begging of your children, you will no doubt once again find yourself devoting an entire evening prior to the actual festivities setting up and ultimately taking part in an alleged fun-filled family event. Not unlike the decorating of Christmas cookies, you will also find yourself amidst a table cluttered with bowls filled with food colouring, an overpriced egg decorating kit, and a dozen or so hard-boiled eggs (all of which eventually have to be eaten by you). With good intentions and the excitement of a dog in heat, the children will stay at your side for at least ten minutes, then one by one they will slowly drift away to the next more interesting matter, such as the cartoon specials on television. And there you will be left alone to decorate the ten remaining eggs, a task you take to heart as you painstakingly apply special effects in order to out-do your mate's egg. When the children are younger, say two to seven, they will rise very early and, like Christmas, feel it necessary to wake their parents so they can witness the hunt. As they get older, they may do one of two things — sleep in a little longer anticipating that the goodies will still be there anyway, or rise early and madly scatter around collecting the booty, eating on the average half a pound of candy, than passing out again due to sugar overload. Either way, consumption is inevitable, and if Sunday services are on the schedule, parents would be advised to take a brown paper bag along.

Although it is a fading memory, I do recall losing teeth when I was a child, and luckily and for the grace of good dentists, I am not yet at that stage in my life again. I remember joyously waking to a shiny coin which somehow magically replaced the blood-clad tooth I had put under my pillow the night before. It was all very exciting. The tooth fairy would flit in during the depth of my slumber and without so much as a flutter of her wings slip directly under my head, sprinkle some pixie dust, then turn my tooth into a nickel. In the morning I would awake to the sheer delight of discovery. Well the concept hasn't changed much over thirty-five years; however, the value of the tooth has increased in our case by some forty percent. Maybe the tooth fairy has some stock tips. As a parent, I was suddenly faced with the palm-sweating, heart-pounding role of the tooth fairy. In the beginning it was easy, sneaking into the childrens' room and making the swap as the tired child slept soundly. Then the challenges started to develop.

My first transcendental trial came when my five-year-old daughter lost her eighth tooth. She, of course, was ecstatic at the prospect of another cash-for-body-part-payout and diligently placed her tooth on the kitchen table, announcing, "I'm going to leave my tooth here tonight cause I'm scared I'll scare the fairy away when I snore."

Finally my husband and I were given a break, no sneaking into her room and running the risk of getting busted. No more staying up until the wee hours of the night, which for most parents with small children is anything after 9:30 p.m. There was a god. So just before I turned in I placed two loonies under the yellowish, blood-crusted tooth and contentedly went off to bed. I slept peacefully until 5:15 a.m. when I was awakened by sobs from my daughter who stood at the head of our bed. Through the gaping hole in the front of her mouth, she half whistled and half spoke the tearful words. "The toof fairy forgot me, thee didn't leaf me any money, mommy woth I bad, why would thee forget me?"

Still partly asleep I lay there dumbfounded. What she was saying made no sense in spite of her obvious lisp. I shook my head and focused on her sweet yet distraught face. Tears stained her cheeks, her hair was ruffled from having just risen, and her toothless smile was down-turned in a pitiful pout.

"Are you sure you looked exactly where you left your tooth? Remember, you didn't leave it under your pillow this time."

"Yeth, mommy, I looked on the kithen table, right where I leaved it, and the toof is there, but no money."

With this explanation came more shoulder-shrugging, head-bobbing sobs, ending in a grand finale of body slamming onto the side of our bed. Her persistence convinced me a crime had occurred and I had to investigate. As I rose from the bed I glanced back at my husband who had an equally confused expression. With a tiny hand in mine, I led my heart-broken daughter back to the scene of the crime, all the while trying to figure out exactly what had happened. I distinctly recalled putting the loonies on the kitchen table and neatly placing the tooth on top of them. As we approached the table, it was evident that the two loonies were gone but the tooth remained. Knowing perfectly well my five-year-old didn't yet have the creative ability to sneak out, snatch the loonies, then make a false claim against the unimpeachable character of the tooth fairy, I phrased my next question very carefully.

"Are you sure you didn't get up earlier and pick up the loonies, then go back to bed, fall asleep, and forget about it?"

"No, Mommy, I waked up when Bwadley came in and thaid the toof fairy didn't come."

Suddenly it started making sense. Considering the still early hour, I returned to my bedroom with Krysta and gently tucked her in between my husband and I, assuring her the tooth fairy had left her some money, but she needed to get a little more sleep. Reluctantly she fell asleep. Approximately an hour later Bradley sauntered into our bedroom heading towards our bathroom. Through inherent parental instinct, I noticed he resembled a fox with chicken feathers on his face.

"Hey, Brad, did you happen to see the money the tooth fairy left for Krysta?"

"Nope,"came a startled reply.

"How come you told her the tooth fairy didn't come?"

"Cause."

"How do you know?" I suspiciously asked.

"Cause I went out to get a glass of water just before Krysta got up and there was no money, so she forgot Krysta, hahahah."

The weak explanation was bad enough, but the cruel teasing laugh set Krysta into a frenzy of tears again.

"Well, honey," I said between gritted teeth, "I'm sure the tooth fairy left some money."

"How do you know, Mom, unless you're actually the tooth fairy just pretending?" came Brad's quick retort.

With that I was speechless. Krysta stopped wailing and my husband managed to sit up and stare at me, wondering how I was going to get myself out of this mess. My few years of experience and my sometimes annoying quick wit managed to save the day and my butt.

"Well, I got up about 4:30 and went to the kitchen to get an aspirin and I noticed there were quarters under Krysta's tooth. So if they were there then but gone when you went out, where do you suppose they went?"

Finally Krysta caught on.

"Bwad, you took my money. Give it back."

"No, I didn't."

"Yeth you did. Mommy, make him give it back."

"I didn't take your stupid loonies."

There was a huge pause, then Brad quickly retreated back to his bed. I followed him and sat down beside him on the bed. He had the covers tightly pulled up over his head.

"I thought you had to go to the bathroom?"

"I changed my mind."

"Brad, why did you say the tooth fairy left loonies even though I had said quarters?"

"I just guessed. I don't know, cause . . ."

When the term "cause" is used at the end of a sentence, it has a slightly different meaning. The child may realize he is suddenly in deep doodoo and can't think of any way to get out of it.

I softened my demeanor. Anticipating a brow-beating would not result in a confession, but more likely an all too familiar mind game played by children who know they are in over their heads.

"Did you take the money, B?"

Despite the covers still tightly pulled over his head, I managed to hear a muffled reply.

"I was just playing a joke on her, Mom. I was going to give it back."

Then a tiny hand slithered out from under the covers and revealed two shiny loonies. I took the loonies, then gently paddled a round lump in the middle of the bed, assuming it to be and extended butt.

"Not nice, B, don't do that again. But more importantly, don't lie."

Ironic words coming from a woman who had been continually denying the truth about the tooth fairy, Santa Claus, and the Easter Bunny. But that is something we do as good parents — we lie to children, lead them on, and then bear the damaging news at a never appropriate age.

"No, Virginia, there really isn't a Santa Claus."

Santa, the Easter Bunny, and the tooth fairy are three larger-than-life figures that fill children's minds with wonder and excitement, all the while filling their hearts with joy. Their greatness is only limited to the willingness of a parent and her own childhood memories of those magical occasions.

For some unexplained reason, the tooth fairy is usually the first mystery to come into question. Perhaps it is because she is economically inept when it comes to the mother-lode brought by Santa, who after all only requires you to hang a sock out for goodies and not leave an actual body part. Nonetheless there does come a time and it most definitely will vary from child to child, where make-believe gives way to reality. Usually schools are the breeding grounds of doubt. Once children are bombarded by sneers and laughter over their willingness to believe versus their friends otherwise wise beyond their years, the smoke and mirrors of childhood magic is sadly revealed. And yet another twist of ironic fate is introduced to a parent's life — the sadness accompanying the loss of sweet innocence combined with the joy over no more pressure to perform what should rightfully be considered the real truth behind making magic and keeping secrets.

While not supported by fairy tales and legendry, there are other occasions in the lives of children which are cause for parents to perform at peak levels. Welcome, Halloween and birthdays.

From my understanding Halloween is mostly recognized with such ceremony in Canada and the United States, and not everywhere in those nations. However, the places that do make a fuss over the All-Hallows Eve do so in a big way. Somewhere down the paths of history a tradition of dressing kids in costumes and sending them begging for candy to every house feasible in a period of five hours has developed.

Thought You'd Like to Know

In case you may be wondering and if you have not already done a little research, I thought I would share with you the information I found on how this now infamous, somewhat holiday of the Western Nations came about. Halloween began as a Celtic Festival in Samhain some 300 years ago. The date commemorated the end of summer and the beginning of the cold, dark winter, November 1. Because winter was often associated with death, the eve of November 1, October 31 was viewed as the point where the gap between the living and the dead became illusive. Ghosts were said to return to earth, and the living would make large bonfires and sacrifice crops and animals to these kindred spirits. When they held this festival, they wore costumes. When Christianity came to Samhain, the day was recognized as important and therefore sanctioned as a Christian holiday, All Saints Day or All-Hallows (Eve) accordingly. The tradition of trick-or-treating quite literally developed from the act of poor people begging for food and being given "soul cakes" in return for their prayers for deceased family and friends. As time moved forward to the new century and immigrants, especially Irish, moved to the Americas, the tradition continued as a form of begging for food. Of course, like everything else in our world, tradition has given way to modernization, and while the need to beg for sustenance is no longer the norm, sending children out in elaborate costumes to beg is today's way of celebrating the festival. As a side note, the celebration has reached enormous proportions, so much so that over seven billion dollars is spent on Halloween. And alas the tradition of dentistry was formed.

Children get as excited over Halloween as they do Christmas. After all, when else can they go to school in a cool costume and party all day, then go out that night and get pillow cases filled with candy. I too remember the excitement of Halloween; the only difference is that the candy we got that night was pretty much the take for the year. My mom used to go the extra mile and always hand-made all of our costumes. So like every good parent with a need to outperform, I took to the tradition of Halloween like a dog takes to a ham bone. Costumes were to be my specialty. Not normally a seamstress, this was my opportunity to show the world, or at least all the other mothers, that I was Lady Singer herself. I began planning the costumes around the first week of October, purchased the shiniest, gaudiest, flashiest fabric I could find, and then adorned it all with sequins, beads, trim, and fur. When my children were old enough to walk, it was time to adorn an elaborate hand-made costume that would not only earn them a handful of candy at every door, but also earn me a reputation for being super-mom. What started out as fun soon became an obsession. The first costumes were pint-sized, stuffed to the brim dinosaurs. Krysta was only two and she could barely carry her own weight let alone the weight of a batting-stuffed tail that trailed three feet behind her. The next year I had life-sized, cute as buttons sunflowers, then a miniature version of an R.C.M.P. and his ice princess, then a beautiful red velvet cape-clad pirate and his wench. But the obsession finally came to a head when my daughter was in Grade 2 and my son in Grade 3.

At their request I would make a lasting impression with a lifelike pheasant costume and a full three-foot-span winged butterfly. What was I thinking? Not only did I stay up 'til the wee hours of the night for four days prior to Halloween, but I never put any thought into how my daughter was actually going to sit in her seat during class. My overly artistic flare, along with my foolishness, had to stop. These worn-once-in-a-lifetime costumes were not only causing me lack of sleep and frustration, they were costing me a fortune. Other moms were content with throwing a bed sheet on their little goblins, cutting out holes for eyes, then sending them merrily on their way. Besides, my kids were getting a little too old for costume overkill. So I caved in and toned down, turning to the basics of Zorro, hippies, army dudes, and witches. I even discovered that the department stores had some pretty promising replacements for my hand-made creations. It's simply amazing what a little hair paint and makeup can do. I still enjoy the challenge of sewing some downsized costumes, but I've learned to let go and settle with the fact that Bradley wants to go as a funky kid this year. No sewing required.

Unfortunately for the children, Halloween falls on a school night five out of seven years. Fortunately for the parents, these nights are limited to three to four hours of trick-or-treating. Even at that children still stay up way past a decent bed time, get loaded on sugar, and suffer from sugar hangovers the next day. Perhaps consideration should be given to making the day after Halloween a holiday; our nation's teachers would be delighted. Like many other holidays, Halloween has become a contest among children to see who can get the largest stash, and highly competitive children need to be stopped at three full pillow cases. After all, they will no doubt never eat all of those goodies, which puts a great deal of pressure on mom and dad to help out. Usually this means being the recipient of all the unwanted candy, such as those very chewy candy kisses (which it so happens I love), chocolate bars that are only classified such by the manufacturers, plain potato chips, and of course all the wrapped hard candy. The rest of the good stuff gets hidden away in the kids' rooms to be found sometime in May when parents are doing a thorough spring cleaning.

It goes without saying that birthdays have become vital celebrations in the realm of childhood. But like any other celebration, the extent of the event depends entirely on the willingness of the parents. At the risk of another "When I was a child . . ." story, when I was a child birthdays were pretty much limited to a party including four or five of your closest friends, mom's homemade birthday cake with nickels strategically placed in it for partygoers to find, pin the tail on the donkey, and gifts that were usually under five dollars. Times have changed and once again, depending on the circle of friends your children draw from, so too has the concept of birthday parties. When my son entered E.C.S. (Kindergarten), the first signs of birthdaymania appeared when he was invited to his first party. Of course he was delighted and equally excited; this was, after all, his first major social outing. I, however, found myself in a quadrant of quandaries. What should he wear? What should he bring? Will he be okay? Will he know some of the other kids? The first two worries were easily taken care of by the invitation. The party was being held close to Halloween, so they could come in costume, and there was a phone number I could call in order to resolve the worry of present selection. When I did call, the host mom was very helpful in supplying a list of items of choice. I thought it appropriate to take Brad with me and let him be part of the gift selection process. Most of the items were reasonably priced, but Brad felt he might look chintzy if he didn't bring at least two action figures and perhaps some trading cards. So eighteen dollars later we had what he thought was an appropriate gift. I decked him out in his Mountie costume and reluctantly took him to his first ever, away from mom outing. I walked him to the door and waited to speak with the hosting mom. I knew the family somewhat and was very assured they were wonderful people, but despite any first-hand knowledge of their good values and kind ways I still felt it necessary to ensure my baby's last minute well-being.

Brad was greeted by the birthday boy and then shuffled inside the house, which was ornately decorated for Halloween and birthday. I stood and chatted with mom for a few minutes, then said my goodbyes and left. Admittedly, I sat in the car out front for a few extra minutes anticipating that my little white-haired boy might come running out begging to be taken home. Four hours later I returned to pick up the partygoer. Once again I walked to the door to retrieve my little buddy. I half expected a battle over wanting to stay and party on, but instead was surprised to see my played-out partygoer waiting anxiously at the door for me. Brad ran to me, took my hand, and said, "Let's go." Before I could extend my hand to the hostess, Brad was pulling me towards the sidewalk. I graciously thanked her for inviting Brad and made Brad do the same. He did so quickly, then ran to the car. Although a little puzzled at his quick retreat and obvious eagerness to be with me, deep down inside I was actually proud to think he missed me that much. When we got home, I questioned him as to who was there, what they did, and did the birthday boy like his gift, etc.

My original last two quandaries were eventually answered. Brad explained that everyone from their thirty-two student E.C.S. class was there except for three kids who were sick or away and the teacher. As well, there were some friends and family. My jaw must have dropped to the floor. This innocent birthday party hosted over thirty candy-induced, runny-nosed, costume-clad, six-year-old kids. He said he couldn't remember if the birthday boy liked the gift he gave him, and when I thought about the dynamics of receiving over thirty gifts, I wasn't at all surprised. When I again asked what they did and did Brad have fun, he quietly replied, "It was fun." I assumed he was very tired and that explained his rather nonchalant attitude. After removing his costume and giving him a big hug, I watched as he fell onto his bed and fell sound asleep. I went to the kitchen table where he had placed the goody bag he got from the party. I sat down and opened the elaborately wrapped treat bag and dumped the contents out onto the table.

Once again my jaw dropped. There were two full-sized chocolate bars, a regular-sized package of bubble gum, a cute note pad, two Halloween pencils, a small action figure, a balloon, some chocolate coins, and a package of stickers. The treat bag alone had to total close to what I had spent on the present. As I marveled over this mom's ability to host such an event and supply such a fantastic party favour, I also began to worry about how I was going to fare when it came to Brad's first party. Adding to the stress was the fact that his birthday is five days after Christmas.

As I sat there pondering this new parental dilemma, the telephone rang. The host mom was on the other end and she thought she should telephone me to see if Bradley was okay. My heart went into my throat. What had happened? Did he get hurt? Did the other kids make fun of him? Did he get sick from the excitement? At my inquest the mom informed me they had planned mixed Halloween and birthday games, and some of the games entailed the children sitting in their dark basement while the dad told scary stories. As well, the children were led around to different unidentified substances which they could touch and feel, then they were told the substances were eyeballs and brains. Of course, this overtly imaginative mother and father were using peeled grapes and noodles, but to my sweet five-year-old whose imagination tended to run wild at the best of times, there was no convincing him that what he felt wasn't the real thing. Apparently he became very frightened. Despite the parents' every effort to calm and reassure him, the rest of the party, for him, was pretty much a bust.

Suddenly it all made sense. Brad's first social outing turned out to be quite a traumatic experience for more than the obvious reason of being away from mom with near strangers in their house, surrounded by many other rambunctious kids. When Brad awoke that evening for dinner, we discussed the difference between reality and games. He tried his five-year-old best to disassociate the two, but still ended up sleeping with my husband and I for the next few nights.

Two short months after that incident, Brad hosted his very first birthday party. The time of the year dictated an inside party, and I was determined not to be outdone. Once again I discarded the warnings of my ever-so-wise husband and went all out. I did not invite the entire E.C.S. class, but nearly all of them. I decorated the house in birthday flair, including streamers, balloons, signs, crepe paper, the whole nine yards. I went with a Happy New Year theme by supplying plastic champagne glasses for the kids' punch, noise-makers, hats, sparklers, bursting streamers, party crackers, and of course, falling balloons. I arranged at least five games, nothing involving unidentifiable substances, and a special craft project for the partygoers to take home for their moms and dads. The invitations were sent out informing party invitees the party would go from noon until four. If other mothers could last four hours, so could I — besides, I had recruited the good graces of my mother-in-law and my wonderful neighbour. The party guests started arriving at 11:45 (those of the wiser parents), and the festivities got well under way. Even though I had refrained from inviting the entire class, I still managed to have twenty-two very excited, very loud, and somewhat overzealous six-year-olds, (most of whom were of the haphazard male persuasion) mini party animals in my usually fanatically maintained house. I sincerely thought I had it under control until one hour into the party when I noticed that two of the more active fellas were using my stairs as an indoor slide and my "rarely sat on" sitting room couch as a launch pad. I calmly walked over to them and suggested they join the rest of the partygoers in the kitchen for lunch.

Lunch was fairly uneventful: hotdogs, potato chips, and ice cream cake, unfortunately all consumed in less than ten minutes, not the hour I had planned. What now? I escorted the now fed and ready to rumble gang downstairs for gift opening, and decided I needed to waste some time if I was going to survive the next two and half hours. So I used a well-thought-out party suggestion of making the gift opening into a game of elimination. Besides, opening twenty-two gifts would or should take up some time. Despite the obvious restlessness of the partygoers, I managed to ward off pleas of, "Hurry up, Brad, open mine," and worked this part of the party into a little over an hour. I did, however, assign my mother-in-law (bless her), the demanding task of controlling the two aforementioned party animals. Sometimes the mere pointing of Gramma's finger is enough.

After all the gifts were opened and Brad did his part in oohing and aahing, I quickly swept the gifts up and placed them on a table out of the reach of some twenty-two very curious, must-open-and-play-with six-year-olds, that was after all the privilege of the birthday boy and his father. I shuffled the now very restless crowd back upstairs to the kitchen where my party helpers had cleaned up and set up for the craft making. My intentions were noble — the partygoers would be occupied for an hour and moms and dads would get a cute handmade craft. My intentions may have been noble, but my experience with a bunch of six-year-old high-strung children was very limited. Most of the active boys finished their craft in a record four minutes, and even though I tried to explain that mom would rather have a beautiful bouquet of felt flowers as opposed to a carelessly cut piece of brown felt glued to a popsicle stick, my argument fell on deaf ears. The girls at the party were more than content to sit quietly while they painstakingly tried to outdo each others' craft, but the boys were a different story. I couldn't just throw them outside to play — it was December 31 and the temperature was in the minus twenties. So I reluctantly let them go downstairs to the family room and just play. To say the least, 4 o'clock could not come fast enough, and by the time parents started arriving, the once neatly tucked-in partygoers were quite literally played out. As the guests started leaving, I stood at the door and handed out my version of a treat bag — elaborately decorated cello wrapping containing a New Year party favour (determined to make a lasting impression on the parents), two pencils, a fancy black-papered notebook, a package of stickers, a cool eraser, a full size chocolate bar, a package of bubble gum, a dinky toy for the boys, and a ring for the girls, all of which was neatly tied with black and silver ribbon. Oh yes, the partygoers got to take home their crafts and their personal plastic champagne glasses. All totaled, including the decorations and food, I figured this homemade birthday party probably cost us two hundred dollars.

As the years passed and I gained experience with young partygoers, I concluded it was easier, cheaper, and just as much fun to invite a few good friends and treat them to a movie, bowling, or something held outside of the home. This does, however, bring me to a point I would like to make regarding birthday celebrations. Parents are faced with enough pressure when it comes to raising children without having to compete for the "Parent of the Year Award" given to the parent who can outdo every other parent by throwing the best birthday bash. I saw it happen, and I too fell victim to its severity. Birthday bashes in the circle I found myself falling into were no longer about celebrating another year in the life of a child, they had become pageantry. My children attended parties that included bowling for twenty, movies for twenty, fun centres for twenty, renting entire swimming complexes, backyard blow-up jumping arenas, and even gymnasiums outfitted with entire castles. I began to think I could never keep up, and as I grew wiser I realized I didn't want to, so I opted for two or three good friends, a movie or movie rentals, pizza, and a sleep-over. The money I saved could and would be better spent on my child's birthday present. Truth be known, children won't remember how great their sixth birthday party was; they will, however, remember that their parents never missed one of their birthdays.

Celebrations will come and go throughout your children's lives, and even if the magic wanes as they grow older, the moments should still remain magnificent. They may trade waiting anxiously for jolly old St. Nick for donning a Santa costume and going to the hospital to visit sick children. They may not believe in fairies that flit through the night, but they will renew your faith in their goodness when they willingly participate in keeping the magic alive in the eyes of a younger sibling or cousin. They may choose to be with friends on their birthday rather than celebrate in your grand style, but they will thank you for trusting them and forgoing your fun for their independence. Maybe the magic wears off, but celebrating the wonders of raising your children never will.

The Joys of Toys

Let's be honest, even as we grow into adulthood we never really grow out of the desire for toys. The toys we have when we get older are simply more expensive, more technical, and likely bigger, but nonetheless are still toys. We have our computers, cell phones, DVD players, fancy home theatre systems, recreational vehicles including snowmobiles, quads, motorcycles, and some might say our cars/trucks and even airplanes. The more buttons we can get the better, the more power they have the better, and certainly the more fun we can have with them the better. So why should it come as a surprise to us when our children seem to value their toys more than the family pet, the house they live in, and in some cases their own family members. Toys, after all, spell FUN, but for parents, childrens' toys can spell STRESS. To begin with, there are literally millions of toys to choose from, ranging from the ever-popular Etchasketch to more elaborate computer games involving eighty-seven levels of difficulty, graphics that would baffle Walt himself, and sound effects so realistic one has to forewarn the neighbours. So parents of today and most certainly the future are facing "Post Toymatic Stress Disorder." Not only are there too many choices, they no longer can be acquired with a five dollar bill and may even require a second mortgage on the house.

As mentioned earlier, our children are inundated with marketing blitzes specifically targeted at a child's sponge-like brain. I am convinced that when some television commercials are played backwards, they contain subliminal messages secretly encoded for the minds of children which make them whiny and whimpering as they sit dumbfounded and pointing at the television, repeating an induced message, I WANT–MUST HAVE–GET NOW. A parent's only hope for bringing their sweet child back is to promptly channel the television to P.B.S. Unfortunately, it may be too late, and the need-to-have seed is already planted. As if this weren't challenge enough, taking these now brain-washed children shopping can be as grueling as cleaning up throw-up that trails from their bed sheets down the carpeted hallway and ends right beside the toilet bowl. I have yet to discover any sure-fire way to avoid these challenges, and must admit have on more than one occasion failed at good parenting by simply giving in and buying the much-demanded item. Sometimes I do so out of sheer frustration, sometimes out of sheer self-satisfaction — after all, there are some real cool toys out there today.

That might explain my daughter's sixty-five piece doll collection, even though she's more of a tomboy and sixty of them are still in their original boxes. I knew I was stepping over the line of collector to fun fanatic the day she approached me with every little girl's question.

"Mommy, why doesn't dolly get married?"

Without missing a beat, my unappreciated, satirical humour jumped in. "I don't know. Maybe she wants to marry a man who has a job and who's hair doesn't look like a rusty SOS pad. I've got an idea. Why don't you introduce her to G.I. Joe, no woman can resist a main in uniform. I know whenever I see a guy in uniform, my heart does a little pitter-patter. I mean, nothing looks as good as a strapping, hard-bodied, twenty-five-year-old, clean cut guy donning an Air Force uniform. It's the ultimate of strength and power and . . ."

I caught myself rambling and glanced down at my daughter who was staring back at me in disbelief.

"Besides, I think the boy doll is really her long-lost brother."

Not the best retort considering Krysta had the boy doll's stiff arms pointed out beside the girl doll's waist and their heads pushed together in a doll-like passionate embrace.

"Oh YUCK!!!"

The last thing I recall was the boy doll being thrown across the room.

Face the piper, new parents, you will now without a doubt find yourself in the toy store or aisle more than you do in your favourite clothing or hardware store. Along with other parents, you will stand bewildered in front of an endless variety of toys experiencing the same gut-wrenching feeling of confusion you get every time you enter the cereal aisle in the grocery store.

Some of Life's Most Embarrassing Moments Happen while Parenting

Once children are introduced into the picture, the constant worry about wearing the right outfit, having your hair done perfectly, or slurping your soup by mistake is totally irrelevant — the true definition of embarrassment is about to rear its ugly head.

The Sound of Pitter-Patter

On what fathers would describe as the rarest of occasions, the familiar sound of the pitter-patter of little feet crossing the hall to your bedroom manages to somehow escape you and suddenly you're faced with every parent's nightmare. Normally mom can hear the sound of ten well-padded toes hitting the thickest of carpet more than sixty feet away, but the heat of a rare moment can create sound barriers capable of blocking out the engines of a Boeing 747. At the foot of passion, literally, stands two tiny eyeballs just barely gazing over the mattress and the box spring. The quiet night air is broken by the innocent request of your toddler.

"Daddy, can I come up and wrestle with mommy too?," or

"Mommy, are you trying to start daddy's heart like the guy on tv?"

I am now.

There really is no graceful or easy way to get out of this entanglement, no pun intended. Some parents opt for playing dead in hopes that the intruder will become discouraged and walk back to his own room. Still other parents perform callisthenic-type moves, distorting their bodies in what would otherwise be sexually amazing in order to assume more familiar positions. Some parents resort to frantically yelling, which eager therapists will conveniently blame for dysfunction later in the child's life. However you do it and despite your greatest effort to make it just go away, this stressful experience will come back to haunt you, either at a family Thanksgiving dinner or in front of all the other parents at the day care when junior exclaims, "Mommy and daddy were playing leap frog in bed last night."

The Family Bed: Kings and Queens Need to Reign
Much to be discussed or discussed much

Games of leap frog do tend to be a lot less frequent when young people are roaming the halls of the home. More often than not these little lost souls are simply looking for a safe place to lie down away from the monsters that haunt their slumber. As a result, you may find night-time intruders standing at the foot of your bed or, more disturbing, right beside your pillow breathing heavily into your face. Such visits lead to an abrupt waking up and are accompanied by pleas of bed sharing. The verdict on bed sharing is still out. Some parents are adamantly against it, making claims of maladjusted children later in life, while others find sharing the family bed a great way to bond and instill security in children. Personally, I leave the decisions up to the family and would never be so bold as to presume that what is good for us is good for everyone else. We did fall victim to sharing the family bed on several occasions, not as an excuse to share special bonding with our children, but because we were simply too tired to address the battle of getting the children back to sleep in their own beds. Sometimes it meant one of us would sedately go and lay with the worried child with the intentions of lulling him to sleep, which often meant falling sound asleep in a mate's bed better suited for the likes of a four foot person. Other times it meant waking up to a tiny, inadvertently placed elbow or knee. In fact to this day there are mornings when my husband and I will wake up and go searching the house for one another. But a person does what a person has to do. As our children grow and reach the tender ages of vanity, the frequency of night-time visitors has lessened, and once again we find ourselves in a position of sleeping together, pun intended.

Hissy Fits and Toddlers' Tantrums

As a parent you should prepare yourself for a number of embarrassing moments. You are more than likely going to be subjected to the indignity of what I refer to as "hissy fits and toddlers' tantrums," the type of behaviour which conveniently or not so conveniently rears its ugly head in very public settings, such as your local grocery store. Depending on the situation and the desire, the performance can be as low key as incessant begging to as high profile as laying in the middle of the produce aisle pounding fists and flailing legs, all to the embarrassment of the parent and the amusement of onlookers. During the first performance, you are simply mortified — your eyes widen and your jaw drops and you can barely do anything but stare in disbelief. The next time you will stand there and perform one of your own hissy fits by yelling at the child and pulling him up by his skinny little arms. But once you become a seasoned veteran, you realize that the best response is none at all. In fact, you may master the art of acting.

First you pretend the child is not yours, looking around as if searching for the parents. You may even embellish with a few untruths such as, "What a spoiled child. Where are the parents?" then quickly and quietly disappear around the corner. Once junior realizes he is no longer the object of your attention and frustration, he will grow tired and soon join you, likely in a frenzy of anxiety at the very thought that you may have deserted him among the bunkers of apples and oranges. Hopefully the anxiety will be intense enough to forestall any further instances, but not so intense that the child ends up living at home until he is forty-three.

with small responsibility; one day alone raising children can feel like a lifetime. A parent's day is filled to capacity and even after the lights go off and the house is still, a parent's mind and heart never really rests. They are always on the job.

Sniff Sniff Sniffles

Why is it that whenever a parent or parents finally have a special occasion planned just for themselves, something they are counting the sleeps until, is when a child suddenly gets sick? You could go for months without ever going out or taking some much deserved time for yourself, and the minute someone calls and sets up a luncheon date, or you get the opportunity for a weekend get-away, that is precisely when a new strain of the flu hits. More often than not you will find yourself making an emergency visit to your doctor's office on the Friday hours before you are due to leave on your emotional escape. I must admit, however, doctors, especially if they have children themselves, are getting wise. Rather than wait for the throat swab to come back or for huge hives to develop, they may instinctively write out a prescription for a cure-all penicillin or antibiotic and give it to you either to fill and begin administering, or just to keep in case the test comes back positive, saving you the inconvenience of another trip to the doctor.

Hats Off to Perceptive Physicians

Dealing with sick children is never an easy experience. When they are babies, the feeling of helplessness is so overwhelming you will likely be calling your physician every three hours after the first sign of a sniffle or sneeze. As they grow your paranoia will wane, and you will become a bit of an expert in the area of your own children's ailments. You will be able to take their temperature without causing them the agony of wrongful insertion, lower a rising fever with the use of a tepid bath, successfully apply a butterfly bandage, administer cough medicine and other distasteful meds, but most importantly you will be able to recognize a sniffle for what it is, a sniffle. Even with your new-found knowledge and skills, there will still be many an occasion for visiting your family doctor.

Anything you don't feel right about always warrants a visit to the doctor. Be prepared, however, because visits to the doctor can be more traumatic than the ailment itself. If you are lucky enough to get in to see the doctor on short notice, you are likely going to have to wait in a very crowded, germ-infested, noisy waiting room where you will no doubt be surrounded by other sick children who are wheezing, coughing, crying, and screaming, and a mix of older folks who glare at them in disgust. After you have read your moaning child the tattered Dr. Seuss *Cat in the Hat* book fourteen times, you will finally hear the frustrated nurse call out your child's name. She will ask you what the problem is and then give you a well rehearsed response of "Uh-huh" and then guide you to a chair in the doctor's office. There you will have an opportunity to read another book to your child, probably four times before you actually see a doctor. Depending on the age of the child, this could be the biggest challenge you have faced all day, even more so than cleaning snot from your new shirt, driving while holding a half-filled barf bag, or listening to the ramblings of delirium. Usually a small child's only experience with a doctor involves needles, or poking and prodding, which is upsetting to say the least. So it is only fair to assume when the person wearing the stethoscope hanging precariously around his neck enters the room, all hell is about to break loose.

Your once passive child now resembles a male Pit-bull with his family jewels stuck to a freezing light post, raging mad but too scared to move. All the distractions in the world aren't going to reassure him, and suddenly those status symbol stethoscopes become a target for revenge. Wise doctors approach with caution and usually request mom or dad to sit the trembling child on their lap. Then the doctor can easily maneuver around the child, using the parent as protection from flailing arms and feet and legs that take on a life of their own, striking at the least opportune moment and at the most sensitive body parts.

After a tiresome game of "foot dodging," the doctor will complete the check-up and announce the news, "Junior has a cold. Give him lots of fluids, bed rest, and children's painkillers. If it persists for longer than a week, come back and see me." Depending on your doctor's keen sense when dealing with children and equally keen sense dealing with overloaded parents, he may offer the forlorn child a treat after a reasonably successful visit. After all, nothing soothes a hurting soul and calms a nervous mind more than a sucker or piece of licorice.

After many a visit to our family doctor both for my children and myself, I began to wonder why adults are never offered a treat. After all, we never bite the doctor, throw up on him, or scream bloody murder when he sticks the popsicle stick down our throat, or react to any of the other atrocities we (most specifically women) endure at the cold hands of our doctor. Forget the sucker, Doc. I think you owe me a steak dinner.

Play Dates and Day-care

One of the most helpful hints on child rearing I ever read was the suggestion that parents should arrange play dates for their toddlers. The reasoning: this gives the toddler an opportunity to socialize with other children and, more importantly, gives parents a much needed break. The theory behind the play dates was that they act as a caregiving (babysitting) exchange program. Whoever hosted the play date this time got a "get out of the house without the kids" free card for the next time. Personally, I thought this was an ingenious idea. Little did I realize how difficult it would be to find parents who actually wanted to take on the responsibility of having more than their own bundle of energetic playdom in their house for a few hours. I guess when it came right down to it, I too wasn't sure how eager I would be to return the favour. It certainly did sound good in theory. Besides, most of the other parents from our circle worked outside of the home, and the only day trade we could work out would be the weekends, and robbing rare family time seemed somewhat unfair. Even more unfair are the consequences of this theory on a stay home parent. It's amazing how quickly your house becomes labeled as the place to go if there is a stay home parent present, by both children and their parents alike. The scales of exchange tend to become imbalanced. Besides, there is always the issue of timing. What may be needed by one set of parents may not be convenient for other parents, and usually involves extensive planning and scheduling. The idea of spontaneous favour-cashing is wishful thinking. If it works, play dates are very useful. Parent and child get a rest from each other and a chance to be with someone else, someone who can relate to their terms of play or their need for outside companionship.

Unlike play dates, daycare may be a necessity of life for parents who work outside of the home. The decision to return to work after the birth of a child is never an easy one, but there may be no choice. To add to this stress, parents must choose a fitting daycare facility to tend to every possible need of their children in their absence. Word of mouth from close acquaintances is the best method of choosing a satisfactory facility; however, new parents may not have access to experienced parents whom they trust. Parents must then rely on their own investigative skills. Once a suitable facility is selected, parents would be advised to make an auditing visit to further determine if the facility is appropriate. Of course, nothing can replace the security and comfort of being at home with mom or dad, but many of these daycare facilities are well-equipped and staffed by capable and caring individuals.

Despite the difficulty of selecting a facility you feel secure enough to leave your precious child in, the most difficult part of daycare is no doubt the first time you have to leave your child there alone. Many parents will attend the daycare with their child for a few hours the first days, hoping this will make the transition easier. While this idea is in good faith, it is in all likelihood more of a hindrance then a help. When the day comes, the reality of separation anxiety rears its rather ugly head. Everything will be normal up to the part where mom or dad turns toward the door and begins to leave. Suddenly it dawns on junior/ette, who was strategically placed on the far side of the room among scads of toys and some new-found friends, that they are being abandoned. Mom or dad is leaving her there with these nice but nonetheless strangers in a big square room with a bunch of little tables and chairs and a bunch of other babies. I can only imagine that she is thinking, "I'm being refunded." And as silly as that may seem to us, the mind of a little person is incapable of comprehending the truth — it can only conjure up scary scenarios that threaten her security. With that thought in mind, she makes a mad dash for the door, falling with a thud to the floor at mom/dad's feet, then with the strength of a boa constrictor, wraps her arms around mom/dad's leg and holds on for dear life. At first mom or dad may be oblivious to what is happening as they try very hard to hold back the tears themselves, and it isn't until they feel the extra thirty pounds attached to their leg and hear the blood-curdling screams of what sounds like their child that they realize they are in trouble.

Parents try desperately to reassure the child, promising only a short time until they return, all the while trying to pry her from their leg. When they finally think they are successful in releasing the grip and begin to take another step, like some spring-loaded eel, the child coils around the other leg. Thoughts cross the parent's mind to stay and hold her for a while, but unfortunately time is running out and if this fiasco continues much longer they will be late for work, not to mention the disapproving stares they are getting from the daycare staff. With one more futile attempt to uncoil the kid, the parent is rescued by the experienced staff member who firmly puts her arms around the child and pries them loose. She wisely advises a quick retreat by mom/dad with no looking back and no last minute "I love yous" or "I'll miss yous." While it may seem cruel, her advice is backed by education and experience — just get out, the staff will handle the rest.

The rest of the day may seem like the longest in your life thus far, waiting and worrying about the well-being of your traumatized child. In fact many parents will telephone the facility just to check up on things and be somewhat disappointed to learn that five minutes after they disappeared from sight junior/ette was gleefully distracted by the antics of "Itsy Bitsy Spider." When you do finally return to retrieve your child, you are taken aback by her sudden lack of interest in your presence, replaced only by her new interest in the sand centre. Every day gets easier once children realize they actually came with a "No refund" policy.

Potty Training 101

Most parents would agree, the greatest invention of the twentieth century is the disposable diaper. Earth parents around the globe may beg to differ, suggesting that the natural feel of cotton is better for baby's butt, and washing reusable diapers is better for our environment. I praise their values while I equally praise disposable diaper manufacturers who have been able to produce a diaper that is ninety-five percent biodegradable, and skin care manufacturers who developed a non-allergenic cream exclusively for use on baby's butt. All this considered, why wouldn't you want to keep your child in diapers as long as you can? Solid foods, that's why. Changing diapers after the introduction of wieners brings on a whole new meaning, and short of waiting until the child is old enough to change his own diaper before introducing solid foods, Potty Training 101 is inescapable.

Depending on your level of patience and your own personal reasons, potty training will begin and conclude at different times. For our boy, it began just before age two and reached entire completion around age three. We read and heard many philosophies on training boys, most of which involved placing targets in the toilet bowl so he could take aim at something, or ringing a bell when the momentous occasion occurred. The latter reminded us too much of Darwin's theory on pain avoidance. Parents learn early the omnipotence of their little guy's wee willy — despite its tiny stature, once loaded it can very quickly become a pistol of pee. This knowledge is first experienced by the unexpecting parent during a diaper change. Parents stand in mouth-dropping awe when they first observe the ability of their little guy's manly muscle to stand at attention. Unfortunately and unwittingly, they often become the recipient of a taste of its perfect aim as well. So it is no surprise when it comes to potty training a little boy that there are great expectations. Dad, as the possessor of first-hand knowledge, desires immediate greatness for his prodigy. In fact dads often think one "hands on" lesson, so to speak, is sufficient and once junior realizes the power he holds, so to speak, there will be no turning back. If only it were that simple. Up to this point junior didn't need to help "Mr. Willy," so the thought of standing and holding him is, to say the least, imprudent. Training can be long and tedious, and requires a lot of patience and a little ingenuity. To begin with, unless your house is equipped with a floor level urinal, junior will need some help in order to step up to the plate, or toilet. Purchasing a little blue plastic step is one option, or dad could use this opportunity to build his own version of a Step Up, and if mom is so inclined she can paint cute little animal characters on it and give it a cute little label like Bradley's Piddling Pal.

Whatever choice you make, it will be totally useless if you don't take the time to stay in the room and coach. Coaching can occur in a variety of ways. Dad may choose to stand looming over junior in a virtual reality demonstration. Freud would say that this may be cause for years of therapy, for reasons obvious and some not so obvious. Other dads prefer to put the primal theory to use and give junior his first lesson on the art of hunting by treating Mr. Willy like a long arm, no pun intended. There is a notion of training in aiming by placing pieces of paper in the bowl, or waiting for the stream of fluid to hit the water at a high rate of speed and thus create natural targets, little yellow bubbles. And, of course, no lesson from dad would be complete without testing to see exactly how far the stream can spew, delighting in the height and the splash factor, and pivoting in order to determine how far one can turn and look at other things while doing their business. Personally, I think there is an unwritten rule among the male species which defines their manliness by the precision with which they can pee on the adjacent walls of a toilet. Maybe the idea of urinals in houses isn't such a stretch. This rule is right alongside the other rule — a man's dexterity is directly attributed to the accuracy with which his name can be written in newly-fallen snow. Moms, on the other hand, prefer a more dignified approach to training junior, such as rewards, better known as bribery. "If you go peepee in the toilet mommy will give you a treat." Like any other form of coaching, if mommy doesn't stay in the room with the trainee, the bribe is fruitless. After all, it doesn't take a Rhodes scholar to figure out that apple juice and pee have similar characteristics when being looked at in the bottom of a toilet bowl. But staying in the room can present some concerns for mom and boy alike. With dad, junior can learn through imitation, but with mom there is something kind of unsettling about having her assist in holding techniques and stream direction.

With Brad, we simply learned to look for tell-tale signs, such as suddenly stopping what he was doing, standing still, and developing that dopey grin and shivers of relief. At that point, we would scoop him up, run him to the toilet, place him on the step stool, pull down his pants, and then point the culprit into the toilet bowl. Our theory was that we could catch him just in time to finish the job in the toilet. Unfortunately, more times than not we grabbed him so quickly we literally scared the pee out of him. Eventually my husband resorted to teaching him how to write his name in the toilet bowl — a habit that continues into adulthood and extends to the wall beside the bowl and, of course, a fresh blanket of snow.

Eventually your diligence will pay off and junior will be peeing outside the diaper all on his own. Soon he too will revel in the joy of being able to relieve himself in the great outdoors on family camping trips. However, don't be shocked when he extends this natural desire in other wide open spaces such as the soccer field, your back yard, the neighbour's front yard, or the artificial plant at the corner of the bank.

Our daughter was a little more challenging. As a result of the female anatomy, girls must sit down on the job. The use of paper decoys posed a whole new dimension of problems as the little one tried to position herself such that she could observe the paper turn colour the minute it was contacted. The most successful way to do this was to squat above the toilet seat slightly off to one side. I needn't paint a detailed picture of where most of the body fluid ended up. Once again we thought it best to watch her and wait to see those tell-tale shivers, then rush her off to the toilet, pull her pants down, place her squarely on the seat, then wait and wait and wait. Patience was once again a valued virtue, so we decided, on the advice of others, to offer distractions such as books or small toys while awaiting the event. After ten minutes, six books, and a well-developed butt ring, we would lift her off and replace her "pull ups," only to watch that dopey grin unfold as our hard work of coaching, bribing, and waiting emptied out into the minimal amount of padding in the diaper-type-underwear invention.

All told, it took both children about six months to be fully trained in the delicate art of urinating in the toilet. The second part of the job was a little more time consuming and to say the least a lot less pleasant. Suddenly Brad had to forget everything he learned about standing up and accept that this part of the job is best done sitting down. Because Krysta had already mastered the sitting down part, she was much quicker to learn. She figured out in no time at all that both duties could be taken care of in one clean swoop or should I say poop. Brad, on the other hand, couldn't be bothered wasting precious time with this job. After all, running into the washroom, unzipping your pants, taking the mouse out of the house, quickly whizzing, then tucking the mouse back into the house and returning to play, involved a maximum of two minutes, especially if you conveniently forgot to zip up again. But the idea of having to actually sit down was just too much bother. Now we were charged with the task of watching and listening for grunts instead of shivers. Brad finally got tired of people backing away from him and that warm mushy sensation, and he too defeated the battle of bowel movements.

Not every child will learn the same way or in the same amount of time, but eventually every parent will be treated to that proud moment in their young child's life when they come running out, pants down around their ankles, toilet paper trailing behind, and declare in front of a room filled with dinner guests, "Mommy/Daddy, come look, I just pooped in the toilet."

New parents should also be aware of the somewhat disconcerting fascination children have with their own bowl of bounties. Most children will stare in wonder for minutes, but there are the few too curious ones who will actually do a "hands on" examination. The latter makes the lesson on flushing a must. In fact, wise parents will teach their children to flush before the tush leaves the seat. Of course, there is an equally interesting fascination with the whole business of "the flush." What could be better than swooshing poop being sucked down a hole the size of a quarter? And thus begins the challenge to see exactly what else can fit through that hole. Combs will fit, a whole roll of soggy toilet paper will fit, dinky toys and doll shoes will fit, but the cat, the cat definitely will not fit. In fact, inquiring little minds soon discover cats don't even like to swim.

The "Too Soon" Road to Independence

Independence Day arrives around the tender age of two, which for most parents is far too soon. Somehow, amazingly, once children are capable of taking care of business on their own, they develop a sudden sense of independence. The first signs appear early one morning as they make an entrance clad in carefully self-selected clothing and proudly announce, "I dressed all by myself this morning."

Once you get over the shock of purple stripes accompanied by red polka dots, accessorized by long Christmas stockings and black patent shoes, you will inevitably respond, "What happened to the nice clothes I laid out for you?"

The urge to keep them babes forever is powerful. After all, like any baby animal, they are so cute during this stage. However, time dictates a child's growth both physically and mentally, and even though each stage in a child's life seems to pass far too quickly, the process of growth is healthy and a welcome sign to all parents. These wondrous little beings begin to take on unique characteristics as they form into their own person and start down the road to independence. Suddenly parental guidance holds less importance to the toddlers, and they stake claims on crossing the street without holding your hand. Or they announce to parents their feat in going to the washroom by themselves at the daycare centre. The crib they once went safely to sleep in is now for babies, not for grown-ups like them, and they plead to denying parents for a real bed. Instead of crying when parents go out for an evening, they bounce off the walls with excitement at the thought of spending an evening with the "way more fun" fifteen-year-old babysitter. Their worlds are expanding as are their experiences and knowledge, and they not only can figure out how to turn on the television, but they no longer need you to put in the DVD and push start. All of those jobs you did for them as a parental right are being taken from your grasp and rightfully claimed by them. The reality behind the terrible twos is not the unruly behaviour described by parents before you — that was merely a cover-up for the true meaning. Twos are terrible because you realize this little person is exactly that, a little person, with little joys and little successes, little fears and worries, little habits and traits — a little person with a little mind of his own, a mind that longs to be challenged and needs to be used. Now equipped with the physical capabilities of walking, using his hands, talking and listening, seeing and understanding what he sees, a toddler's next step to independence is realizing the power of thinking on his own and consequently being given the freedom to do so.

This is not to say parents can send them off to figure out this big world completely on their own, but that parents need to accept that children won't always reach for their hand to guide them on their way. As parents we will always be there to catch them as they fall and steady them until they are solid on their feet again. This stage in a child's life is the first of many changes for both child and parent. It is not, nor should it be, viewed as an end. Rather, it should be seen as a curve in the road which gently takes us into the next unknown stretch of our lives.

CHAPTER THREE

Where Are You Going, My Little One, Little One

I recall many of my predecessors telling me to enjoy my babies/toddlers while I could, and not to rush the wonder years of sweet innocence. Now as my children develop into independent young people, I appreciate the advice they offered, and I offer it to you. Rearing children never gets better or worse, it simply gets different, and now those frustrating moments of potty training or stroller toting seem a distant memory. This chapter describes a new era in the life of parenting which takes the child away from the security of parents or chosen caregivers and places them out into the cold world of school years and new fears.

I Baked a Cake Once: the Early School Years
Children, welcome to E.C.S. (once referred to as Kindergarten)

Just when you thought you were over the worst — the terrible twos, the terrifying threes, the foreboding fours — and you are part way through the fatuous fives on your way to a small slice of freedom, the horror of the school years begin. But this should be a delightful time in yours and your children's lives. They are taking their first big steps towards autonomy and as a parent you can, after four and a half long years, bask in some normality in your life again. Wrong. You see, it is not as simple as dropping off the precious package like the UPS guy. There are unwritten regulations that impart parents with the duty of bringing the child into the E.C.S. class. Once inside, you are promptly dismissed, and adding insult to injury, you are not allowed to look back. Suddenly those feelings of joyous freedom turn to heinous guilt. You have just left that sweet, innocent child who once terrorized the sanctuary of your home in the hands of a seemingly terse stranger, a Kindergarten teacher. Many a tear has been shed outside the closed door of a Kindergarten classroom. Otherwise mature adults are reduced to babbling cells of the most pathetic sorts. The walk to your car is long, but it is nothing compared to the wait in your car until the lunch bell. My theory on this matter is that they should provide on-grounds counselling for all those poor lonely soles now riddled with the onset of "First Day of School Blues."

It takes several trips to the school before the gut-wrenching feelings begin to dissipate. By then both parent and child have settled into their new lifestyles, after which comes the next big shocker. You get a telephone call from a fellow Kindergarten parent to inform you of your scheduled times as a "parent helper." A what? You see, due to recent cutbacks in schooling funding, it is necessary for parents to share the duty of attending the Kindergarten classroom to assist in any way the teacher sees fit. But the fun doesn't end there. You are also expected to bring a healthy snack befitting thirty children, ages four to five. Bear in mind that it is a rather difficult task to combine healthy and yummy, and did I forget to tell you that along with your snack schedule, you also get a list containing all the food allergies in the class? Imagine my terror when I realized that the only cookie I knew how to bake and I was sure would meet the approval of thirty of the toughest critics was now on the endangered list. In what could have been one of my darkest hours, I was rescued by a fellow parent. During one of many PKCWR (Parent's of Kindergarten Children Waiting Room) conversations I was enlightened by the knowledge of a *Snacks for Fun* book that existed.

The very mention of the book generated a frenzy of "Oh, it's a great book," "I love that book, it saved my life," "It's got great ideas for birthday parties," "You'll love the frogs on a log idea," "It's a must have." A book on children's snacks — who would have guessed. It wasn't long until *Snacks for Fun* had taken up residence on my book shelf, right beside *Gone with the Wind*, which was basically the direction my life had taken. Try as I may, my snacks never seemed to measure up to the works of art some earth mothers were capable of preparing. In my years I have seen cookies that should be framed rather than eaten, cakes that took hours to decorate, and vegetable trays that could be auctioned off on e-bay. But I digress, there is still so much more a parent needs to know about the responsibility of the helping parent.

When your scheduled day arrives and you have prepared a healthy yet popular snack and purchased four litres of juice along with cute napkins that cost more than your last manicure, you are ready to face the crowds. You will no doubt experience a mild case of first day jitters as you enter the room using your four and a half year old as a shield from the eager onlookers. Just when you think you have blended into the background and all attention is no longer focused on you and your snack, the teacher announces, "Let's all welcome Mrs. Larsen to our classroom. She is our parent helper today." The heat is on again as all sixty eyes turn and zone in on you, who, I might add, are sitting very uncomfortably in a chair that was not designed to hold over sixty pounds, your knees almost even with your nostrils. Do you wave, do you smile, are they expecting a speech? What horrific pressure. The teacher speaks again, this time requesting everyone to stand for the National Anthem, but be prepared if you are a proud patriot like myself and choose to bellow out the words, you will soon be the centre of "dropped jaw" attention again. Later your child will take no time at all to tell you, "Mom, please don't sing so loud next time, it's embarrassing." And so begins a lifelong pursuit of you controlling behaviour you once regarded as okay but your child regards as mortifying. After the National Anthem, the children are instructed to go to their pocket charts (a cute little hanging device whose instructions on how to make them are included with your list of supplies when you first register your child) and find out which centre they are supposed to be working (and I use that term loosely) at.

I feel it imperative to tell you about the pocket charts, thus providing you with some advance warning. These delightful little creations are designed to hold index cards instructing the children on the purpose of each centre. They hang somewhere in the classroom, and in our particular E.C.S. class they were on the back side of a bulletin board. The teacher had asked me to help the children at their pocket charts, and being somewhat intimidated by her five-foot-one 105-pound stature, I gladly complied. I didn't realize what surprises waited around the corner of the bulletin board. You see, the instructions I mentioned earlier on how to make the pocket charts included size, suggested material, name of child, and anything else you wanted to add to make theirs special. I let my son pick the colours — imagine orange, brown, green, blue, and yellow all within the same vicinity — and then I painstakingly embroidered his name at the top and sewed on a few sequins, fish and stars. I must say I was very pleased with my project. So I went around the bulletin board and the rest is pretty much a bad memory. There before my eyes were the most spectacular displays of handiwork I had seen since the last church bazarre I attended. There were more sequins then an Elvis Presley costume. Most pocket charts were not only colour-co-ordinated but also included some form of petit point or advanced embroidery. The materials ranged from felt-backed silk to a really creative piece that was made of different pieces of cloth from the child's outgrown clothing. And amidst all of these works of art hung a coloured, painfully obviously homemade creation with the name Bradley unevenly embroidered across the top. My first inclination was to tear it off the bulletin board and stuff it under my shirt. I could make up some lie — maybe it got stolen (like that would ever happen), or maybe it fell off and the janitor swept it away, but it was too late. The children had already joined me at the bulletin board, so all I could do was pray that my son would not have to take too much teasing about his mother's feeble attempt at handicrafts.

After the children have located The Centre (see Glossary for complete definition) they are supposed to be at, then begins the next challenge. The teacher or aide will ask you to be the helper at a specific centre, and it is usually the craftiest and, I might add, the hardest. The children are gathered around a two-foot-high table, each occupying one of the miniature chairs. On the table is a collection of scissors, glue, crayons, construction paper cut into cute little bells and bows, and delightful little decorative objects, like tiny coloured cotton balls and sprinkle glitter. All of this can not add up to good. The aide will give you an abridged version of instructions on the purpose and ultimately end result of this centre. Then you are on your own with six little unfamiliar faces staring at you, depending on you for guidance, and putting the fate of their project in your hands. You will soon discover that saying, "Okay, kiddies, you know what to do. Now get at it, and keep the noise down 'cause we don't want the teacher to get mad at us," just won't cut it.

You see, a group of four-to-five-year-old children have a very difficult time staying on task. So you will find yourself squatting beside the miniature chairs ready and willing to assist any of the little people left in your charge. And let the games begin. Suddenly there is a frenzy of hands grabbing, pushing, cutting, pulling, and slapping. Glitter and cotton balls are airborne, some actually landing on the designated cut-out bells and bows. White glue bottles are getting the life squeezed out of them, resulting in litres of glue being poured onto a 2x3-inch piece of construction paper. Sleeves on wonderful lace-trimmed dresses are being dragged through mounds of glue and glitter, even attracting the odd cotton ball. Most of the children work feverishly in an effort to complete the project as fast as they can so they can move onto the more interesting centres, like the sand or water centre. But the odd Picasso will painstakingly measure each location for one dab of glue, which more often than not dries before he has chosen which decorative object to place on it. So then he starts all over again. Watching a child take care in creating the perfect project wouldn't normally be an issue, except half way through your duty the teacher tells you the children must finish this project today because it is going home with them. But that's not all. You still have three groups of children to run through. Ahhhhhhh. Well, Picasso, whether you like it or not, this parent helper is going to give you a little hands-on guidance. You snatch the glue out of his hands and dab ten spots, all the time encouraging the blooming artist to select his decorations quickly. You meet your quota of processing eighteen children and miraculously finishing eighteen craft projects, some of which still resemble the original shapes of bells and bows, when the teacher tells you the children are going to gym now to play some games, etc. Wow, you think to yourself, now this could be fun, playing in the gym where the acoustics are more conducive to the unyielding voices of thirty, four-to-five-year-olds.

But your hopes are soon dashed when you are politely told that your duty entails staying behind and cleaning up the craft table and then preparing thirty places around the tables for snack time, which includes pouring juice into thirty plastic cups, but only half way, and then setting one cup at each place. Oh, and did I forget to tell you, you have twelve minutes to complete your task, otherwise the teacher may just self-destruct. Here's a tip: if you put the cups on trays really close together you can pour the juice much faster, and any spills can simply be washed away when you clean the tray. However, these tips don't come easily — it took me two commissioned snack days to realize there had to be a better way than running back and forth to the pouring counter ten times.

The children return from twelve minutes of steady running and they are thirsty, hungry, and a little edgy. Once they take their places and are quieted down at the request of the teacher, you and your child are ready to hand out the snacks. But wait, out of nowhere the teacher asks your child this question: "What are your snacks made of?" For most mothers, this wouldn't pose any anxiety, but for a mother who opted to take easy street and go to the local grocery store where they make the greatest mini muffins, this is a moment of terror. Never dispose of the plastic packaging until you have memorized the ingredients. I was lucky this time; I had ensured the muffins contained none of the endangered food groups, and the rest I simply ad-libbed.

After snack is finished, your final duty for the day is to clean up. Despite the fact that the children are strictly instructed to dispose of their own garbage and put their own cups into the sink, there are the odd few (twenty out of thirty) who are just too used to mommy or daddy taking care of business. So you meticulously pick up all the half-eaten muffins and crumbs, along with the barely used overpriced napkins, and toss them into the wastebasket. The cups are gathered and placed in the sink ready for you to wash and, as instructed, rinsed with very hot water. The runny noses are a testament to the need for near-sterilization. As you approach the sink, it hits you — like every other piece of furniture in this room, the sink is designed to suit the needs of an average height of thirty-four inches. You have two options. You can stoop over and consequently go home to lie on a heating pad for the rest of the night, or you can kneel down and consequently go home and doctor the bruises on your knees. Either way, the cups will get washed. The final moments of your first snack day are nearing, and you begin to wonder how these two women, the teacher and her aide, can do this day in and day out. Are they crazy, are they in desperate need of employment, are they hard of hearing, or do they simply come from a military background? After putting two children through Kindergarten and having the privilege of getting to know the teacher and the aide, I came to my own conclusion: they really are devoted to the growth and well-being of all of those wonderful little children. **Hats off to all Kindergarten teachers and their trusty sidekicks.**

So Much to Learn

Parental helping commitments do not normally end at the completion of Kindergarten. Unfortunately, our wonderful teachers are bombarded with heavy curricula, outside classroom commitments, larger class numbers, and fewer class days, the end result being a growing need for parental assistance in the classroom. Some teachers welcome you with open arms and will literally embrace you as you volunteer some time; others are a little more reluctant, perhaps worried that you are there to audit their performance or secure your child's learning environment. I have been very fortunate with all of my children's teachers; they have not only welcomed me in the classroom, but have gone the extra mile to show me their gratitude. The commitment is time consuming and not practical for every family, but in my opinion it is a very rewarding experience despite some of the little idiosyncrasies you are challenged to endure. For example, with the exception of the teacher's chair, all other seating arrangements are designed to fit the average seven-to-nine-inch tush, fourteen-to-thirty-inch legs, and thirty-five to eighty-five pounds. The area designated for parental assistants is usually located at the back of the room at a table that sits fourteen inches off the ground. The end result is, to say the least, uncomfortable and can solicit an array of curious looks from the children. Some of the more fastidious teachers will supply a list of "Things to Do," and may even include detailed instructions. Unfortunately, every experience I have had with instructions has confused me more than enlightened me. However, you are usually left on your own as the teacher continues her masterful duties of not only teaching twenty-five children, but trying desperately to keep them on task. For this reason there is a certain amount of anxiety that accompanies any need you have to request clarification, which is amplified by the size of the seats and the environment. So you may be inclined to read the instructions over three or four times before you finally muster up enough courage to interrupt the teacher. How you go about this will vary according to your degree of boldness.

At first I was timid. Having taught for fourteen years, I could empathize with the frustration of distraction, but realizing the limited time and the number of items on the "to do" list, I finally made my move. Like a lioness approaching a lion, I circled around the room looking for the perfect opportunity, and then I walked towards the teacher, bobbing my head in and out similar to a pigeon, all the while avoiding direct eye contact. I remained at a safe distance until the teacher recognized my presence, then waited for her signal to speak, at which point I quietly excused the interruption and sheepishly admitted I was unsure of the instructions. The whole fiasco took about five minutes and must have appeared quite odd to the children, who at some point became more interested in what I was up to than what the teacher had to say. Through observing much bolder parents who simply yell from their seat, I have learned to take a little more assertive approach to the whole matter, and consequently I am able to quickly finish the tasks at hand, one of which has become all too familiar, cutting out objects.

Once again, my first experience was less than pleasant. I had been assigned to cut out some beautifully laminated leaves, each of which had several finely shaped facets on them. The instructions were to cut around the facets, but to leave approximately one-quarter of an inch, thus avoiding the devastating possibility of ruining the adhesion. As the teacher handed me the example along with five others, I felt assured that this was going to be a breeze. I began carefully cutting around each tiny facet, all the while ensuring the lamination stayed in tact. My first leaf was completed in the record time of three minutes and looked wonderful. As I selected the next contender, the teacher approached the table and set down a stack of lamination paper, all of which contained ninety-five more intricate leaf forms. I looked up at her in disbelief as she grinned back. It was at that point that I knew my fear of making a mistake was soon to be overshadowed by my fear of not completing. I finished the stack of leaves by skipping the invitation to join the teacher in the staff room during recess. I learned a valid lesson that day: I needed to stop worrying about getting chastised by the teacher. After all, she wasn't grading me, she wouldn't keep me after school, and she certainly wasn't going to call my mom and tell her I didn't do very good in school today. If anything, she was just plain grateful that I showed up at all.

Once I had relieved myself of this tremendous pressure, most of the tasks to follow were much easier, except perhaps photocopying. No matter how much experience I have with photocopiers, I am still intimidated by them. Single page copies I can handle, but when the teacher starts talking about coloured, double-sided, reverse to front, back to reverse, sixty percent reduction, and multiple copies on one page, my head begins to spin and I break into a cold sweat. Embarrassed to admit my incompetence, I slowly trudge down to the photocopy machine and face the beast in terror. I have discovered that if I wait long enough or go into the administration office with a forlorn look on my face, the school secretary and sometimes even the maintenance staff will come to my rescue. God bless them all.

Two of my pet peeves regarding parental assistance involve other parents, and the sudden personality changes in my children. On the rare occasion another parent may be scheduled to help in the classroom at the same time as you. This usually occurs when there is a party or centre-based learning is being used. Normally I am a fairly social individual, and I have managed to comprise a select group of parents that I enjoy working with in the classroom. Unfortunately, every once in a while you luck upon a Chatty Cathy who uses this time as a social event and prefers to spend the duration of the classroom visit talking continually. Even more unfortunate and by some sardonic coincidence, this parent also happens to have the loudest speaking voice in the entire community. I have tried an array of rude responses such as nodding but not replying, looking away, even walking away, but like metal to a magnet, these parents somehow affix themselves to you and end up earning both of you a polite glare from the teacher.

Even more frustrating, however, is the drastic change in my children's personalities. They are on their own turf and they know I won't go ballistic on them in front of their teacher and classmates. So they tend to become the class clown or worse, the class problem, or they cling to me like some sort of fabric softener sheet. It has gotten to the point where I request any children but my own on class field trips or in centres. This may seem cruel, but I think the old adage applies: your own child always behaves better for someone else, and so be it.

As the children grow, so does the parent helper responsibility. In the latter years of school, the amount of field trips increase, and the need for parent drivers becomes more relevant. After signing your life away on the "Driver's Form," you will become inundated with requests to drive the maximum capacity of passengers to and from a multitude of events. Of course, in most cases your responsibility does not stop when the last passenger exits your vehicle at the desired destination — be prepared to be asked to stay and help supervise the students. I strongly believe that teachers feel a looming sense of danger once they are off their turf, the school grounds. Let's face it, three teachers and ninety Grade 5 students contained in an otherwise meticulously manicured curling rink would cause anyone reason for concern. So now your duties have taken on new challenges. Your responsibilities include: helping explain the rules to the inattentive, ensuring there are no physical altercations amidst the competitive boys, keeping the girls focused on the objectives and not their hair, all the while acting cool but not too cool at the request of your child. As well, you are expected to play hip music on your car stereo (country and western is taboo), not sing along, and definitely do not attempt to engage in conversation during the ride there and back. In other words, act like a devoted and loyal, underpaid and over-criticized family employee.

Over the years of class visits, I have learned a valuable lesson that I would like to share with you. Teachers are wonderful, gracious angels of knowledge. They devote their days to the betterment of children, big and small, short and tall. They exhibit a tremendous amount of energy, patience, and flexibility, and tend to see the light that shines behind every child's eyes. They are not afraid to correct and equally not afraid to cherish. Their wealth of wisdom is shared selflessly in hopes it will spark a flame in a child's curiosity and imagination. They give attention to an otherwise starved soul and give love to an otherwise empty heart, and expect little in return.

I have witnessed behaviour by students that would tarnish even the gentlest of minds, but have been fortunate enough never to witness an unkind act at the hand of a teacher. Despite hours filled with restless energy, constant inquiries, runny noses, and exasperating efforts, I have never seen a teacher turn down a student's request for extra help or a compassionate ear. The frustrations I know in twos, for them is multiplied by ten, yet they manage to compose themselves for the amelioration of the cause. They too know sorrow, joy, and confusion; they too have families they love and are devoted to, yet we tend to overlook this and expect them to treat our children like they are their only concern. So the lesson I have learned is simple: if giving up an hour or two of my time by lending a hand or offering a friendly word to someone who doesn't hesitate to support the growth of my children means her days will be eased and a little bit brighter, then I will without hesitation endure the discomfort of a chair that's too small. *Hats off to the teachers who give so much.*

Ladies and Gentlemen, Start your Cameras

One of the proudest moments of a parent's life, and there are many, has to be your child's first appearance at a school assembly or concert. This is a time for child and parent alike to shine in front of an audience composed of fellow students, teachers, support staff, and forty other fervent parents. I suspect the pattern is pretty much the same in most schools: the school gymnasium is set up with collapsible risers centre stage, a microphone pole that stands four feet high set off to one side, and a piano strategically placed on the other side. Then there is a huge gap of empty floor space towards the back of the gym where three to four rows of uncomfortable wooden chairs designed to withstand a maximum of ten minutes of sitting are lined up. Above the middle of the floor hangs a rubber room divider which I am told weighs over 500 pounds yet appears to be held up by something resembling a kitchen curtain rigging. During the entire assembly you will find your eyes shifting back and forth between the stage and the ominous room divider.

It is my experience that arriving a little early and enduring the wooden chairs a little longer pays off in the long run. Having the front row end seat enables you to view your child's performance (the most pivotal, of course) without any obstructions, all the while providing you with the least conspicuous place for moving back and forth for photo and video opportunities. Once you are seated and you have placed a mass of equipment, ranging from 35 mm cameras with zoom lenses to a video camera that may require an outlet in the event of battery failure under and around your seat, you can settle in for the show. About one minute after the principal's P.A. announcement beckoning students and teachers to the gym, you will be overrun by the total student, teacher, assistants, support staff, and otherwise school body. The students are instructed to sit in order on the floor space directly in front of the parents. A wise school official discovered that mixing Grade 6 students with E.C.S. students is a recipe for disaster, and therefore proposed an order of hierarchy starting with the little tots closest to the stage and ending with a gap between the Grade 5 and Grade 6 students who are as close to sitting on your feet as humanly possible. Most assemblies last around thirty minutes; any more than that and the troops become restless.

The E.C.S. students usually begin to fidget with everything from their shoelaces to the student's hair beside them, turn around to face the parents, and in extreme cases get up and shout, "Are we done yet?" On the other hand, the Grade 5 and 6 students are a little more sophisticated in their restless antics, including games of wad-spitting and eye-rolling and, for the more talented rabble-rousers, acts of ventriloquism. The time can also seem lengthy to the parent, who has sat patiently through announcements, the school song, presentations to well-wishers, and the performances of other students, to be privy to fifty seconds of your own child singing or dancing with twenty other over-actors. If you are lucky, the program will be announced, but more often than not you will find yourself day-dreaming or staring up at the room divider when they introduce the only reason you are there. In a fit you scramble for your cameras, lens covers flying, and not so discretely make your way to the front of the gymnasium in order to snap off two photographs of your child and approximately forty-two seconds of video zooming in and out. When the film is developed your still pictures will likely be the tip of your child's head behind that other child who kept jumping in front of him, and your video will have you wondering if there was an earthquake during your filming. But that doesn't discourage you from repeating the same process at the next school assembly or concert.

The Regrettable Pink Slip

During the elementary years of school, almost without a doubt you are bound to find the regrettable pink slip in your child's backpack. Like every other notice they are charged with bringing home, you will most likely find it crumpled up, shoved down, or possibly folded into a paper plane at the bottom of his backpack, but this particular notice is worth digging for. It is not a notice of suspension, a notice of misbehaviour, or even one requesting parental assistance. No, this notice is far more distressing. This is the "Head Lice" notice. It generally reads: "A case of head lice has been discovered in your child's classroom. We suggest you carefully check your child's hair for any of the offenders. If you discover head lice, use the following procedures to remove any nits or live animals from your child's hair. Once you have treated your child, be sure to continue checking his hair for a two to three week period. We appreciate your co-operation in this matter."

Suddenly a wave of horror goes over you: there are live animals in my child's hair! You find yourself rationalizing: but we wash our hair and keep our clothes clean and have a very clean house. How could this happen, what will people say? Of course, until you actually check your child's hair, you can't be certain he even has any offenders, as the notice so eloquently put it. Along with the notice will come a three page leaflet explaining what head lice and nits looks like, including a black and white picture enlarged five hundred percent, making the creature look like something out of a sci-fi movie. There are also detailed instructions on the search for and ultimate removal of the offenders, including the purchase of a very expensive but highly effective shampoo.

As a concerned parent, you immediately drop everything and summon your children to the kitchen table. With a bright light and a fine-toothed-comb, donning rubber gloves you begin your inspection. As you catch a glimpse of your reflection in the glass patio doors, you envision yourself with long red hair covering your entire body. You have become a mother orangutan. After a twenty minute inspection of each child, you may conclude they have no offenders, but you will more than likely go into a twenty minute spiel about how they should not use other children's combs, brushes, toques, coats, mitts, or anything that may carry lice. If your children are in higher grades, they will more than likely look at you like you are some kind of a freak. "Mom, who in their right mind would wear someone else's clothes, or use their brushes, that's just sick." Their reasoning makes perfect sense; after all, I could barely get them to comb their hair at home. What would possess me to think they were secretly grooming themselves at school?

The unfortunate flip side of the inspection is that you discover some offenders in your child's hair. The nits range from a light grayish colour to a dark colour and are usually the size of the tip of a pencil. The live animals are much larger and there is no mistaking their identity. If you are lucky enough to see one move, it will take everything in your willpower to not run screaming out of the room. Instead, you should calmly inform your child that he has some lice and will need to be treated. You will immediately go to the nearest grocery or drug store and purchase a bottle of the expensive shampoo as mentioned earlier.

Be sure to read the instructions carefully, noting that they recommend all people in the household be treated. The shampoo has a potent odour like a mixture of tar and mint. Once applied to the hair and scalp, it is meant to be left in for a period of approximately ten minutes. When you feel a sensation that must be similar to being burned by dry ice, it is time to remove the shampoo. I concluded that the shampoo works because something that smells that bad and tingles that much can't be good for the likes of micro-sized lice. They recommend only one treatment, and then after a seven day period, if there is no sign of offenders, discontinue use. We were lucky we nipped it in the bud on the first application.

However, my paranoia didn't end there. Worried that the offenders may have jumped ship before the shampoo treatment, I decided our whole house needed "de-lousing." I rented a rug shampooer and proceeded to do forty-six loads of laundry. Everything from all of the bedding and towels to coats and toques and mitts and scarves were washed in hot water. What could withstand bleach consequently was bleached. Our house smelled like a hospital, my back ached for days from shampooing every inch of carpet in the house, and the kids were warned (threatened) not to touch any other person or person's items in the school. We had officially become anti-licers. Once again overkill, no pun intended. After two weeks of being lice free, I was beginning to settle down and feel rest assured that we had rid ourselves of the nasty offenders. Almost to the day, I checked my child's backpack for notices, and was mortified to see another regrettable pink slip. Not again. This time upon inspection, no offenders were discovered. I suppose the constant drill of "Don't touch anybody's hair, clothes, books, etc., and don't, whatever you do, use their combs, and put your coat and mitts and boots and scarves in your backpack, don't hang them beside anybody else's, and if someone scratches their head get out of their way and don't touch their hand," had actually paid off.

Much to be Discussed or Discussed Much

Head lice do not discriminate. Despite popular belief, they do not thrive in unclean environments and do not prefer unkempt hair. So no matter how much you think your children couldn't possibly carry head lice, don't be fooled into believing old wive's tales. Check your children thoroughly upon notice and if you do discover head lice, don't be shell-shocked, simply treat the problem immediately. I researched the topic thoroughly once I discovered lice on my child, and was amazed to learn that they can only survive on the hair and will not start multiplying in your couch. They will lay eggs then subsequently die; the eggs are referred to as nits and can be removed very effectively with a nit comb. Washing articles of bedding or clothing that have been recently in contact with the affected hair is wise; hot water wash is really all you require. The most common occurrence of head lice is in October to December and for no apparent reason the occurrences of head lice dissipate once children are in Grades 5-6-7 and up. One final word of advice from the queen of paranoia: the less intense you are, the better off your children will be, and chances are you can avoid costly therapy sessions if you accept that this too shall pass.

As, Bs, Cs. Please, No Ds, They're Moving On

At the end of every school year comes the much anticipated news, promotion to the next grade level. A parent would have to be living in the closet to have no idea whether or not their child(ren) are being advanced to the next grade. However, this moment still comes with a degree of trepidation, so much so you find yourself attending the last day of school so you can whisk the manila envelope out of your darling's hands, then speed-read through the technical stuff and get right to the nitty gritty: Bradley has been promoted to Grade 5, Krysta has been promoted to Grade 3. Thank the heavens above, I think. There is a small part of being a parent that wishes children could be babes forever. Tucked inside the same manila envelope is also a school supply list for the next grade level.

In the beginning this was an all-new concept to me. I assumed things were still the same as when I went to school. In September Mom would buy us each a new pair of shoes and that was it. Oh how things have changed. This list usually consists of a neatly-composed, typewritten page with no less than twenty-five items which are specific in nature right down to the preferred lead type of pencils and pencil crayons, the recommended amount of glue sticks, Duotangs, erasers, lined/unlined paper, whiteout pens, tape dispensers, and calculators, to the size of the rings in the binders. Not to mention that their school supply list includes not one but two pairs of running shoes, no black soles please. Remember those cute runners you bought for them when they were toddlers? Well, feet have grown, tastes have developed, and hand-me-downs are out of the question — forget about the new linoleum for the bathroom. To newcomers the list can be mind boggling and is often tucked away in a safe place until the bank account is lofty enough to handle the purchase. Years of experience have taught me to never, never wait until a week or even two before school starts to go shopping for supplies. Mortgage the house if you have to, but as soon as school supply flyers begin appearing in your mailbox, which is usually about the second week of July, get to your local "has it all store" and buy, buy, buy. Another helpful hint: do not take your children with you, despite what child psychologists suggest about giving children the responsibility and allowing them to make decisions. Spending four hours in the school supply aisle arguing over the colour and style of a pencil case is truly a waste of time.

After you have purchased the suggested supplies and subsequently sacrificed that new pair of shoes you needed or that night out together, you will more than likely feel possessed to purchase each child some new and funky clothes for the onslaught of September and the new school year. Heaven forbid they should be seen in the same tired $50 pair of jeans you just bought them in June. By about Grade 3 kids start to develop a sense of fashion. Some parents do unfortunately experience this earlier. This sense of fashion is not necessarily the child seeking out their own individuality, but more likely happens as a result of peer pressure, not to mention the bombardment of advertisements and music videos. So begins the continual battle with your children over what is cool and what is affordable. If you are brave enough to go out and purchase new clothes for them by yourself, be prepared to ward off a battering of fits and tantrums. You may also wish to arm yourself with some lines of reasoning that are capable of standing up to their not so reasonable pleas: "I can't wear that; I will look like a geek."

"Mom, maybe those worked in your day, but I wouldn't be caught dead in them." "Obviously you don't care if I get beat up." "That looks like something Grampa would wear." "Everybody else will have a pair." "Those are so-o-o-o not cool. Where's the label?" "Pleeeeeease, Mom and Dad, pleeeeeeease."

The list is endless, as is their tenacity. What I have learned over the years about dressing older children may be of some assistance. For starters, be up front with them and tell them you are on a budget. If you tell them that they have $100 for new clothes and they can buy whatever they want within reason, it will amaze you how prudent they can be if they really want something. For example, if they absolutely must have the $40 jeans, then they may be willing to settle for some $10 t-shirts. Or you could give them some options such as: you will have to get some of these more expensive clothes as a birthday or Christmas present. If all else fails, you can offer to purchase the more expensive items when they go on sale. Of course by then they will be out of style, despite the fact that they will go on sale approximately one week after they first hit the shelves. Face the hard facts, once kids reach this age of obstinacy, they will not wear clothes you like. Even if you dress them and send them out the door, there is a good chance they have what they refer to as more acceptable garb stashed somewhere at school or tucked way down in their backpacks. As soon as they are out of eyeshot, they rip off that shirt Gramma gave them and replace it with a t-shirt that has some unrecognizable symbol or a message that you would otherwise wash their mouths out for repeating. In defense of the children I have to say that it seems somewhat hypocritical for us as parents to be particular over our own attire yet expect our children to go out in public in something they feel totally egregious wearing.

NOTE: Parenting tends to be the epitome of hypocrisy. For example: parents who forego all other duties to catch the next episode of *Survivor* yet hastily turn off the television for the good of homework, parents who swear and yet threaten to wash mouths out, parents who pig out on chocolates yet scold their children for eating junk food — you get the drift. The list of "I can do anything you can't do" is endless and is better left for the next book, *When Pigs Fly: Living With a Teenage Alien*.

Try as you might to control your child's wardrobe, you may as well face the hard facts that at that certain point when they develop a mind of their own, they will only wear what they want to wear. If that happens to be a frayed pair of baggy blue jeans and a plain black hoody, then that is what they will don day in and day out, taking them off only long enough for you to put them through the wash. All other items will remain in closets and drawers with the tags still attached. When you do finally get fed up and decide to return the other items, be prepared to argue with a sales clerk, not much over fifteen years old, about getting a full refund for that great sparkly shirt that just two weeks ago they assured you was all the going rage. You see, besides all of the pricey name brand items, every six months there is an introduction of new fads and crazes that every child must simply be part and party to, most of which come at a cost. In a short ten years, I have seen the following come into the stores and go out in garage sales:

Bell bottoms (flares)
Skate-boarder jeans
Neons
Cargo pants
Platform runners
Paint-on tattoos
Non-pierced nose rings
Embroidered jeans
Tear-away pants, then Zip-off pants
Beaded jeans, t-shirts, shoelaces, etc.
Toques with several octopus trailers
Hoody's (better known as sweat shirts with hoods)
Baggy jeans with underwear showing (boxers only)

Then there are the items of clothing that bear logos from popular television shows and the latest Disney movies. Of course the "I'll just die if I don't have it" sentiment is not limited to clothing. The manufacturers of toys, gadgets, and electronics have also cornered a healthy market using our children. To name a few: video games, disc players, computer games, remote control anything and everything, robot pets, life-like dolls, virtual reality computer and television set-ups, BMX stunt bikes, roller blades, mountain bikes, 10-20 speed bikes, and DVDs, not to mention the return of yoyos, skateboards, snowboards, scooters, lava lamps, disco balls, and other items we begged our parents for but which have quadrupled in price. If we'd only known.

Purely Peer Pressure: The Hard Realities

The whole unfortunate consequence of wearing and having the latest is the real and often painful pressure it places on our children and families. Some children develop the ability to be cruel at very early ages and will make fun of any child they deem as not cool. Cool, in their tiny minds, is defined as having the newest and best of everything. I have been witness to some heart-wrenching acts of unkindness when my own children have been ostracized from groups of friends because they didn't have the most expensive bikes, or they wore a pair of running shoes that didn't have a recognizable logo on the side. You can sit with your children and explain that it isn't what they wear that makes them special, but when you are nine years old, all the explaining in the world won't make the hurt go away. The best you can hope for is that your child grows thick skin which protects her self worth and when the pressure becomes too intense she has the sensibility to defend what she sees as right.

With girls it may lead to the "new best friend" syndrome; with boys it will inevitably lead to a fight. When your son comes home sporting his first black eye or cuts and bruises earned from an altercation at school over his "ugly" coat, it is difficult as a parent to avoid patting him on the back and proclaiming, "I only hope the other guy looks worse than you." Instead, the mature thing to say is, "Honey, it is better to walk away than to fight." Of course, we all know it's a line of bull dung, but condoning physical confrontations won't get you grades towards your degree in parenting. Dads are especially prone to congratulating the contender rather than correcting the behaviour. I am positive it has something to do with primitive male rituals such as, "Me man, me protect what's mine." Our first experience with Bradley's demonstration of passive-aggressive behaviour happened in Grade 3. One of the other boys in his class had been pestering him off and on for a few weeks, and finally one day in gym class, Brad saw his window of opportunity. The boy was allegedly pushing Brad while they waited in line and Brad decided a quick backward kick was in order. So he pulled his knee towards his chest and let his leg fly out straight behind him, resulting in a good swift kick to the young fella's . . . let's just say that at that age precious parts are in the direct line of fire. When the boy crouched over and began sobbing in pain, Brad was busted and busted good. The teacher sent both to the principal's office, and the consequences were a little more devastating for Brad, and rightfully so. He not only lost his recess privileges for three days, but he had to face the wrath of mother. Dad's response was to be expected: "Well if he was bugging you, he had it coming, but next time don't go for the family jewels," which, I might add, had to be explained later by myself. I, on the other hand, was mortified. My precious son was showing signs of violence. I didn't sleep for two days conjuring all sorts of scenarios of Brad's soon-to-be life of crime.

Finally I took the bull by the horns and made an appointment to visit the principal. Of course I wanted to apologize for my son's barbaric behaviour, but I also was hoping the principal could offer some sort of solace for what I deemed to be a sign of further trouble. To say the least, the principal was prepared for my visit, with pen and pad in hand. I suppose he was ready to take down notes as advised by solicitors hired by the board of education for when irate parents come to complain about unfair treatment of their avowed innocent child. Much to his dismay and evidenced by his felled jaw, I was there to seek forgiveness and beg that my son not be sent away to "bad boy school." Overkill, to say the least, but as a mother who believed she had taught her son not to fight, I was distraught and more concerned about my own failure as a perfect parent. The lesson was hard but timely. Brad was beginning to feel his own sense of being and he struggled with some issues during this year.

Against the better wishes of my husband, I arranged for Brad to talk to the school counsellor. A follow-up telephone call from her not only reassured me, but set me straight. Brad was a normal eight-year-old boy who was simply and with no other hidden personality defaults, feeling his oats. Her interview with Brad concluded that he regretted what he had done, but would more than likely defend his right to be left alone again. She also added that he was a very pleasant boy and by all regards was happy with his family and life in general. Phew . . . what a relief! I could put all the sharp items back in the house where they belonged. I also learned a valuable lesson, that what I was teaching my children about self-esteem was paying off.

The school years are filled with self-esteem missiles, from cutting comments by fellow students to failed grades and rejected notions. The pressures are real, and in many cases intense. Girls shoulder the pressures differently; they rarely resort to physical conflict, but pride themselves in the art of emotional combat. "I don't like you anymore, and you're not my best friend." "So and so thinks you are stupid and she doesn't want to play with you." "I get to go over to so and so's house and play, but she didn't invite you." The weapons in word war are as varied and as perilous as the tiny little soldiers that are armed with them. Dealing with a kick to the crotch is in many ways easier than healing the wounds of emotional warfare.

I guess the only saving grace to a parent's constant and consuming toil through the school years is that the children will be smarter and wiser and capable of standing on their own two feet. The lessons they learned both in and out of the classroom will enable them to make sound decisions that positively affect the outcome of their lives as adults and ultimately parents. The acquaintances they make will provide them with experience about the diversity of our world, and in some cases give them a wonderful support system of invaluable friendship. But most importantly, these years will empower them to stretch for stars that may have otherwise been beyond their reach.

Friends and fun should be forever.

Pardon Me, Miss Manners: More Embarrassing Moments

Chapter Two discussed some of the times in parents' lives when the sweet innocence of their babes can be the source of some embarrassing moments but many a good chuckle, especially later in life. However, the moments discussed in this chapter are more about Direct Hits taken by parents at the lack of manners, and sometimes intentional "get evens" of their now blossoming children.

No Truer Words were Spoken

Thanks to the excellent work of our school systems, our children develop an extensive vocabulary and critical thinking abilities at a very early age. Combining the two can result in some fairly powerful and likewise hurtful statements made by the likes of an eight year old. Of course, the blame for some of their not so thought out soliloquies should fall on parents as well. The child psychiatrists warn parents to choose words wisely, otherwise they may come back to you at the most inappropriate and consequently embarrassing moments, monumental advice that tends to fall on deaf ears until your child mimics your vivid description of a fellow driver in a way which seems all too natural.

Speaking from experience, I am now convinced that until the age of five my children thought that all other people driving vehicles were better known as "freaking idiots" or some other equally descriptive term. As well, tender-aged children have not developed the ability to differentiate between what should be repeated outside the home and what should not. When referring to people you come in contact with, parents should speak only niceties in the presence of their children or otherwise be prepared for Mrs. Smith to approach you and ask you why your son/daughter thinks she has way too much to say about things. Your only hope for salvation is to blame it on your spouse or plead total ignorance and then pray Mr. Jones doesn't mysteriously find out what you really think of they way he combs his hair forward. Usually after the age five children do begin to develop a little conversation savvy with much coaching from parents, but heed my warning and enjoy those younger wonder years, because their verbiage is about to turn into a weapon in their fight for independence. For example, when you go to help them with something you assumed was your parental responsibility, such as escorting them into school, birthday parties, public washrooms, etc., or picking out their clothes, hair styles, and playmates, you're kindheartedness may be met by such cutting remarks as: "I don't need you." "You always treat me like a kid." "I can do it myself, just leave me alone."

Their words make you realize your two worlds have suddenly come to an abrupt impasse, and though not so eloquent, are painfully true. The silky-skinned, wide-eyed child has sprouted up to the height of your shoulders and is no longer walking head to hip with you. His attitude has also grown — your secret vocabulary is no longer viable and your reasons better have substance. "Because I said so," just won't cut it any more.

Please and Thank You

I have come to another conclusion after ten years of rearing children, which I concede is a cakewalk compared to some experiences — courtesy is not a standard feature of children. Of course I should have realized this. After all, I have met many an adult with manners that would cause Heloise mental anguish. The first lesson in courtesy begins with the token pleases and thanks yous. Once children learn how to speak, it is imperative to teach them these two simple idioms — before requesting, say "please," after receiving, say "thank you," and anything and everything deemed necessary in between. This comes so naturally to parents that I find myself correcting anyone's ill manners: "I need to see your licence and registration."

"What do you say first, Officer?"

This is officially classified as parental obsessive-compulsive behaviour, and so much for the warning. As children grow they begin to question the validity of using idioms, insisting that they are simply rehearsed and lack sincerity, and you may find yourself agreeing with their reasoning. After all, thanking the doctor for sticking that needle in the arm does lack good common sense. In their minds the only reasonable use for them is to sugar an otherwise implausible request: "Please, Mom and Dad," or place a little insurance on the next request: "Thanks, Mom and Dad, you're the best."

Huh-Um

The next lesson in courtesy involves the dos and don'ts on interrupting. Once children learn how to speak, they have an uncontrollable need to do so on any occasion and with little consideration for anyone else. Therefore they must be taught when and how to be party to conversation. The ultimate goal is to halt that annoying behaviour when they come rushing up to you and other people in conversation, tug at your pant leg, and shout in their loudest voices. You can try to ignore them, but eventually you will find yourself clasping your hand over their mouths and retorting some generic command, "Please don't interrupt, it is very rude." Your command will likely be met with wide eyes of confusion. After all, they do have something important to say, like the dog is eating poop again. Unfortunately, teaching children not to interrupt and to patiently wait their turn to speak is a very trying task and notwithstanding the reality, explaining to them that they have many more years to be heard than you do makes little to no sense to them. But you shouldn't be discouraged. The message does eventually sink in after three or four times of having their mouths held shut by your hand. Maybe it's the heavy odour of freshly cut garlic on your hands, or their lack of patience, that convinces them it is easier to just do as you request and speak when appropriate — either way they do learn. However, the lesson doesn't end there. Once they learn when to take part in a conversation, they must also learn how, especially when addressing other adults: "Hey lady/mister," or worse yet "Hey you," is an all-too-familiar salutation which spouts from the mouths of babes.

Ironic, isn't it. We spend countless hours coaching, bribing, demonstrating, and ultimately encouraging our children how to talk, and when they finally utter those wonderful first words we video the monumental event and ensure we announce the news to everyone we know. After this we spend more countless hours increasing their vocabulary, showcasing them for family and friends with something that resembles parlour tricks: "Say bye bye to the nice lady," and constantly questioning their new-found skill: "Can you say hi to Mrs. Peters?" So we needn't wonder why they have the urge to speak, what we should wonder is where the sense is in now silencing them. Nobody ever said raising children wasn't a maze of contradictions.

One RingaDingy, Two RingaDingy

Once you have somewhat successfully managed to teach children courtesy when speaking with people, particularly elders, you are faced with another phase in the courtesy curriculum: properly answering the telephone. Children are simply fascinated by the telephone. After all, what other object rings a warning and with one quick swoop allows you to speak to people who aren't really there, or should I say here. Her first experience with the telephone will leave the child bewildered and perhaps even somewhat intimidated, unsure exactly how Gramma managed to get herself stuffed into the little plastic contraption. After some trying hours of explanation, the child will finally catch on and realize that the person isn't actually inside the telephone, but in fact her voice is being transported via the tiny little lines that connect these devices. Who wouldn't be fascinated? More hours of explanation are bound to follow regarding the proper use of the telephone, including the "no calls to Europe or 911." Once the mechanism is understood, the need for manners is imminent. Before the arrival of children, answering the telephone was only challenged by your location in the house and how many rings until the answering machine took over. Once children enter the picture, this task becomes much more challenging and you rarely need to worry about the machine picking up any unattended calls. However, you should concern yourself with the manner by which the telephone is answered. In the hurry to beat out any other contestants, children will often scale couches, speed up or down steps, and literally tackle one another in order to be the answering game successor.

Unfortunately the event does not end with the removal of the telephone receiver. The loser is bound to sport some ill feelings about being shut out, and just as the talk button is engaged, the loser will scream at the successor and may even go as far as to knock her down and retreat with the victory trophy, the telephone receiver. Then he will continue screaming, "I got it, I got it," victory cries as he parades through the house holding his trophy above his head in a fashion comparable to the winners of the Stanley Cup. Once he realizes that he has the prize but someone else wants it — namely you — a chase ensues as he frantically runs about the house like the dog with your best leather shoe. As if it weren't bad enough, you forget your situation and begin yelling threats and possibly other undesirables at the child, all to the interest and often amusement of the caller. When you are lucky, if you are lucky, you will finally get the telephone and as you place it towards your own mouth and ear, in a fit of final words, you shout, "When I get my hands on you, you are going to get a good spanking."

Suddenly you remember the caller and you hope and pray that it isn't the strict school principal, some perverted tele-marketing person, or worse, your family clergy. You could hang up or feign a wrong number, or you could just chalk it up to another stressful experience among many in the raising of children. After some stern warnings about telephone tackling contests, you need to further advise your children on telephone courtesy.

Begin by familiarizing your child with your first name to avoid any mistaken identity hang-ups. The next step is to provide your children with a list of appropriate responses to the frequent inquiry, "Is your mom or dad there?" If you are unavailable to take the call, tell the children to say just that, otherwise the caller may be in for unwarranted, lengthy, and often way too detailed explanations as to exactly where you are and what you are doing. "Mommy/Daddy is sitting on the toilet so they can't come to the phone right now 'cause they've got really bad diarrhea." Putting up with the frustration of telephone combat is a necessary evil of parenting. After all, the telephone is one of the greatest inventions of this era, and to add to its indispensability some very wise person made it cordless. Stretching the coil of stationary telephones usually only provided the user with a minimum of two extra feet of movement. Not any more. The world has become party to the "Communication Movement," or, more aptly put, the movement of communication.

NOTE: A word about the Communication Movement of our ever-changing and ever-wowing world of technology: This movement has brought about some mind-boggling new conveniences in the way we go about everyday life, with fabulous inventions such as digital computer imagery, faxes, the Internet, and of course, the cell phone. But with every new era of advancement comes some pitfalls. The use of cell phones has become an everyday, everywhere, anytime occurrence. So much so it has taken over some of life's meaningful gestures, such as conversation during dining, face-to-face shopping, and time better spent driving responsibly. My point: "STAY ALIVE, HANG UP AND DRIVE." Obviously this is a pet peeve of mine, one I discuss at length and with a bit of wit in my book entitled, *You're Driving Me Crazy.*

Now back to the matter at hand. I'm convinced the cordless telephone was invented by an upset parent who was the unknowing victim of "Occupieous Misbehavous " (glossary term). Trying to have a conversation on the telephone is open season for Occupieous Misbehavous. The second the parent gets the receiver to her ear and begins conversing with the person on the other end, the children go into a frenzy of misbehaviour, ranging from crawling up on counters to all-out fist fights in the case of more than one child. Their voices become twenty times amplified and they suddenly need the answer to every question they ever had, like, "Does the tooth fairy leave a whole bunch of money for Gramma when she puts her teeth in a cup every night?" Before the existence of cordless telephones, the parent was constricted to that two foot area mentioned earlier, and more than likely subjected the caller to the ghastly noise when the base was pulled off the table in an attempt to grab the offender(s) as they passed by just barely out of reach. Now in modern times the parent is capable of moving anywhere within the range of the radio waves provided by cordless telephones, and in some cases this may include outside and across the street to the neighbour's house. The little offenders are no longer just out of the reach of a swat. Unfortunately, even equipped with that knowledge, children still partake in Occupieous Misbehavous, and despite all your efforts to move to every area of the house in search of a quiet place to converse, they can and do search you out.

Dinner Table Sound Effects

Once a child has watched his first Ace Ventura movie, any hope for a stylish existence is pretty much out the window, right along with the wafting odours and the unrecognizable sounds that seep from your once-innocent child. The first burp is hilarious, the second is somewhat funny, but after that it is pretty much annoying, especially when it continues at the dinner table or in church, or when you're standing in line at the grocery store. But the minute you laugh is the very minute the child thinks he is a stand-up comedian, and performing any sort of body expression is good for a laugh. So you have just set yourself up for years of unexpected mannerless bloopers at the hands, or whatever body part, of your children. While these are natural physiological occurrences, they aren't necessarily welcome when released without warning, but more importantly, without any concern for other people. As if these transgressions weren't enough, they have to be brought to everybody within earshot's attention by repeating the act with cheesy imitations. Any effort to silence the now out of control entertainer will be next to impossible because he has more than likely acquired an audience who not only find the act amusing, but are delighted by your obvious mortification.

In their tiny lives, they also somehow manage to pick up some other very grating unnatural noises. I suggest that some of them are introduced via the media, particularly television, some occur as a result of childhood friends, while others are discovered purely by accident. A six-year-old can get hours of merriment out of the sound of a new running shoe squeaking on a freshly polished floor, or be totally enthralled with the sound an almost empty ketchup bottle makes. And of course, they are not totally satisfied until they have repeated the gag so many times that you finally snap and frantically remove the offender and his props.

Besides the sound effects, children quickly discover their bodies' ability to emit some not-so-pleasant nonetheless natural body odours. When they first realize the odours are actually seeping from their own bodies, the thought is somewhat frightening, but they soon revert back to the very basic of animal instincts, and when they release odour they throw their heads in the air and take a huge whiff, then howl with delight. After drawing all attention to themselves, they run around in a mad fury yelling, "Whoa, you should smell that one, it's a doozey," as if proclaiming their territory. Of course they also delight in passing gas while lying in bed, usually with you, then pulling the covers over their heads. Apparently this is not just a husband tradition.

If there is more than one child, these beyond-embarrassing habits become fair play for what I refer to in parental Latin as, "Competition Ignoramus" (glossary term), an ongoing battle to see which child can out-gross the other one and all the unfortunate bystanders. These antics are rude enough on their own, but what makes them even more unacceptable is the fact that they more often than not arise during meal time. Competition Ignoramus scores big if you can make mom gag on a spoonful of peas by describing how some kid at school eats his own boogers. Don't be fooled, either, by the alleged sweetness of the so called fairer sex; girls have no problem stepping up to the plate for a good round of Competition Ignoramus. It never ceases to amaze me how many new places a child can find to stick a couple of straws. Like so many issues in child rearing, I really have no advice, but I can offer some tips for dealing with Competition Ignoramus. Laughing at the child's silly behaviour is not necessarily a bad thing to do. While it may send the message of condoning, it also sends another very important message — you are not just a temperamental, rule-wielding tall person in your child's life, you are actually a cool person with the ability to find some fun in things that may be classified as taboo. So enjoy a good chuckle and when Competition Ignoramus becomes habitual, learn to smile and walk away and accept that the root word for ignoramus is "ignore."

Always Remove the Tags: Sibling Warfare

The story goes like this. In a family of three children, the eldest a boy, which is of no consequence, had been given the opportunity to travel to England on an exchange program. This was an opportunity of a lifetime, one that may never present itself again, so the family was very excited and all agreed to make some sacrifices so this opportunity could be realized. Unfortunately there was one factor overlooked — the feelings of inequality it created in the two children left at home. The parents did manage to offset some of the ill feelings by overcompensating with trips to the local water park, special luncheons and dinners out, and abundant purchases of treats, toys, and other trinkets. The trick appeared to be working until the return of the eldest child who, despite the cost of the trip being over $2500 including spending money, did not hesitate to make remarks about the injustice regarding all the special treats the other siblings received during his absence. The concept of fairness is grossly understated in Child Psychology 101. Where there is more than one child, there is bound to be protests of inequality. "It's not fair," is the first phrase children are able to form.

Sister got her ear pierced, it's not fair. Brother got to go to a birthday party, it's not fair. Sister got to go on a field trip she's so lucky, it's not fair. Brother got a bigger piece, it's not fair. Sister got more in her stocking, it's not fair. Even dear old Santa gets accused of acts of discrimination. The only reply I have managed to come up with in a feeble attempt to ward off combat is, "Life ain't fair kid. Wait 'til you're my age and body parts gravitate, mortgage rates escalate, hair falls out in masses in some places and grows uncontrollably in other places, you can remember what you got for your fourth birthday thirty-four years ago but you can't remember where you left your car keys ten minutes ago, then you can talk to me about what's fair and what isn't."

The urge to purge made me feel better. However, I lost the kid right after the words, ". . . wait 'til you're my age . . ." Apparently they can't even wait until my next breath, and they manage to squirm away. Not all is lost, however; I do manage to evade a battle between the soldiers of "it'snotfair" combat.

When children are younger they rate fairness by the size and quantity. If you purchased one child a $700 inter-active hand held computer game with all the bells and whistles and the other child got a tricycle, two Tonka trucks, a package of dinky toys, a jumbo colouring book and pack of sixty-four crayons, all totaling $169, the first child is bound to cry injustice because the second child got more. When they grow older and develop some business savvy, they rate fairness on price and price alone. In the same situation the second child would be crying injustice, claiming you owe him another $531 worth of monetary attention.

There's a reason most products come in even numbers — because they are easily divisible. Of course if you have an uneven amount of children, it does make it a little more challenging, but you are not left without options. You could take the leftovers and keep them for yourself, especially wise in the case of chocolates, or you could have another baby and even things up again. If you do have an even amount of children, like two, there is bound to be "it'snotfair" combat, and don't be fooled by otherwise sagging math marks — when it comes to who gets what, their math is so exceptional that they are capable of counting the number of fruit loops in each other's bowls. One needs to be cautious here. Remember the uneven chocolate solution. Well, it could be hazardous to your health. After all, eating until you even things up can weigh, pun intended, heavily on your hips. While "it'snotfair" combat is inevitable, it is usually easily resolved by ensuring everything is kept in equal balance.

Combat can get very ugly when the battle isn't over things, but over parental affection and attention. "You love him/her more than me." "You never do anything with me." "You think she/he is smarter, cuter, better at, more fun than me." "So and so is your favourite."

Ouch. These words hurt coming from your child, the child you brought into this world with as much anticipation, excitement, and love as any other child. Your heart may break when you hear these comments, but you have to bear in mind that they are more often than not made as a result of unfounded resentment or feelings of insecurity and hurt, and are sometimes the only way a child has of expressing these feelings. I am no expert and I have no sure-fire advice for dealing with this type of "it'snotfair" combat, but one thing I do know is that it should never be ignored and left to fester. I agree with the pros in that you should qualify their feelings by listening and offering understanding as opposed to solutions, and although it may be difficult, avoid telling them that it is simply not true and they are being silly. Anger is not the way to handle this either. After all, your anger is simply a manifestation of your own feelings of hurt. While it is tempting to agree with the complainant in hopes that reverse psychology will bring him to his senses, take it from me, those tiny minds aren't equipped with the resources to differentiate between what they think is true and what really is true.

They will not only use word weapons against you, but they will also use them against their siblings. "Mom/Dad loves me more than you." "Mom/Dad does more with me than with you." "Mom/Dad thinks I'm smarter/cuter/better at/more fun than you." "I'm their favourite." You can count presents, calculate value, divide pies evenly, but balancing the scales of affection equality is far more delicate. Handle with care.

Experts say sibling warfare is as natural as childbirth itself and even claim that to some extent it is healthy. They say it teaches children to defend their opinions and rights and builds character. I say, give them soft boxing gloves and let them really build character. I guess it may be natural and may even be to some degree healthy, but one thing I know for sure, it is one of the most frustrating and likewise exasperating things a parent must deal with. Whether you have two or five children, whether they are thirteen months or six years apart, the outcome is the same — children fight and they do so almost constantly. If you are lucky, you may be blessed with children who get along famously, but everything I have ever heard from an array of parents would indicate that this is not usual, and would further agree that fights usually begin over the most ridiculous matters.

Some Examples:

Front seat of the vehicle, battle of '92. You can attempt to solve this by scheduling front seat passengers, assigning the front seat to only those over twenty, professing the law requires it, purchasing an eight-passenger not-so-mini van and assigning each passenger a row, or you can always threaten them with: "If you don't stop, you will have to walk." Of course all of these solutions bring about their own separate issues. For example, if you put them together in the back, be prepared to endure battles over space, and you can be sure those seat belts aren't nearly tight enough, allowing for just enough mobility for little arms and legs to flail around like a bound frog.

She's in my space, battle of '91. Body parts as minuscule as an eyelash still constitute invasion of privacy in the mind of a child. Their rooms become the grounds for many a "You're bugging me," battle. You can warn the offending child and request he leaves the vicinity immediately, but the minute you are busy with other matters, the culprit will quickly make his way back to the border of off limits and taunt his sibling by placing his toes in and out of the room. The next thing you are about to hear are the wails of a child, "Mom, brother is in my room again, he's in big trouble." As though you needed to be reminded of the warning you had given earlier. Now the pressure is on, and you not only have to go back in and arbitrate another battle, but you must also follow up on your threat.

It was an accident, battle of '90, '91, '92. What wasn't meant to be is always an accident, and when it comes to siblings pushing, shoving, hitting, biting, tripping, or even touching one another, it was never meant to be. Unless, of course, you are the recipient of such behaviour, then it was always meant to be. Although there is no scientific reasoning, it is impossible for two children (yours) that total twenty-four inches in width to pass in a ten-foot room without making unwanted contact. Then the fight is on, beginning with a host of accusations. "Mom/Dad, so and so touched me." "Mom/Dad, so and so just pushed me into the couch." "Mom/Dad, so and so hit me." "Mom/Dad so and so took a breath of my air." Honestly, sometimes I wonder.

I had it first, battle of '95. The television remote control, the Nintendo or computer controls, the alleged perfect seat on the couch, the soccer ball, the only green cup in the cupboard, the dog at the end of a leash, the bathroom, the shower — the list of desires is as endless as the fights that occur over them. But one thing is certain: if one child had it first, the other is bound to want it more. The same theory applies to the "last one" battle. There could be one orange left in the fridge and as

> **Tip:**
>
> *If you are going to use threats, especially in the presence of the other children, be prepared to carry them through or you will soon lose what little power you have. Idle threats are never advised. After all, who really wants their children living in their rooms in your house for the rest of their lives. Sending them to the moon requires a great deal more than the end of your fist, and there are very few gypsy caravans living by the river bottoms any more. You may also wish to choose your descriptive words wisely when threatening. For example, Big Trouble to the non-offender may mean that the sibling will be tarred and feathered, but to you it may mean that they can't go out and play after dinner.*

soon as one decides she wants to eat it, by some twist of fate the other child wants it as well. The results are screams of injustice: "Mom/Dad, so and so just ate the last orange and she knew I wanted it." This may hold some truth. However, the fact still remains that the orange sat in the fridge for over three weeks without so much as a second glance and now appears to be the last orange on earth.

He's bugging me, the longest battle in child rearing history. The "He's bugging me" battle is usually the premise behind every war as indicated earlier in the "She's in my space," battle. Where there are more than one there are going to be nuisance claims. To some degree, this is part of human nature — people tend to get on each other's nerves, so it should be expected of children. The difference between the "nuisance battles" of adults and children is determined by three main characteristics: the matter over which the irritant develops, the unbelievable quantities in which they occur, and their ability to cause more grief to the uninvolved bystanders.

Attitudes Anonymous

By now you may have guessed that the years of growing up may seem painfully slow to the child, but they are painfully quick to the parent who often gets caught up reminiscing about the wonderful days gone by. I stretch out my hand in hopes of feeling the warmth of a tiny palm placed into mine, but I am sadly disappointed as my little buddy makes a wide sweep, totally passing my outreached hand. Suddenly it dawns on me: public shows of affection are no longer cool. I choke back tears, knowing how much I'll miss the tiny gesture and knowing that the years to come hold even fewer outward signs of love. I fight off the quivering lip as I realize that my need to show love with hugs and kisses will soon be reduced to the opening of my wallet. Grade 3 seems to bring about a fluctuation in acceptable parental behaviour. Seven- and eight-year-olds are torn between still needing the warmth and security of their parents and acquiring the approval and acceptance of their peers. Unfortunately, because of their youth and lack of experience, children don't possess a great deal of finesse. Often their signs of disapproval are quite boisterous and sometimes hurtful, and you find yourself, a thirty- to forty-year-old otherwise seemingly mature adult, pouting and feeling sorry for yourself. Amazingly, you revert to behaviour you once found very annoying in your child. You'll make up the most unreasonable theories, such as,

"I'm your mother/father, I have rights." "You can bet Josh lets his mom/dad hug him still." "It's all I have to remember you by, and I miss you so much." "Come on, your teachers think it is so sweet when you hug me good-bye." "All you care about is what I do for you and what I give you." "I went through forty hours of hard labour so you could be in this world; the least you can do is show me how much you appreciate all my sacrifice." "Hugging is a great source of vitamins and will help you build strong muscles." "In some countries hugging is performed by the great warriors as a symbol of power," and if all else fails, "You don't love me anymore."

At this point you realize just how pathetic your emotional well-being has become, that you rely so heavily on an eight-year-old's hug. Unfortunately, along with the sudden withdrawal of affection comes an attitude that is sure to make you start wondering who stole your sweet baby and replaced him with this contemptible stranger. The child you gave life to will suddenly know more than you, have more sensitive feelings than you which you couldn't possibly understand, and will manage to make you feel like you did in junior high gym class — a freak who knows nothing about the real world. Your requests are met by a series of rolled eyes, audible grunts, over-exaggerated arm movements, unnecessary foot stomping, and possibly total disregard. Any attempt to assist the child in success is often viewed as over-protection, distrust, and totally unnecessary worrying. This higher road to independence is frustrating for both child and parent alike. Support groups have never been more necessary than through the next ten years or so of a parent's life.

My son first introduced me to the change in our relationship one day when I was scolding him for not concentrating on his homework. It wasn't as though this had been his first scolding, but it was the first time he had ever responded with such a blatant demonstration of disrespect. After I had finished my well-rehearsed monologue of, "If you don't focus, you'll struggle all your life. I'm not doing the work for you, it is time you put more effort into it," which I am convinced sounded more like blah blah blah blah to him, I stopped and gave him one of my what I thought to be looks of disappointment but which he interpreted as a bitter beer face. Without as much as a blink of his eye, he began mimicking me with strange noises that copied my tone, but didn't even remotely sound like my words. "Nah nah nah nah nah nah."

My husband was sitting at the table and I could see a grin begin to form at the corners of his mouth. I instantly became furious, not so much at my son's exhibition of disrespect, but at the very thought that my husband found the whole situation amusing. I knew if my son saw his father's disconcerting reaction, I would lose what little control I still had, and from that day forward my attempts to discipline would be turned into a forum for my son's comedy routine. I turned my attention towards my husband and gave him an all too familiar "You stupid ass" glare. As he left the room, I thought to myself, "Boy, if the tables were turned, it wouldn't be so funny." By this point my son had totally lost his focus and was now making demented faces, to the amusement of his sister. I began to repeat his name and my message only to be mimicked once again, this time accompanied by some not so flattering physical actions, including hands pressed tightly to his ears, eyes rolling back, and side to side tilting head movements. As his pretentiousness continued my voice got louder, my teeth clenched, and I began to shake my fist. Then it dawned on me that neither of us was actually getting anywhere and we both looked pretty foolish. I stopped and stared at him, curled my lip at the corner, and raised my eyebrows, expressing my sentiments of "What a goof." The very idea that I was no longer spewing but instead was turning the tables on him caused him to angrily shove his chair away from the table and leave in a huff. I looked at my daughter, who at this point was unsure if she should actually make eye contact with me. "What a dufus," I exclaimed, and then proceeded to mimic him. The very sight of her mother stooping to the level of an attitudinal eight-year-old was too much for her to handle and she burst into a joyous fit of laughter, as did I. Had the perpetrator still been in the room observing the fun his sister and I were having at his expense, he surely would have gone into a foot-stomping, bitter-beer-faced, arm-flogging over-dramatized episode.

Many more of these moments would follow; this was the fork in the road to higher independence. One of my children's teachers, an extremely reliable source of information and parental guidance, warned me that when they were around the middle of Grade 5 I would no longer recognize them. I asked her if they would begin growing body hair, or sprout five inches, or suddenly catch on to the differences between boys and girls. She grinned and replied no, actually they would become self-indulgent, you-can't-touch-me, only-in-your-dreams, pre-teens. Pre-teen, I thought, but they barely just learned how to tie their own shoelacess, or so it would seem. And as though it were planned almost to the exact day, in 2001 it happened; a new person moved into our house and it appeared as though our little boy wasn't related to us anymore. This wise teacher was right, and when this period of your child's life occurs, you will wonder if your child even cares about you, or understands that you are a person with real feelings. *Thank you, Robby, for your wise words, shoulder to lean on, and valuable friendship*.

Days will become filled with ineffectual arguing, outright refusals, and constant challenges to your wisdom and authority. You will find that once-eloquent vocabularies will turn into desultory passages consisting of, "As if." "What-ever." "Don't have a cow." "Not gonna happen," and of course, "Do I haveta?" Any thoughts you had of inadequacy are now compounded by the fact that your child thinks you are a complete moron. You will be told in no uncertain terms that you are completely out of touch with things and your way of thinking is stupid and antiquated. Your thirty to forty years of experience and knowledge will be vanquished with one quick and thoughtless, "As if." These tender years are riddled with painful emotional growth. The struggle to keep your child close to you while at the same time letting him move away is undoubtedly the hardest you'll experience.

Growing Up Pains

The pain of stretching body parts can be healed with a massage, a warm bath or shower, perhaps some medicated cream, but the pain of stretching emotions and growing self-esteems can be much harder to attend to. When children are young the most they worry about is whether or not there will be a Popsicle left in the freezer when they get home from a grueling day of Kindergarten. Unfortunately, as they grow, so too do their concerns. Their worries are sometimes bigger than life itself. They often feel frustrated at their inability to cope with matters and even more frustrated at their inability to understand them. As caring parents, we try our hardest to explain the ways of the world to them, and help them grasp an understanding of reality, but it is like teaching them how to ride a two-wheeler — unless we let go of the back, they will never really know how to ride on their own. This is the breaking and making point of all good parents: knowing when we need to let go, and when we need to hang on. There is no specific age, time, or symptom to go by. This challenge in the task of raising healthy, well-adjusted children will come to light the day

moments. I am certain she was debating whether to sit down and cry or just walk off to the change rooms. I yelled, "Way to go, Sweety," but she didn't turn and flash me her infamous "melt me" smile. Instead she bravely began climbing the stairs to the three-metre board. This time she politely turned down the coach's offer to assist her, walked to the edge and looked over, hesitated, then stepped off into a straight jump. When she resurfaced she wasn't smiling, she simply looked defeated. The lesson ended and she slowly walked to the change room. After a while, longer than usual, she came out with a red cheek and a sore back. But most devastatingly, her spirits were broken. Her coach came to say goodnight and did what any great coach should do. She commented that Krysta's back might be stiff, but she would be okay for next week when she tried the three-metre front fall-in again. Krysta smiled slightly, then walked over and wrapped her arms around my waist, burying her head into my side. She had fallen from that high level of self-esteem to the bottom in one big splash.

This was no doubt her first huge disappointment, but certainly not her last. Disappointments will continue to come as sure as the days continue to come. When we are older and somewhat wiser, we begin to appreciate that disappointment is part of building a strong sense of self, and patience will heal the wounds. To a seven-year-old whose back is sore and whose confidence is crushed, only the comfort of a loving parent's arms can help make growing up pains dissipate.

Is Who I am Okay? Life's Toughest Lesson

It usually begins with the clothes they wear or the style of their hair — the age will vary from child to child — but the worrying over whether or not they fit in is imminent. Discrimination begins at very early ages and children are less than discreet at letting their opinions be known. Whether it is through the media, parents, older siblings, or peers, the hurtful act of labeling and consequently making fun becomes your child's first experience with image development. Frankly, I view such behaviour as nothing more than another form of bullying. Mirror magnitude takes control of a child's self-image after he is teased and made fun of for wearing clothes that are considered out of style, which in today's society occurs the minute the fashion hits the shelf. Suddenly a child who felt good about himself is made to feel abnormal and hence the self doubting begins. No matter how hard you try and how many loving parental skills you have acquired, there is little you can do to ward off or soothe over these horrible feelings. All you can do is listen and love them, and hope that your love is enough to pull them through and make them realize that who they are really is okay.

In the meantime, be prepared to endure constant pleas for over-priced items that bear certain names and logos, hair tinting, body piercing, and other extravagances that you can hardly afford for yourself. Teaching children to be socially responsible should be as vital as teaching them their basic math facts. Fancy clothes, the latest hair style, or the money that pays for it all does not guarantee social graces, and in fact more times than not, having all the best makes it very difficult to notice the advantages of just being the best one can be. Sadly, our children are knee-deep in a society that bases self-worth on who has the best and who plays the best, and it is extremely difficult as a parent to not want your child to be the best. I know I have pushed my children to try harder and be the top scorer, or have purchased something far out of our budget just so they could feel that they fit in. But as they grow and develop skills and talents I never could have imagined, I realize that the beautiful people they are inside is good enough for them, so, it's likewise good enough for me.

Independence versus Indifference

As children grow towards independence the lessons get tougher and tougher, and so, too, do the rules. For parents the easy route would be to just let it pass and work from the theory of getting by with little to no hassle over who is right and why they should listen. But raising children isn't like that nor should it be; as parents we are wholly responsible for assuring that our children grow healthy and strong at the same time they respect the norms of family and society. Independence is bound to be accompanied by shows of indifference, doubt, and confusion. All parents will bear witness to their children's continuum of questioning their worlds, and more particularly authority. Never will the need be greater than now for parents to take a strong hold on security and enforcing order in their children's lives. Some may argue that adolescence is when this is of most importance; however, setting standards now will likely alleviate any surprises in the trying times of teenhood.

When to say no and knowing how to say no should be a mandatory course for all parents. I am no expert, and likely there are no experts in this fine art, but the necessity of standing your ground, all the while allowing children their independence, is a delicate and often difficult task. Rules may seem drastic and unfair to children who simply want to spread their wings and soar off the cliff by themselves. To growing children, rules are simply boundaries, but some day in their adult lives they will be seen for what they really are — safety nets intended to protect them from harm. Independence day is the beginning of the era where parents may have to resign their position as best friend and resume their position as best caregiver, offering their children all the protection, love, and support a parent can give, even if it means hurt feelings on both parts. Knowing when to say no is hard, but knowing when to say yes can be equally challenging because this is the point where parents accept that children must experience life and must be trusted to do so.

Oddly enough, they beg for freedom to stay home alone, but in the next breath plead with you to crawl into your bed after a bad dream. They will argue that they are old enough to make their own decisions about what they wear and who they call friends, yet they have no idea on how to improve their math mark. They will tell you in no uncertain terms that you are wrong, yet act like a baby when they discover you are right. "You never let me do anything," is ironically countered by "You expect me to do that by myself." Without independence, children, as do adults, miss out on a world of self-discovery and wonder. Independence affords children the opportunity to become the best person they can be and introduce to the rest of the world the wonderful person they are, even if it is accompanied by a little indifference.

CHAPTER FOUR

Honey, Did You Pack My Razor?

In loving memory of our dearest friend, husband, and father, Les Patton.

Just a Little Dab will do it

The man's most important role in the miracle of childbirth happens at the point of conception and lasts approximately twenty-three seconds, give or take a few. The rest is left up to the athletic abilities of millions of microscopic sperm and the power of genetics. Once one of those mighty soldiers penetrates the uterus wall, the man's arduous task is, loosely spoken, completed. Not to diminish the importance of such an admirable donation, but one has to wonder, when this contribution can actually be made by sharing a special moment with a laboratory test tube without ever having to make physical contact with the donor. Today's modern world of medicine has even made it possible to choose the donor, providing a gene pool rich in selection from hair and eye colour to brain weight and body fat mass. One might say that the man's most important role has been replaced with test tube shopping. The mere mention of the word shopping may very well eliminate a high percentage of women from choosing the old-fashioned alternative to pregnancy. Once the seed is planted, the man would be well advised to step back, way back, because the next nine to ten months will be the true test of patience, will-power, and devotion to the woman he once claimed to be the love of his life. For her these months will be filled with all of the manifestations mentioned earlier in Chapter One. For him they will be filled with the likes of the following:

- constant inquests into his love for her, and damned if he does, damned if he doesn't inquiries about her weight gain versus her beauty;
- middle of the night cravings for cheezies, mushroom soup, ice cream, and other not readily available foods that he would be wise to make every effort to obtain;
- no less than twenty-five mid-sleep interruptions as the mattress shifts and moves when she gets up to relieve her bladder or plays mattress monopoly trying to find the ideal location of comfort which, according to her not so under her breath comments, does not exist;
- sudden but frequent outbursts of uncontrollable and inconsolable, no matter how hard he tries, emotions ranging from shoulder-shaking sobs to dish-breaking anger which are almost always followed by "no right answer" inquests: "Do you still love me?" and critical comments and remarks that include, "This is all your fault," "You only think of yourself," "You've got to be kidding, that's what got me this way in the first place," "Don't you touch me ever again," "Sure, you go ahead to the gym and check out all those tight body gorgeous women, I know you think I'm fat," "You had all the fun, now I have to do all the suffering," "If I were you, I'd keep one eye open while you sleep from now on."

Some of these remarks actually instill fear into men and for good reason — pregnancy can be P.M.S. amplified for two hundred and seventy days. Be forewarned that the bittersweet terms of endearment don't stop at the end of the gestation period; the man must still endure labour and the actual birth. Lamaze classes should come with Husband Advisories.

Men of the new Millennium and a few decades prior have wisely chosen to be present when the big event takes place, and I say wisely because a "no show" in the delivery room is being lobbied as legal grounds for divorce. The onslaught of fathers in the delivery room brings with it some good and some bad. If your spouse is of a mechanical nature, he will likely get busy playing with all the buttons, levers, and gadgets in the room. He will become fascinated with the delivery bed, managing to maneuvre it into a variety of different positions, resulting in mom-to-be being hoisted into callisthenic type moves that are not only uncomfortable but virtually undoable by a woman who is carrying forty or so extra pounds concentrated in the midriff area. The tools of delivery will also attract his attention as he attempts to pick up your pillow with the forceps or pry open the side stand door with the uterus clamps. The fortunate part about your spouse's curious behaviour is that it amuses him, therefore keeping him occupied and out of your hair. The unfortunate part is that his behaviour annoys the hospital staff and can put them in a contentious mood prior to the delivery, and there is nothing worse than an agitated nurse wielding needles and scissors.

Spouses are encouraged to assist moms through labour pains by coaching her breathing, rubbing her back, and even sitting with her in the shower, none of which are really appreciated by a woman who is crouched over in pain, squatting in a shower, or doubled over in a hospital bed with six other people in the room. Some spouses come into the delivery room equipped with video and still cameras prepared to capture the event for posterity. These spouses should be warned that a woman who is straddled into stirrups, whose body is swollen to four times it's normal size, and who is grunting and groaning like a moose in rut is not interested in making her debut on Family Vision tv. There are few delivering moms who can endure such an invasion, and wise spouses would have a waiver signed before they even think about visually recording the occasion.

The man's presence in the delivery room is cleverly disguised as a show of strong devotion and a sincere attempt to begin the father/child bond early by offering to cut the umbilical cord. But the true intentions of the "about to give birth" mother are to have the culprit present at the point of impact. A woman who is experiencing gut-ripping, pelvic-splitting, back-wrenching pain doesn't want the gentle caress of her dearly beloved, what she really wants is a whipping stone that she can throw obscenities at and stare down. With every contraction she wants to be able to dig her nails into the flesh of his tender palms so that he can really be a part of the experience. With every push that feels like a basketball travelling through her sinuses, she wants to wrap her loving hands around his throat. The final push which brings with it the creation of life along with an unappealing mixture of other body extractions, a vision guaranteed to make even the strongest of men weak, will bring about her final words of wisdom: "If I were a black widow, I'd be having you for lunch right now."

As though instinctively, the doctor hands the proud papa the wondrous joy, and for a very intense moment the woman's heart mellows as she looks on at this strong man, a protector of the child, cradling the tiny, precious life. The image of his mightiness being driven down to the very depths of his soul by the helplessness of this child reminds her of all the reasons she fell in love with him in the first place.

Papa's New Role

In the beginning many men play the role of *en vogue* father to the full extent, in hopes that the world, including his wife and himself, will see him as the hip dad who would have gladly in comparison peed out a sunflower seed in order to bring this child into the world. And to some degree their efforts are honest and well intended. For example, dads will offer to give the new babe a bottle during feeding and even more excitedly offer to hold the breast if mom is nursing. However, a good deal of plea bargaining transpires as fathers opt for feeding instead of changing, coddling instead of bathing, or introducing them to channel surfing instead of singing a lullaby.

Fathers of this generation and, I suspect, many generations to follow, are finding themselves in new roles which are no longer simply defined by financial support, but are clearly marked by more affectionate duties, some of which include: feedings, diaper duty, on-call cuddling, and emotional pacifying. Daddies are no longer the silent partners. They are willingly and much more importantly happily involved, and in some instances assume the position of both parents as a single parent. So I am in no way deprecating the roles fathers play in the lives of their children, I am simply stating the obvious — more often than not fathers spend a great deal of their time providing sustenance because society dictates it as such.

Despite the recent changes in paternal responsibilities, many women still find themselves as the primary caregivers. Some experts may argue that this occurs because of the mother/child bond created when the child is still in the womb, while others feel it occurs as a result of nursing. Until they can perfect a nursing contraption that is strapped to the man when the test proves positive and remains there until the child is weaned, women will remain fundamentally responsible for insuring the first eighteen to twenty months of nurturing. To some degree society still puts a great deal of expectations on the mother, and it is not unreasonable to assume that fathers feel pressure to comply with society. This alone would explain what can be construed as otherwise less male participation; they are, after all, just following suit. My first experience with the apparent injustice of shared parenting came by way of a comment, and once I actually thought about it, became quite a thorn in my paw. It came to me on a rare occasion where I found myself out for an evening, child free. Amidst the joy of freedom from the demands of my two children the comment was made in innocent passing.

"Is John babysitting your kids tonight?"

Without hesitation I replied, "Yes, he said he would look after them while I went out." I continued to enjoy my evening, not giving the comment any more thought until a friend of mine, another mother, made a similar comment but with a much different tone.

"So John is finally getting a real taste of parenthood tonight."

It was then that it hit me; the first comment implied that fathers are babysitters as opposed to parents. I began to wonder if I had to pay John the going babysitting rate, if I had given him an emergency number where he could reach me, if I had left some snacks for him, and would he have a girlfriend over, when it dawned on me — fathers don't baby-sit, they parent. But sadly there are some very archaic attitudes out there regarding the roles of fathers, one of which requires the mother to stay at home with the children and sacrifice her social position in society. Going out with the "girls" is less likely to occur. However, when such a joyous occasion presents itself and mom finds herself in the luxury of some time away, she should be prepared for some shocking side effects of leaving dad in charge, all of which will vary depending on the length of absence and the age of the children.

Dads may view the duty of minding the children as putting the baby in the playpen, or sitting her on the floor of the family room. Dads reassure themselves by telling the children not to get into anything and to play quietly. With this base covered, the road is clear to turn on the television, place the channel changer and portable telephone on the table beside the sofa, then lay down and ultimately become fully engrossed in the sports channel or a nap. They convince themselves that they are in control of the situation, which for some reason would not explain the condition of the house when mom finally arrives home. In the case of a baby the little one is probably weighted down by a moist diaper and will appear to be in some sort of trance watching WWF. A half-empty bottle and all play toys lay mysteriously five feet away from the playpen. If the children are anywhere from three to ten years old, the scenario could be almost anything. The kitchen may look like the 41st regiment ate there. The fridge door may be decorated with raspberry jam, some other mysterious substance stuck to the counter tops, and there may be a lengthy trail of crumbs from the counter to the kitchen table (if you are lucky), and dirty dishes stacked in the sink which is conveniently located right beside the dishwasher. Other rooms in the house may take on a similar appearance. Once precisely made beds now resemble the remnants of a lemur slumber party; strategically placed toys, books, and other annoying objects now litter the entire family room floor; and the toilet paper roll is no longer hanging on the device intended to house it, but is more than likely either in the toilet bowl or decoratively hung throughout the house. If mothers are wise they will hide crayons, markers, pens, pencils, paints, silly putty, and all other creating equipment before they leave the house. Otherwise be prepared for some unique art work to show up anywhere but on paper. Many a wall, shower, bathtub, table top, and other places have become a young Picasso's canvas. Mom's first reaction is a gasp of horror, her second is to turn around and run.

Instead she begins to pick up the scattered debris and vigorously throw it into its large plastic container which was turned upside down in order to double for a handy table in exact reaching distance of the sofa. There will be nothing accidental about the way each item is thrown into the container making a loud noise. The intention is to wake the dead, or at least the peacefully slumbering caregiver who took solace in thinking that the children would be fine as long as the door was locked. Of course as the children get older, they develop the ability to unlock doors and escape to the curious world of the outside. Then when mom arrives home and begins the ritual of cleaning up, she is suddenly struck by the incredible sound of silence and a thought crosses her mind, "Why can't I hear the children? Where are the children?"

Mom's night out is now a distant memory and the prospect of another childless evening seems fruitless. Perhaps it is the lack of experience, perhaps it is genetic, perhaps it is even a skillfully calculated plan developed by the first dad charged with minding his own children — whatever the cause, the outcome is the same. It would have been easier to stay home. At some point moms begin to realize that even though they have officially given birth those children are somehow in some inexplicable way still attached to her. The evidence of this mounts as manufacturers introduce new contraptions designed to strap the child to the mother under the guise of convenience for mom as she shops, cooks, cleans, runs errands and, yes, even works out. Face it, mom, your freedom has been altered. Dads, for the most part, resume life as usual. It would seem after the token days of cooing and toting the baby around like some gloating Silverback gorilla, dads can't wait to go back to work. They act like a wounded puppy in a feeble attempt to convince the mom and themselves that they really wished they could trade places. But these attempts are quickly unveiled for what they really are as dad leaves the house in record speed.

I Truly Choose to Stay Home

Not all moms stay home after the birth of a child. Many return to the outside workforce and like their spouses manage to juggle hectic jobs and share in the maintenance of the home. By the same token there has been an increase in the amount of stay home dads who are more than content to be the main caregivers. So at this point I would like to take an opportunity to pay tribute to all stay home parents. They have no specific recognition or status in our society, like doctors, lawyers, teachers, CEO's, entertainers, etc., yet they play a significant role in the growth and wellbeing of our society. They choose to be available to the children in an exclusive manner, not allowing outside distractions to take their attention away from the needs of the children. They forego fancy luncheons for alphabet soup, grilled cheese sandwiches dipped in ketchup, and bananas with brown sugar. They trade engaging conversations with other career companions for scintillating stories about recess antics, math class, and how the teacher's zipper was undone all morning. Despite popular belief, they do not spend their days watching soap operas and eating bonbons. Instead they use the time to run errands, clean and maintain the home, do laundry, prepare meals, answer desperate calls of forgotten homework, and a multitude of other less than news-breaking tasks. Stay home parents are not the dull-minded lost people of our society who have nothing to talk about other than the escapades of the children. In fact, they are often well-read and versed in a variety of topics including politics, art, technology, and the plight of the world. In their minds they don't sacrifice anything but are fulfilled, with the understanding that where they are is where they need to be. Not unlike their outside workforce counterparts, their days are filled with time management, constant inquiries, variances in their learning curves, and vital decision-making. Unlike their outside work-force counterparts, their days are also filled with hugs, kisses, and unin-hibited laughter. The pay they receive for a hard day's work does not come in the form of a bank deposit, but is amortized over years of patience and finally realized in the face of a happy, well-adjusted grown child. **Hats off to stay home parents.**

NOTE: Whether out of necessity or as the result of personal choice, stay home parents are vital and honourable, and our world should embody sincere admiration for them.

I Came Home for This?

Parenting isn't any easier for moms than dads and vice-versa, it is sim-ply different. Ironically, moms complain that they spend way too much time with the children, and dads complain that they never spend enough time with them. All you can ask for in the end is balance and a shared sense of pride and relief that you got the job done, and you got it done with little to no injury to your own relationship.

If one parent decides to stay home and devote her attention to child-care or attempt to run a business from the home, this becomes an even more demanding position. I can safely speak from both sides of the sit-uation, as I worked outside of the home for the first eight and a half years of my childrens' lives and have recently taken up a home busi-ness. The benefits of staying home are immeasurable to both child and parent, but the eventual feelings of being taken for granted are inevitable. Until the school years, the days are filled with feeding, changing, cleaning, playing, reading, feeding, changing, cleaning, resting, cleaning, playing, and then preparing for the arrival of your spouse. Once the school years begin there are a few, and I emphasize a few, spare hours to tend to your own business. However, as I so discovered, what mathematically works out to be seven hours of "kidless" time, in reality works out as follows:

7 a.m.: Rise and shine. Time to get the kids up, dressed, and fed breakfast, backpacks ready, clad for the weather conditions, and out the door by 8:10 a.m.., and, depending on whether or not you drive them to school, may include a ten minute or more trip to and from the school. Included in this time is a quick load of laundry, emptying the dishwasher, combing, curling or otherwise preparing hair, and brushing off and starting the car if necessary. Oh, yes, and one day of the week carrying out the trash.

8:25 a.m.: Stretch those muscles. Like so many health conscious North Americans, many stay homes feel it of great benefit to fit in a fitness program. I chose this time right after the children were settled into school.

9:15 a.m.: Shower. Despite the popular image of stay homes walking around in curlers and fuzzy slippers all days, most choose to shower and do their hair. You never know when you may receive a Loomis delivery, and with any luck it will be some hard-bodied twenty-five-year-old delivering. But I digress.

9:30 a.m.: It is time to sit down and get some business done. All the while you will answer any incoming calls, check the stocks, clean up things like bowls and cups left from the night before, put in another load of laundry, and manage some time for a quick cup of java or tea.

11:15 a.m.: It dawns on you that the children will be home soon for lunch so lunch must be prepared. You have the option of throwing a bag of chips and a banana on the table and saying help yourself, but the novelty wears off after a while. In all seriousness, you prepare a well-balanced, nutritious lunch for your charges. Unfortunately, despite attempts to be creative and prepare a variety of meals, after a while the routine loses its glamour and no matter how hard you try, even carrots sticking into a thick mixture of dip intended to resemble people sinking in sand, the vote for most popular lunch inevitably goes to a can of spaghetti.

11:30 a.m.: Leave for the school to pick up the kids.

11:40-12:30 p.m.: Lunch is served.

12:30 p.m.: Return the children to school.

12:40 p.m.: Return home and clean up after lunch, sweep floors, tidy bathroom, and do yet another load of laundry.

1 p.m.: Back to work.

3:15 p.m.: Drive for school pick-up. You are well advised to leave a little early so you can get a good parking spot because most schools are not designed to accommodate the rush of time-starved, crazed mothers and some fathers who have a plate full of other things and places they need to be immediately after the children are picked up. The result is the worst display of traffic violations and lack of driving etiquette that can possibly happen in an area that measures less than one-tenth of a kilometre.

3:30–6 p.m.: Can vary and may include taxi service to an array of different activities ranging from gymnastics, piano, hockey, soccer, karate, diving, singing — the list is endless. In some rare instances, however, this time may mean a quick trip to the grocery store to pick up last minute items, then home to the kitchen table to complete all homework requirements.

5–6:30 p.m.: The time to prepare dinner, set the table, go over spelling words, listen to reading, and, oh yes, do another load of laundry.

6:30–7:00 p.m.: Eat dinner and clean up after. Sometimes it is simply quicker and much less stressful to do the cleaning yourself than to argue for ten minutes about whose turn it is and then have to clean up the mess incurred during the rebellious clean-up.

7–8:30 p.m.: The time reserved for larger school projects that require mechanical expertise, family sharing time which can consist of a heated game of Yahtzee, some quality tv time, or just plain catching up.

8:30 p.m.: Time to tuck the angels in, kiss them goodnight, and listen to about twenty minutes of whispering, giggling, and general winding down noises, often accompanied by the occasional parental interruption, "You guys get to sleep."

9 p.m.: All is quiet, but the ironing pile is looking ominous, your spouse is looking amorous, and your bed is looking glorious. And may the best man win.

Of course, schedules will vary from person to person, but what I am getting at is that those wonderful seven hours you thought you had, really factors out to be about four. So when your spouse arrives home and wittily inquires, "Soooo . . . what did you do all day?" his sense of humour is about as welcome as his timing.

If you are brave enough to confess that you had a pretty rotten day because the hot water tank went on the fritz, the kids were especially querulous, the dog got out of the yard, the letter carrier delivered somebody else's mail, your A.T.M. card didn't work at the grocery store, and your son called in a fit because he forgot his library books again bequeathing you with the duty of driving them to the school immediately, you will more than likely receive a rather unsympathetic reply of, "Well, at least you didn't have to deal with a bunch of whiny people all day." And so begins the battle of: *My day was more stressful than your day.*

As a stay home you feel huge pangs of guilt complaining about your day spent in the comfort of your home, compared to your spouse's day out in the jungle world. This brings me to a most important issue, the "Acceptable Welcome Home, Honey." As attested to in a 1959 High School Home Economics text book, the time right before the much anticipated arrival of your spouse should be spent tidying the house, keeping a deliciously prepared dinner warm, quieting the children, and primping yourself so you look just right. Well, we've come a long way, baby, and it is more likely that there will be rollerblades strewn in the entrance way, backpacks flung on the floor, coats laying under the hooks, a dinner resembling breakfast (french toast), kids arguing or fighting which in turn has you shouting or crying, and you wearing a pair of blue jeans with a t-shirt bearing the ironic message "No Fear" and hair pulled back with cute little butterfly clips, face au naturel, all the while toting a dish cloth. Suddenly "Welcome Home" feels more like "Whycome Home," but that's the reality. It sort of makes you long for the days before kids when the arrival of your spouse called for a passionate kiss, a romantic dinner, and . . . well that's what got us into this circumstance in the first place.

Days off can be somewhat of a challenge as well. The stay home may declare this as her day off as well and an impasse is bound to occur. Sleeping in is an option only for the "work outside the home" spouse. The regular routine as illustrated earlier must continue as normal, and is still the job of the stay home. If the children are of school years, then once they are dropped off, there is some time for the couple. However, crawling back into bed is not practical, despite how much promise it may hold for your mate. The day must go on, the laundry done, the house tidied, the meals prepared.

Sick days are another bone of contention among stay homes. When they feel under the weather, unless it is strategically designed to happen on the spouse's day off, life simply goes on. Once again, if the children are of school age you can manage to slip back into bed after they are secured in school. Lunch may not be as well prepared as usual, but nonetheless is prepared. If the children are not of school age, the situation is a little more complicated and a lot less appealing. Migraines, flus, colds, or any other illness take a back seat to the care of the children. Nothing is more difficult than caring for an unsettled baby while battling a migraine. On the other hand, the "work outside spouse" not only gets entire bed rest as well as the service of the stay home, but is actually paid for sick days. I find it amazing that there has never been a union formed for "stay homes."

As well as sick days, holidays are defined differently by the stay home and the outsider. The outsider earns his holidays by putting in a set amount of hours with the company while the stay home is often perceived as being on permanent holidays. So when holiday plans include out-of-town getaways, the stay home is, perhaps rightfully so, charged with packing. Whether it be the holiday trailer or suitcases for that dream vacation in Hawaii, the stay home is responsible for having things ready to go the minute the outsider gets home. A well-prepared stay home will have a light lunch packed for the trip, the kids waiting not so patiently in the car, the house cleaned and secured including a key to the neighbour, the lawn mowed, the newspaper cancelled, and all holiday necessities neatly and compactly packed.

In some instances, the outside working parent is afforded the luxury of overnight away from home for meetings or conventions. To the stay home the thought of getting away from it all, spending a night or two in a hotel room, eating out in restaurants, having someone clean up after you, and best of all having someone else pay for it all, is to say the least, spectacular. To the outsider such trips are unconvincingly dreaded. So as the outsider heads for the door, suitcase in hand, and stops to make a pathetic attempt at making the stay home feel guilty because she gets to be home with kids, it is important to note that, "I'll miss you, honey. Oh, by the way, did you pack my razor?" will not at all be appreciated.

Me, Mate

When I was still working outside the home I was given an opportunity to attend a four-day conference. I was delighted yet apprehensive; I would, after all, have to leave my husband and children at home. My husband is a very reliable and intelligent individual more than capable of holding down the fort in my absence. However, it is a mother's prerogative to assume that we are the only ones really capable of taking care of the children and maintaining the household, then with a twist of irony complain that our spouses never help around the house or with raising the children. I think this is directly related to hormonal imbalance. Disregarding my unfounded apprehension, I opted to go and enjoy the time away by myself, something my husband had done on several occasions. There was, however, a noticeable difference.

Whenever my husband left for a business trip or one-week hunting trip, he would do some quick preparations, then out the door the day of departure with hugs for the kids and a reasonably passionate kiss for me. During his absence I would still manage to get the kids to and from the sitter's, work a full day, come home and prepare dinner, then do homework and all the other tasks required to keep the household running smoothly. I may have received the odd sympathetic, "How's it going?" but for the most part people felt little appreciation for my temporary single parent status. When the tables were turned, the situation was noticeably different. I, in my attempt to prove I was the perfect wife and mother, prepared some make-ahead meals, arranged for day care services, did all the laundry, ironing, and cleaning, then before I left turned around several times to hug and kiss my children and assure them I loved them. Unlike with my stint of single parent status, my husband was

> **Tip:**
> Stay home parents are wisely advised to have the name and phone number of an alternative caregiver on hand as well as putting aside fifty dollars a month for emergency caregiving services. Such services can then be used by stay home parents who do not have the indulgence of family or friends to attend to children during their own ailment.

offered dinners at friends and family, including my own parents, extensions on baby-sitting services with no extra cost, delivery service to and from the school by sympathetic mothers, and was continually monitored by concerned people. Once again, I have grown wise, and now when my husband takes a leave I call my faithful mother-in-law, who happily comes to my rescue by offering to stay with me. I don't expect her to drive the children back and forth or cook or clean for me, but I can never tell her how much I appreciate having the company, not to mention someone who appreciates my temporary single parent plight. **Many thanks, Edith.**

You Need to Speak into my Good Ear

Communication becomes somewhat strained once children are introduced into the relationship. When the children are infants, communication is often interrupted by cries for attention, and once the baby's needs are attended to, the flow of the conversation is likely lost. When the children get older and are capable of talking, their constant desire to chatter leaves little to no time for mom and dad to converse. I, however, in my need to keep the communication lines up and running with John, found a perfect solution, at least for myself. Once the rest of the household was in quiet slumber, John and I could speak freely and without the constant inclusion of a five-year-old reciting the goings on of "Hey Arnold." Unfortunately John did not nor does he share the same definition of a "quickie" at night. The thought of a little physical communication along with some good verbal communication wasn't entirely out of the question, but the order of business had to be established: first some serious talk, then some pillow talk. My reasoning being that in anticipation of the pillow talk John would remain semi-conscious; otherwise I would find myself speaking to the rhythm of his snoring.

There is no denying the importance of communication in any relationship, but the need becomes even more prevalent after children, if not for the mere fact of having a conversation that doesn't begin with the words "I spy." Of course, keeping communication alive and well can be met by more challenges than just the children. While there is no scientific proof or medical explanation, spousal selective hearing is a known and experienced fact for couples. Spouses often claim that they can only hear out of the ear opposite to the one their mate or children are speaking towards, with the result, "You never told me that." This may also explain the ability of a spouse to sit and watch television despite the glass-shattering screams of the children. He may have to adjust the volume a bit, but he does so without even flinching. With selective hearing your plea to be taken out for dinner, your request for some quiet time, or your lengthy account of how badly the kids behaved, how nagging your boss was, how your nylons ripped twice, and how the car got dinged in the shopping mall parking lot may be slightly diffused. What they choose to hear is more like: "Dinner will be ready soon so take some quiet time, honey, you deserve it, the kids will behave, later I'll slip into those fish-net nylons you like and you can pretend you're my boss, I fixed the ding in your car and I never want to go to the shopping mall again." I must confess, though, that over the past few years I too have been guilty of using selective hearing as my husband recounts a rendition of his day. "I had the worst day, I had to break up an argument today, the cash terminals were on the fritz again, I didn't get to go for lunch so what's for dinner and I really could use a back rub," translated through my selective hearing becomes, "If the kids argue I'll take care of it, here have some cash so you can go for lunch tomorrow, I'll cook dinner tonight then I'll give you a long back rub honey, 'cause you deserve it so much."

There's a lot to be said for hear what you want to hear, then do what you have to do. I'm certainly no relationship expert; heck I still get mad when the toilet seat gets left up, but one thing I am sure of — in order to hear each other you must first learn to listen. As our children have grown and we find ourselves lucky enough to have some couple time, John and I have developed a habit of sitting in the front room or on the deck with a cup of tea and doing some quality communicating, which includes a little conversation with a whole lot of listening.

How will They ever Learn

An area that causes constant dissension in any parental relationship is the discipline of children. In many situations both parents usually have fairly similar ideas regarding discipline of the children; however, there are also numerous occasions where the directors of discipline may not see eye to eye. The result — a deadlock that leaves the parents second guessing each other and the children confused and insecure. Nothing is more annoying to a parent than having her partner mimic or contradict her attempt to discipline. For example, mom tells junior he is grounded for back talking, then dad lifts the ban for the sake of tickets to the monster truck show. On the other hand, dad chastises junior for using and consequently losing his tools, to which mom chirps, "He's only trying to be like you." To a parent there is something oddly soothing in blaming the child's behaviour on the other parent. Other minimizing statements that blurt from the mouths of dueling directors of discipline include but are not limited to: "Spanking them doesn't teach them anything." "I think you're being a little harsh." "You're being so dramatic." "You are taking their behaviour way too seriously; they are, after all, just kids." "What do you know; you are never around to help discipline." "I suppose you think this is my fault." "You spoil them." "Well, the strap worked when I was a kid." And, of course, my all time favourite, "Don't mind mommy, guys, she's PMSing."

However you approach it, discipline is hard to handle, and a split jury makes it even more difficult. Children are quick to take advantage of parents who agree to disagree when it comes to being disciplined. They are masters at playing one parent against the other all in an effort to save their own hide. "If mom said yes and dad said no and we tell mom that dad said no and tell dad that mom said yes, then mom will get mad at dad for saying no and dad will get mad at mom for saying yes, and hopefully they will forget about being mad at us." Sadly, their crude attempts at reverse psychology sometimes work. So we have learned to agree in the presence of the children or to remain neutral until we have consulted with one another. We will still come to crossroads on how to handle discipline, but we have managed to convince our children we are a strong unit, not to be fooled with.

How a parent disciplines is personal choice and will likely vary according to the crime. In our household lying is never acceptable and can earn the culprit loss of privileges, a stern lecture, and depending on their response, a possible spanking. Disrespect is intolerable and comes with a week's sentence of loss of privileges, a lengthy lecture about how we are the adults, and some much-deserved time in the isolation chamber, their room, which for older children is often no more of a punishment than telling them they have to stay home instead of going to Gramma's house. Fighting with siblings is such a repeated offence that we decided if it didn't involve bodily damage then it was best left to the participants to hash out. The punishment for damage to personal property is weighted on whether or not it was a willful act or accidental and usually results in a monetary fine involving loss of allowance or treats, up to the replacement value of the property. Minor infractions such as teasing the dog, backtalk, door slamming, etc., are punishable by one day incarceration and loss of privileges. All disciplinary action is accompanied by well-rehearsed lectures, evil-eye looks, and of course threats of what a second offence will earn them. Disciplining your children is without a doubt the greatest oxymoron of raising them. You will find

yourself riddled with guilt because you must punish someone you love for something they did wrong. It is not an easy task, so it is not surprising that it is one that has the potential to cause friction with your spouse.

Take Two Aspirin and Come to Bed

Sex after babies is a highly debated subject between man and woman, and has the potential to become a contentious matter causing some bent and even hurt feelings. The recommended six week waiting period after the actual birth is not only healthy but extremely wise. After all, mom's body and mind are both healing, and in most instances her sexual drive is stunted by her need to return to some degree of normality. Dad, on the other hand, is in "booty withdrawal" and while innocent onlookers may mistake his sappy grin at the hospital for a smile of delight, moms should be forewarned it is more likely a weak attempt at some perverted flirtatious "come on" that is not only unwanted but unreasonable. Once you are physically capable of returning to a sex life, there is always the issue of mentally returning. Caring for a newborn child is, as we have discussed, very trying on both parents, but more so on the mom. If mom chooses to nurse the baby, then she becomes inundated by several other, more life-concerning requests for the breast. And I feel the need to reiterate that while some contest that breast feeding is sensational, let's face it, after a woman has had thirty pounds of pressure per minute strapped to her breasts for fifteen minutes per side, the last thing she likely wants is a round of nipple nuptials. Even if mom doesn't nurse the baby, the wear of getting up several times in the middle of the night to tend to the baby along with the actual physical strain on the body from pregnancy and childbirth tends to deplete the drive. So while hubby continues to grovel for a little "lovin," mom continues to heal in hopes that her hormones will one day return to normal and she will become more amorous. My advice: be patient, the wonderful day does come and like a trapped kitten discovering the opening of a brown paper bag, hang on, daddies, you are about to have your socks rocked off. Those same hormones that raged inside mom when she was pregnant and then lay dormant for months after the birth suddenly and with very little notice become inflamed, infuriated, and infectious, looking for some willing host body to take their vengeance out on. On the rarest of occasions mom is totally oblivious to even the wailing cries of baby and daddy alike.

The occasions are rare and the sad reality remains: sex for mom after a baby is, albeit still exciting, more often than not controlled by the constant message in her brain that the moment could be interrupted without warning. Despite dad's ability to stay in the moment, a crying baby or wandering toddler has a way of putting a damper on the mood for mom. These interruptions tend to get mom thinking this is what got us here in the first place, instead of this is a beautiful moment I want to share with the one I love. For this reason and for the sake of maintaining a loving relationship with your partner, any offers by sympathetic family or friends to take the kids for a night should never be turned down.

Locker Room/Luncheon Therapy

Male or female, it doesn't really matter, each has its own idiosyncrasies, and neither is any more annoying or ridiculous except, of course, to the other sex. So it goes without saying that this chapter wouldn't be complete without some mention of locker room/luncheon therapy.

If men are from mars then women must rule the earth. Or so they would have men believe. After all, they are the chosen sex given the fortitude to bear childbirth. In return for replenishing populations, they vow to make men's lives miserable, or so men would have other men believe, in what I refer to as locker room therapy. Topping the men's list of grievances:

1. She is always nagging. "You never help around the house or with the kids." "We never go out." "You watch too much sports." "All you ever think about is yourself." "Yadda Yadda Yadda."

2. She rarely wants to have sex. We used to do it at least twice a week. Now I'm lucky if it's once a month, and I tell you right now, I am not begging.
3. She says I never romance her, yet just last week I bought her a fishing licence so she could come with me.
4. She has no idea how hard I work all day. Is it asking too much to have some time for myself to golf, watch sports, hunt, read the paper.
5. She rarely gets all decked out any more. It's always blue jeans or sweat pants, no make-up, and hair pulled back. I wish she would look like she did when we were dating.
6. She spends way too much money.
7. Her job must be too much for her, because she is always complaining about being so tired and having to do everything else on top of working.
8. She's put on a little weight.
9. She reminds me of her mother.
10. She's never happy. It seems like I can never please her any more.

On the flip side of the coin, women spend countless hours and enormous energy trying to analyze and subsequently out-think their partners. The pending result is usually a vat of guilt and a field of self-pity. Women tend to pride themselves in taking on every emotion in the household and have a hidden sense of responsibility to turn themselves inside out in order to make everything okay. Unfortunately, no one human can handle such pressure, and somewhere down the line the mate is going to pay. But before the stinky, sticky stuff hits the fan, women have learned to first seek support and agreement from fellow females in what I refer to as luncheon therapy. "Hi, Sheila, can we meet for lunch? I just have to talk to someone."

Their top ten list of grievances:
1. He says all I do is nag, but he forgets all the listening I do when he complains about work.
2. He thinks I can just drop everything for sex; he's always begging for it. Like I have time after I have cleaned house, made the meals, toted the kids back and forth, done the laundry, not to mention my job. I say just lift up my skirt while I'm doing the ironing.

3. He never holds my hand anymore or kisses me goodbye. Where has the romance gone?
4. He has no idea how much I do all day; I am sure he thinks I just sit around watching television and eating bonbons.
5. He is always admiring younger women and commenting on how nice they look. I can't remember the last time he told me how good I looked.
6. He complains constantly about how much money I spend.
7. He works way too much, I never see him, and he is rarely around to help out at home.
8. He thinks I am fat.
9. He is turning out to be just like his dad.
10. He never seems happy any more. I am worried he doesn't love me.

If the lists seem similar it is not by coincidence. Odd, isn't it, that what concerns us also concerns them. Such issues don't always arise at the onset of children, but often begin rearing their ugly heads as a result of the intense commitment of raising children, thus causing us to fold somewhat on our commitment to our mates.

Lest We Not Forget

When all hell is breaking out in the house and it feels as though the walls are vibrating with sibling rivalry and you have picked up your twenty-sixth piece of clothing, frustration may hit an all time high when your life partner magically escapes inside the television set with a sudden new-found interest in the game of tennis or curling. On the other hand, he can walk in the door after an unbearably bad day for him and automatically shoulder the misgivings of your day, allowing you to escape to the comfort of his arms held close to his heart, a place where you've longed to be since the first argument by the children the minute their feet hit the floor in the early hours of the morning. Life partners, as they are now politically correctly called, are a mixture of emotional escapes and emotional escape artists.

The purpose of this chapter is not to undermine the role of any one partner, but to make clear that we are together for reasons much more profound then perfect compatibility. I can speak for myself when I say I love my partner for who he is and what he gives to me without my asking. It's impossible to share close quarters with another human being and not feel differences and express frustrations. At some point both parties are bound to feel a sense of unfairness. Add to this the extreme pressures of raising children, and the unproductive result will be conflict and laying of blame. One of the most challenging elements of any relationship is to accept that we may not always get what we want, but to recognize that love almost always gives us what we need. Despite all the difficulties, despite all the differences, being partner to the growth and success of a child is one of the most rewarding ventures two people can share. After children are introduced, a loving relationship is no longer defined by nights filled with passion, long seductive looks across a table in a fine restaurant, days off spent cuddled up together sleeping in until noon, or extended evenings spent partying with other childless couples. A loving relationship is defined by falling asleep together on the couch, on the odd occasion eating a home-cooked meal alone even if it is ten p.m., laughing hysterically when your child releases gas in the bathtub, looking at your child and seeing your mate in his smiling eyes, or remembering to say I love you even if it is just once a month. But mostly it is defined by the very fact that you can tough it out together. So take it with a grain of salt and reap the rewards that come in the form of hugs, kisses, and smiles. Hold your partner's hand more often, kiss him every day in spite of any ill feelings, and thank him for being part of your life and allowing you to be part of his.

CHAPTER FIVE

Take My Hand, Touch My Heart

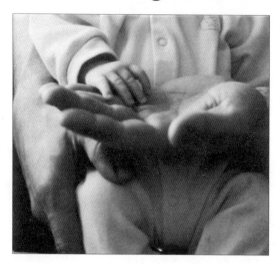

Where have You been All My Life?

When all is said and done, there is no denying the other feelings you experience as a parent which overtake your heart and reside deep in your soul. These feelings can stop you in your tracks, wake you from a sound sleep, cause you to choke back tears, and ultimately well up inside you. Read this chapter slowly and know that each written word represents a piece of my heart, the real place where my children live.

Right from conception a strong, nonpareil bond is born between mother and baby, and thanks to the increase of father involvement, father and baby as well. Inside grows the most marvelous consequence of two people sharing tender moments of love, creation so wondrous it has rightfully earned the title "Miracle." Your first ultrasound reveals the shape of a one-inch person with tiny moving parts, as precisely engineered as the finest Swiss watch, and so the love affair begins. Tended by love, care, and proper nurturing, the child grows and his once imperceptible movements become more and more visible to the outside world. With each impression of a little foot or hand, reality begins to sink in and feelings seem to come from deep within your being. All the parodies of pregnancy are bearable because the good really does outweigh the bad.

When the long awaited day arrives you finally understand that all the events that come with this blessed gift are the best you will ever experience. Is it a boy or girl? What will he or she look like? How big will he or she be? Will he or she know who I am? Will they know how much I love them? And once baby enters the world all your questions will likely be answered. Boy or girl, doesn't matter: they are whole, they are absolutely the most beautiful babies you have ever laid eyes on, they are unbelievably tiny, they only coo when they see mom or dad. Your eyes will tell them how much you love them — they will never have to wonder. The nurse gently lays the new life on mom's tummy and mom welcomes the babe to the world with a teary, "I've been waiting a long time to meet you." And for some reason the first thing mom does is take a tiny hand and engulf it with her own. As the physical cord is cut, the bond becomes stronger, and for the years to follow every time the child places his hand in yours, it connects to the heart and the bond is reinforced.

Now I often think to myself, as I am sure most parents do, "What was my life like before my children came along?" besides the stress, worry, and frustration? What used to make me sing songs like Rudolph the Red-Nosed-Reindeer, Purple People Eater, and John Jacob Jingleheimer Schmidt all the while laughing and giggling? What possessed me to make goofy faces with my nose pressed up against a window? What caused me to stick straws on my upper lip and do a really bad imitation of a walrus? In fact, the only recollection I have of getting excited at the prospect of The Grinch Who Stole Christmas or savouring red licorice dipped into a glass of chocolate milk was when I was four years old. The thought of eating a whole bag of blue candy floss rarely crossed my mind any more than the joy of falling into a blanket of fresh snow, arms and legs flailing, in order to create a perfect snow angel. These were all distant memories until the birth of my children. Suddenly I was given a licence to enjoy life as a child again along with all its bonuses.

The Perks and Benefits

On a day when you feel exasperated by it all, challenged by every breath you take, even unsure if you can go on, your child surprises you with a cup of tea made all by himself. Oddly, that cup of weak tea with no cream and way too much sugar is the best you have ever tasted. The water was likely not brought to a boil, but in its lack of heat that cup of tea warms you to your soul. The perks of raising children are endless and as varied as the parents who benefit from them. I have taken the liberty of including some of my favourites:

- Jumping in puddles;
- Eating at fast food places;
- Buying outrageous clothes;
- Collecting dolls, dinky toys, etc.;
- Pitching a tent in the front yard and sleeping in it;
- Going into the local convenience store and buying jawbreakers, pixie sticks, candy necklaces, potato chips, and so forth;
- Sitting in a kiddie pool;
- Endless art and poetry;
- Homemade cards for every occasion;
- Riding on the bumper cars and not worrying about being the geekiest driver there;
- Owning a pet, even if it is only a fish;
- Eating Cheese Whiz on celery and admitting you like it;
- Cheap entertainment;
- Playing with toys;
- Laughing out loud at ridiculous movies;
- Attending soccer/hockey/baseball/basketball, etc. games without having to pay outrageous admissions;
- Bouquets of every flower imaginable and some not so;
- Appreciating the beauty of a dandelion;
- Riding a bike, rollerblading, tobogganing, riding on the open tail-gate of a truck;
- Eating burnt marshmallows;
- Sloppy kisses received and given;
- Unwarranted and unsolicited hugs;
- Caring unconditionally for another person;

- _____

- _____

- _____

- _____
- _____
- _____
- _____

Use the last lines to fill in your own. This exercise will not only help you realize how much joy your children really do bring you, but will also take you back to the joys of being a child, something we could all use now and again.

What's in a Name?

Mama/Dada, Mom/Dad, Mommy/Daddy, Mother/Father — by any other name is still the same, a title bestowed upon a person giving them the power of greatness. The origin of this comes from a young tot attempting to put to speech an identifying pseudo for those big people claiming the right of parents. The first time parents hear one of these, their hearts fill with a sense of incalculable worth. You have suddenly become the most important person in another person's life. The only other title which even comes close is that of King or Queen. What other accolades have a day reserved in their honour, complete with the giving of specially selected gifts? These are gifts that keep on giving, such as: hand-painted t-shirts bearing the letters MOM/DAD in brightly printed fabric paint; ties carefully selected from a pile marked to clear for a reason; ornaments that only a mother could love or identify, like that orange ceramic elephant with painted toenails; a vast array of coffee mugs also bearing the letters MOM/DAD; not to mention precious hand-picked bouquets, hand-written cards, hand-crafted gifts, and hand-cooked breakfasts served in bed at way too early an hour. Of course, as the children grow so too does their taste in gift selection, which is often monitored by the other parent. Homemade meals are replaced by a list of choices for dining out, topped by the most popular fast food places. But even the most fragrant red roses or most popular brand of fishing ties will never replace the home-made calendar complete with pictures of stick people and spelling only a parent can decipher.

Prior to children, you're likely used to hearing your given name: "Lori, can you stay later at work?" "Hi, Lor, it's Mom, why haven't you called lately?" "Lor, are you coming to bed?" This all changes with your new title. The minute you have a baby all previous identities become forgotten, even by your spouse: "Hi, Daddy, how was work today?" "Mommy, the baby needs changing." "Can Mommy and Daddy bring the baby over tonight?" The change is difficult at first and parents will find themselves looking around for their own parents, but eventually they grow accustomed to their new designations. Of course there are some perils, the most common of which includes seventy-five parents standing up in the middle of a movie theatre yelling, "What's wrong, honey?" in response to an anonymous cry of, "Mommy/Daddy." Not only will your given name be replaced with this new title, but you are about to hear it no less than fifty-eight more times a day. "Mom/Dad, Krysta's bugging me." "Mom/Dad, can I go swimming?" "Mom/Dad, where's my book bag?" "Mom/Dad, can I sleep in your bed?" "Mom/Dad, you should see what Jenny did in Kindergarten today." "Mom/Dad, we got to eat worms in class today." "Mom/Dad, will you read me another story?" "Mom/Dad, I can't wait to tell you all about the movie we watched today." "Mom/Dad, where did I come from?"

Lori Larsen is now referred to as mom or Brad/Krysta's mom, my past identity temporarily replaced. I often wonder if I should renew my licence to read MOM LARSEN, 5'7", blue eyes, blonde hair, and 130 pounds? (A girl can dream.)

We may strive hard to obtain letters behind our given names; some may even earn the distinction of PhD, MA, or BSc, but none are more esteemed than that of MOM or DAD.

To this day I still find myself in awe when one of my children calls me mom, wondering if they are really referring to me, wondering to myself whether I can live up to the expectations of this entitlement.

Fridge Art and Wondrous Treasures

A real estate agent once gave me some invaluable tips on preparing a house before selling, some of which were obvious, such as cleaning, painting, and getting rid of clutter. However, there were two that I thought odd: remove all personal photos and whatever you do, take down the fridge art. After all, you are selling a house, not a home. I could only guess that the reason for removing the photos was to take away any personal attachment to the house and allow the "would-be" buyers to envision the space as their own. But fridge art is just another perk of parenting.

It can be as elaborate as a field of green grass with colourful flowers, eight-legged cows, and a very large sun, or as simple as a green and black blob in the top right hand corner of an eight-by-ten orange piece of construction paper. Most fridge art is a mystery, and wise parents learn early to have the young artists give the piece a title, thus sparing them the shame of having to reply to the child's innocent inquiry, "Can you guess what it is, Mommy/Daddy?" After all, a rose is a rose, if by no other name, but a boy riding a horse is definitely not a rose. No matter what the subject matter the thought is the same — this masterpiece is a present from a tiny heart and is just one of the many precious gifts of gratitude a parent will receive.

Appreciating the simple joys.

Other gifts come in the form of withering bouquets collected on the way home from school, pigeon feathers found on a walk through the park, lizards and frogs that were unable and therefore unfortunate not to be able to escape, heart-felt poetry which only rhymes when the parent reads it, hand-crafted collectibles, store bought items that would otherwise remain on the shelf for a lifetime, and, of course, carefully wrapped toys painfully selected from their own private and most valuable collection. Displaying all these treasures poses a bit of a dilemma for parents who are totally aware of the precious feelings that accompany such gifts but are also aware of the spatial factor of the family home. The fridge, after all, is only so big. Upon the realization that the bookshelf can only hold so many trinkets, wise parents may choose to have a special plastic container capable of storing all the treasures. Along with this container should be a smaller version which is saved specifically for hand-made cards. In the beginning when children are babes, moms and dads take on the responsibility of purchasing and giving store bought cards from the kids. Suddenly any reasonably special day is fair play for a homemade present.

Once children move into Kindergarten, they are guided by tenacious teachers in the craft of making cards and gifts for special occasions. Depending on the creativity of the teacher, these prizes can range from a piece of coloured construction paper, chosen by the craftsperson of course, adorned with glued-on cotton balls, sequins, broken popsicle sticks and other such items, to clay plates which bear the craftsperson's handprint along with a well-chosen poem typewritten on a piece of paper and carefully glued to the back. By no surprise or coincidence the crafts don't vary much from year to year, making room for a little friendly sibling competition, the judges of which are the unfortunate parents. Once again a parent finds herself the master of diplomacy, fastidiously pointing out the unique qualities of each masterpiece. The craftiness may continue through Grades 5 or 6, once again depending on the teacher, after which the giving of treasures usually becomes limited to Mother/Father's day and Christmas. If the child has an inherited knack for craftiness the potential for home-made gifts is unlimited. Even in junior high and high school the excitement of creating another treasure is heightened with the introduction of Woodworking, Metal Works, and Home Economics classes. Not every work of art is reserved for special occasions. Armed with a box of crayons and some recycled paper, a child can create no less than twenty-three masterpieces in less than an hour on a rainy day. The expectation — all should be proudly displayed on the refrigerator. The reality — it only fits ten before it becomes impossible to open the door.

The Other P.M.S.: Parental Mental Syndrome

As indicated earlier, there will be whale days and there will be pig days. Sometimes when you really are at your wits' end you will wonder why you took on this job in the first place. At moments like this you are suffering from what I now refer to as the other P.M.S., Parental Mental Syndrome. This syndrome is accompanied by symptoms such as extreme mental fatigue, confusion, temporary insanity, physical exhaustion, an overwhelming sense of failure, and intense pangs of guilt. Pangs of guilt are not only a symptom of P.M.S., but are typically a parental trait. The pangs will vary in intensity according to the situation over which the parent feels guilt, and the situations are never-ending.

To begin with, there are the feelings of guilt over the ever so occasional evening out. The feelings are the most intense when the children are still babes, but lessen as the children grow and actually look forward to getting rid of the parents so they can harass a babysitter for an evening. There are guilt feelings about what you can and cannot, should and should not, be buying for your children. Many of these feelings are a result of societal pressure, a parental version of the Jones's and the Smith's. This situation is intensified by the often whimpering demands of the children, which only go to increase the parent's level of anxiety. Then there are the guilt feelings that accompany the decision to work outside of the home, and it doesn't matter whether it is mom or dad or both, these feelings are real, profound, and sometimes debilitating.

Amazingly, there are also feelings of guilt over whether or not you are providing the child with enough and proper stimulation in order for them to grow both physically and mentally. You put yourself through a punishing list of questions. Am I a *good* parent if I don't begin with flash cards as soon as they are old enough to hold their own heads up? Am I a *good* parent if I don't read ten chapters of a selected series of previously approved children's literature to them every night? Am I a *good* parent if I don't spend four late nights preparing the best science project the Grade 2 teacher has ever seen, including actual rotating planets, precise dimensions and, of course, night display capabilities. Am I a *good* parent if I don't always make them home-made cookies, feed them nutritious meals, strictly control their junk food intake? Am I a *good* parent if I don't volunteer for everything humanly possible at the school? Am I a *good* parent if I don't sit with them every night to ensure their homework is done and corrected? Am I a *good* parent if I don't always sacrifice a new pair of shoes for myself so they can be enrolled in at least five outside activities? Am I a *good* parent if I don't keep extremely tight tabs over everything my child watches on television? Am I a *good* parent if I don't always have the laundry caught up? Am I a *good* parent if I don't keep the house in show-home condition? Am I a *good* parent if I don't always hear every word of my child's rendition of the antics of the day's recess? Am I a *good* parent if I don't always pretend to be a *good* parent? Am I a *good* parent if every once in a while I fall victim to the symptoms of P.M.S. and lock myself in the bathroom just so I can cry? Good is relative; normal, however, is commendable.

Parenting through Discipline: This hurts Me More than it does You.

To me there are no truer words said. Disciplining a child, while necessary, can also be one of the most disconcerting elements of parenting. Being angry at someone you love so much is a true indicator of the delicate design of emotional balance in the human species. Unfortunately for our world, there are humans who are incapable of recognizing when the emotional scales are tipped too far to one side, and the sad result is child abuse, a subject I can't nor wish to broach.

However, I am experienced enough to address the feelings parents get when they do rock the scales of emotional balance. As I grow older I grow less patient, but thanks to wonderful literature, I also grow wiser. Perhaps this is well planned out.

I recall an incident where my daughter and I were sharing a delightful moment of reading while laying on my bed. She had placed a glass of juice on the night stand next to the telephone, contrary to my many warnings that having drinks and food outside of the kitchen was neither neat nor wise. As could be expected, the telephone rang and she immediately lunged for it, a reflex reaction both her and her brother had learned in an attempt to be the victor of the answering game. To no one's surprise (including yourself I'm sure) the juice glass became airborne and did a triple gainer, finalizing its journey down the front of the night stand and onto the carpet below. The accident may not have been a surprise, but my reaction was. I instantly saw red, my veins bulged, and sharp hurtful words spewed from my mouth. I jumped out of my cozy retreat and flew angrily into the bathroom to get a towel. All the while she stood frozen, staring at the mess, making no attempt to even help clean up. This angered me more and I proceeded to throw more sharp hurtful words in her direction. The telephone was now in her hands and she began to weep soft pleas into the other end. "Hi Daddy, I'm sorry, I just spilled my juice and Mommy's mad at me, I'm sorry."

I took the receiver from her hands and cursed at my husband who was still somewhat oblivious to the entire goings-on. As I frantically cleaned the juice from the carpet and the top of the night stand, I noticed that the bottom drawer was slightly ajar. I opened it to discover that the juice had run into the drawer and had completely soaked the contents as well as the bottom of the drawer. I pulled the drawer from the stand, told my husband I had to go and clean up a huge mess that his daughter had just made, and hung up the phone.

What followed next is still like a bad dream, with someone else playing the part of me. I took the drawer and dropped it onto the floor. My daughter, as though instinctively, had already moved to the other side of the room, but nonetheless now stood in complete silence and fear. She then disappeared. I sat down and cried, not because the drawer was now broken, not because I had to wash the contents, and not because I still had a sloppy, sticky mess to clean up, but because I had truly breached my promise to my daughter — at that point she did not feel safe. The wiser me finally kicked in and instead of going to find the culprit I got a hammer and banged the drawer back together. I am sure the soft particle board didn't require the blows that would be necessary to build the Titanic, but the need to relieve the rest of my tension was ultimately satisfied. After I had repaired the damages to the drawer, the more important task was still at hand — I had to repair the damage to my daughter.

I found her in her room sitting quietly on her bed, cheeks stained with tears. At first I didn't speak, but simply walked over and sat beside her and began to cry also. She stopped crying and moved close enough to me so our bodies touched, and I wrapped my arms around her little shoulders and uttered the hardest words I'd ever spoken, but none truer: "Mommy is so sorry she got mad at you, Krysta. It was both of our faults that the juice spilled, we both know we shouldn't have the juice in there in the first place. I'm sorry I yelled and scared you. I scared myself too. Let's just go and clean up the rest of the mess and be friends again."

We hugged and kissed each other gently on the cheek, hoping the kisses would evaporate the tears. After the spill was totally cleaned up, we resumed our position on the bed and not another word was uttered about the incident.

I am sure there have been other tense moments such as this, other times when my fly-off-the-handle temper led me into untenable incidents. But this one was different somehow. For the first time I really saw the hurt my words caused, really felt the fear children must feel when they are unfamiliar with their parent's behaviour. For the first time I truly understood the intense battle of emotions when deep committed love meets raging anger. I made a personal promise to myself that day: I would try very hard to use words wisely, and I would always allow myself the much-needed time to release the anger on anything but my child.

A child's love for a parent is indisputably unconditional. They get chastised, criticized, ignored, spanked, and yelled at by parents, yet they never really stop loving. As they grow older they begin to seek retribution in the form of pouting, arguing, fighting with siblings, yelling, and playing spiteful tricks, but I can only say that they learned from the best. And as parents we can take solace in the thought that despite the times our parents made us feel hurt, or spanked us, or yelled too much at us, we grew up healthy and reasonably adjusted, and we still love them.

Sometimes the truth just plain hurts, and parents find themselves once again writhing in a vat of guilt over a bout of disciplinary duty. On the other hand, parents also have a nefarious habit of using children as their tiny whipping stones. I am certainly no exception. If our days have been filled with cranky bosses or employees, irresolvable problems, rage at the hands of someone completely indifferent to us, then it is likely that the last thing we want to do when the day settles in is to have to listen to a five-year-old's impersonation of some annoying cartoon character, or thirty verses of Mary Had a Little Lamb. So we snap at the unsuspecting innocence of an otherwise sweet child whose only intention is to try to add a little joy to our day. Sometimes when our children repeatedly do things we perceive to be in defiance, our good sense is so blurred by our own issues that we raise our voices or, more destructively, our hands to them. Time Outs may better be spent by parents in their moments of desperation. Knowing when enough is enough is the vital lesson in parenting through discipline, realizing that these precious little people are never the cause of our distress, but most certainly can be the effect of it.

Parental Voodooism: Feeling their Pain

The strength of the parent/child bond is tested as parents are automatically turned into some sort of psychics the very second their child is hurt, whether physically or emotionally. Personally, I think it is parental voodooism. The pain they feel is somehow transposed directly to your heart and subsequently when they react, instinctively so will you. You find yourself gasping for air, suddenly incapable of making sense or reasoning. But by some powerful outside force you react, and strength quickly comes from a place deep within you, a strength capable of supporting your trembling muscles and worthy of lifting twice your body weight. My first experience with this came when my first-born was only fourteen days old. I was sitting on the couch feeding Brad and watching the world broadcast of Desert Storm. The irony was undeniable; I held one small life in my hands while the pilots of war jets held the lives of many in theirs. I remember thinking that those pilots must have to shut down their hearts the very instant they press the bomb buttons. As soon as I thought it my son began choking. Suddenly there was nothing else around me except my helpless son and I was plunged into a spinning black hole of fear. I stood and instantly recalled the "football hold" for choking infants. But by then my tiny baby wasn't making any sound and a horrifying new reality sunk in — he's not breathing. I gently tapped on his back again, all the while racing up the stairs to put on my boots preparing to flee to my neighbour's. As I pushed the front door open, Brad coughed, then spit up. I slowly raised him towards me, ensuring all matters had been dislodged, then lay him gently over my shoulder. I placed my hand on his tiny back and on shaky legs walked back downstairs and collapsed onto the couch in a flood of tears. Brad wriggled around and made the most beautiful cooing sounds I had ever heard. I was somewhat reassured, but still felt the need to telephone John and cry some more. That night I slept very little, finally pulling his crib so close to the bedside that I wasn't sure who was actually behind the bars.

As time has gone on and with two children to tend to, I have learned not to panic, but the feeling of sheer terror still lingers in my soul at the very thought of them being hurt. I am now aware that as parents we are equipped with a whole different set of emotions that give us the ability to rationalize and do what is needed. These emotions will automatically force us to sacrifice our own lives in exchange for our child's. They will also factor in the moments after a crisis when your whole body begins to react to the situation. This set of emotions can best be described as an overwhelming sixth sense, which when flared up expends an enormous amount of energy capable of taking on any threat to your child's well-being.

These emotions are equally powerful when your children begin to experience their own emotional pain. This pain is often more challenging to deal with than physical pain. A broken arm can be treated by a visit to the doctor, resulting in an unprecedented amount of attention given to the bearer of a cast. But broken hearts aren't so easily fixed. The pain is as real and the scars can be as deep, but the treatment requires much more sensitivity and an uncanny ability to delicately reach inside of them and hug their hearts. To make matters more difficult, you can't actually see the healing take place, and if your child is the silent type, which many are, he may leave you on the outside for a very long time. I have come to discover that part of the key to nursing them back to emotional wellness can be summed up in three words — patience, support, and love. A child who is bullied, made fun of, left out, or a multitude of other heart-breaking, esteem-crushing incidents needs only to have her feelings of despair validated, not unlike adults. The difference is that children don't have the experience to help them deal with it, so they depend solely on a loving parent to guide them through. Ideally what we wish for our children is a life exempt of broken-heartedness, so the first time our child comes home in tears because, in his words, "No one at school likes me," we can only think of two unreasonable choices. We could go and tell off all of the other children, or we could home-school.

As the years pass and issues arise causing your child different grief, you come to realize that protecting your babes does not mean living their life for them. So you allow them to experience the high-wires of life; you will always be there to provide a safety net for them. It may consist of a warm smile acknowledging their feelings, a long-lasting hug that reassures their sense of security, soft shoulders for them to lay their burdened minds on, or just the right words giving them hope and encouragement. Whatever it takes, you will find it in you to give even when you feel totally drained, totally exhausted. The last ounce of emotional energy comes from somewhere inside you and is tenderly poured over their wounded souls. The duty of protecting hearts and providing support never stops, for which I am eternally grateful when I find myself at thirty-nine breaking down in sobs to the willing and loving ears of my mother. And more times than not, the minute I have reached for the telephone to call her it rings, and by now you can probably guess who is on the other end. The only logical explanation — parental voodooism.

Hugs for Sale
Prior to children, hugs and kisses in adulthood are usually reserved for intimate moments with your partner. There are, of course, the odd

exceptions to the rule. I still crave hugs from almost anyone I feel is receptive. Unfortunately, at our "mature" ages we adults, generally speaking, rarely express our affection outwardly. But that soon changes when children enter your life. One needs no excuse to cuddle them. In fact, when they first arrive in your life, you find yourself making excuses to pick them up and steal a squeeze or two. The feeling is so overwhelming that you have to contain yourself while they sleep to allow them the much needed rest. As they grow in length and strength, their own ability to hug becomes apparent, and with the coaching of open arms and twitching fingers, you can suddenly be wrapped in a flurry of little arms and legs. A child's hug, knowing another person feels loved and secure in your midst, gives you a deep sense of worth. The only drawback is that as your children get bigger they can actually catch you off guard, testing your ability to catch a sixty-eight pound projectile equipped with whirling attachments as it comes flying at you from every direction. But the ends definitely justify the means as you balance yourself against a counter top, enabling your heart and soul to get the rejuvenation only a child's hug can provide. Up until a certain age, your children will crave your hugs, and it's always okay to hug them because it provides them with a sense of security and reassurance. It draws them into your heart as close as physically possible. Kisses often resemble that of an overly anxious puppy, wet and never precisely aimed, frequent and dripping with love. But it's the thought behind their hugs and kisses that mean so much. This is the gift they give you to show their unconditional love, to let you know that no matter what else anyone says or does, you are the most important person in the world. And I'll lay testament to the fact that when the world feels like it's coming down around you and your heart is heavy with anguish, a child's sloppy kiss and over-exuberant hug can heal all.

Nothing Good About Goodbye

Whether it's the kiss at the Kindergarten classroom door, or waving at the airport gate, saying goodbye to your child is never an easy task. No matter how good the free time will feel or the silence will sound, the truth remains that you will be apart from your child, and that moment carries with it a huge sense of emptiness. But the moment is inevitable for all parents. For some it will come sooner, as they return to the workplace leaving their beloved child in the hands of a caregiver, and for some it will come later, as they listen to the echo of the classroom door shutting them out. I returned to work immediately after my son's birth, so I learned early that there was nothing good about goodbye, and that the word was far too hard, too un-giving, too final. So as I drove off in a cloud of tears, I made a pact that I would never say goodbye. I could say see you later, have a fun day, mommy will miss you, only six hours 'til I see you again, but never goodbye.

Goodbye seems to be reserved for a far less meaningful departure, like when your family leaves after a two week visit, the paperboy takes a new route, or the neighbour you barely know moves away. To say goodbye to a child would insinuate that it is good to be apart. All the liberating time in the world could never be as glorious as being with someone you love with all your heart and, even more importantly, someone who loves you with all their heart. So the farewells are tough, but the hellos make up for it.

Whenever I hear or read about the loss of a child, I stop, and I think, and I cry. You see, I firmly believe that there is nothing more painful then the loss of a child. Oddly enough, when I hear or read about it, I can't help thinking what if. At that very instance an emotion so powerful and so overwhelming comes from as far deep inside me as any particle can travel. It is an emotion that has no descriptive value, has never been put to words, and yet while it remains unfounded, it is still there. The emotion grips at your breath and leaves you feeling numb, aggrieved, and terribly afraid. The only hurt more unimaginable than the thought of losing a child would be the actual loss of a child. But for some reason not substantiated by science or explained by any written collection of knowledge, there is a built-in mechanism that makes you ask what would it be like, how would I feel, what would I do, and in the very same moment of thought you pray you will never find the answers.

CAMP: ITSA-BLAST: "Now Pleeeeeeeeease Take Me Home"

If your children are ever afforded the opportunity to attend a summer camp you will surely find out just exactly how hard goodbyes can be. Despite your child's unruly excitement over the prospects of spending a week or so away from the demands of home and any perceived sibling inequality, and despite your excitement over the thought of having a reasonably quiet household, the pangs of summer camp goodbyes are unthinkable. My first experience with them came when our son was eleven and a half years old. One might say he was a grown boy. I, however, still thought of him as my first-born baby. Brad was a member of the Cadet Corps and throughout his year with the club he earned badges and the right to attend a summer camp in the mountains. We forked out the $225 for him to attend and anxiously awaited the week in July. The house was abuzz with excitement, and every day for at least a month we all heard about and spoke about Brad's great adventure. Finally the day came to pack up and drive him to the camp location, which was only an hour and twenty minutes away from our home. As far as I was concerned, this day couldn't come too soon. I was tired from packing a two page list of required items and was equally tired from breaking up horrendous battles between him and his sister created by some animosity about him getting to go and about her getting to stay. A parent will never figure out those oxymorons. I loaded up the back of my SUV with what appeared to be enough gear for twenty kids, although I admit it did include the gear for his friend Peter, and loaded two little campers and one reluctant sister into the back seat. The hour and twenty minute drive seemed like an eternity as my husband and I were subjected to spats, teasing, physical confrontations, name-calling, and a variety of other not so pleasant sibling battle cries. We should have realized that this road trip wouldn't differ much from the many others we had endured over the years, but somehow we thought there might be some magical sense of "made for tv" sibling love that would come over our children, considering they weren't going to see each other for a week.

We arrived at the campsite, a beautiful Boy Scout camp tucked into the majesty of the Rocky Mountains. There were volunteers and staff everywhere directing us to the proper places in order to get these two campers registered and settled in. We unloaded the gear at the designated areas, got the registrations completed, then found ourselves driving aimlessly around with the two campers still sitting in the back of the car. Finally we stopped and asked for directions, an occasion all too familiar when travelling, but this time I too found myself somewhat embarrassed when inquiring about exactly where we had to leave the actual campers. After some not so discreet rolled eyes, the Camporee volunteer informed us that we were supposed to drop them off when we registered. Now that I think about our confusion, I have reason to believe it was more like a subliminal effort to keep these boys with me where I knew they were safe. But alas, my husband drove around the site again, this time stopping in the only place available due to the hundreds of other misled parents driving large SUVs and vans on tiny dirt roads, and we shooed the little campers out of the vehicle. With cars lined up behind us awaiting the same fate, I was only allowed a quick goodbye, including a somewhat reluctant hug in the eyes of many other mature eleven-year-olds, and there he stood, my sweet baby boy and his little buddy, on a dirt road amidst a million tall evergreens, all alone, excepting of course for the 300 adult volunteers and staff members. As we slowly drove away, I watched them turn around and face their biggest challenge yet, how to find their designated camp without mom holding their hand.

The drive home was filled with unscheduled stops at waterfalls and picnic sites in order to appease my daughter and make her feel as lucky as she felt her brother must feel. Once home the away time was filled with restless nights worrying constantly about the well-being of my child, several type-written email messages to him, and indecisions about whether we should make the hour and twenty minute trek up to see him on the family day. Deep in my heart I knew I had to go, I knew I had to see my little boy, and hoped he would still recognize me even though it had only been three days, but I didn't want my husband to think I was being paranoid. Why this time should be different than thousands of paranoid moments before I didn't know. My husband was the hero; he gently suggested on the Friday night, two days before family day, we should go see if B, our endearment for Brad, was having a good time. My relief was incredible. I was going to get to see my little guy, but more importantly I was going to get to hug him and tell him how much I loved him. Once again on the Sunday, three days after dropping him off, we found ourselves packing up the car, this time toting along a best little girlfriend for our daughter.

We made the short journey to the mountain campsite, arriving just in time for the big guest luncheon. I had sent Brad an email telling him of our intention to come for the visit. So I anticipated that he would be madly searching the two acre area amidst thousands of campers, volunteers, and now family members in order to find us. After several minutes of expectation, I became restless when I didn't spot my boy despite my effort to discreetly look under every orange ball cap. I was amazed at how after only three days every eleven-year-old began to look like Brad. As I began to wonder if he was actually going to come down to the big tent for lunch, our daughter's friend calmly stated, "There he is." I looked down a row of little campers and saw a lonely little figure walking towards me. He was wearing the cadet uniform required of him for Sunday services, his orange ball cap was tattered, and his beautiful tanned face was rather dusty. He walked straight towards me and my resistance to grab him and hug him weakened. All I wanted was to feel his tiny arms around my waist, and feel reassured that he still thought I was the best mom in the world. With my arms tightly around him he raised his head up and his big blue eyes looked into mine, and he quietly said, "I told my buddies, hey I recognize that t-shirt, I think that's my mom, and I was right, it was you."

I asked him if he got my email saying we were coming to visit, and he replied no in a cracked voice. I then realized I should never have ignored my deep feelings of parental love and should have been the one to suggest we come for the visit.

Nonetheless, we were there, and I could tell by the wrinkly smile lines around his fragile eyes that we had made one of the best decisions. We spent a wonderful three hours with B visiting his campsite, meeting his new-found friends, and exploring all of the great activities he was doing. But the time went fast and at the request of the Camporee officials we were due to be off the site by 3 p.m. Around 2:30 we went back to the Big Tent and sat with Brad, enjoying a refreshment. I had made many inquiries into Brad's well-being — was he sleeping okay, were his clothes still dry, did he like his counsellors, was he eating enough? All were answered as typically expected, Yes, Yes, Of course, Yes, and so on, but both John and I were surprised to hear that he was actually pretty hungry at that moment, even though the camp had provided a huge roast beef dinner at noon. Brad was more interested in the rather boring tuna sandwiches I had packed for us. He gobbled down four sandwiches and at his father's inquiry over why he didn't want some of the left-over beef, he solemnly replied, "I wanted something Mom made."

Suddenly I knew that this was going to be a very hard departure. The time came for us to walk B back to his campsite, a choice we thought would be easier than leaving him sitting at the big tent. We strolled back up the hill to his site and when we arrived we were greeted by his counsellors.

I was delighted to see how nice they were and how well they treated Brad. We chatted with them a few minutes, then told Brad we had better get on our way. He rose from the picnic table and slowly came towards me; I pulled him into my chest and gave him a quick peck on the head, quietly whispering that I loved him. He walked over to his dad with his hand stretched out, but John pulled him into a tight hug and kissed his head. Brad turned quickly and sat back down at the picnic table, pulling his ball cap down so the rim covered his eyes. Despite his effort to hide his emotion from the inevitable teasing of the other campers, I could see his eyes were reddening. The four of us turned and began walking down the dirt path which led us away from B's camp toward the site exit. John, Krysta, and Erika managed to get about fifty feet ahead of me; I attributed my slower pace to my reluctance to leave B, when I felt a tug at my arm. I turned to see my son standing there with a desperate look on his face. My heart began sinking and finally plunged to the depths of my being when he struggled to say, "Mom, I forgot to tell you I love you." Then he threw his arms around my waist and buried his face into my chest. I felt his small shoulders shake and knew that he was weeping. My arms locked around him in a grip so hard it hurt. I, too, was crying, but was wise enough not to remove my sunglasses in order to provide him with what little strength I had left. I noted several counsellors looking at us and could tell by their empathetic expressions that they knew I was in trouble. Before anyone had a chance to approach us and add fuel to Brad's anxiety with sympathetic and well-wishing coos, I released my grip and did one of the bravest things a mother can do, I let go. I reassured Brad that I loved him very, very much, but he would have two more days of great fun and then I would be there to pick him up. I knew it was the right thing to do for his sake and mine, but I can honestly say it didn't feel that way at all. I could only muster the courage to use some well-timed humour and said, "Now you go and have fun, but not too much fun." He turned and ran back towards his camp. I, on the other hand, could barely walk. All my strength seemed to have disappeared.

I caught up to my husband who was waiting and wondering where I had gone. After I explained what had just happened, his only response was, "I'm glad I didn't see it, I probably would have just taken him home." I noticed his voice cracked.

I picked Brad up on the Wednesday as scheduled and resumed the tight hug I had reluctantly released two and a half days earlier. As it turns out, Brad had a wonderful last two days at camp, and we were both very proud that he managed to ward off his homesickness. I, too, was proud of myself — I had kept my promise and never did say goodbye.

The Sadness which Accompanies Great Joy

I spoke earlier about post-partem depression only briefly because I lack any medical background and fortunately any real experience in this debilitating condition. That, however, is not to say I lack experience in the sometimes unprecedented sadness that comes with the true joy of raising children. So parents be forewarned about the moments when you feel an incredible emptiness inside an ironically busy life, feelings of despair and anguish despite the incredible amount of love and admiration you get from your children, which is far more evident when they are still young. Maybe it's because of the overwhelming concerns parents have about totally ensuring their child's well-being, yet realizing it may not always be in their control. The worries we endure when raising children are never-ending — beginning at conception and continuing through the entire span of our lives. Complications during pregnancy and birth, SIDS, physical or mental challenges, injuries, abduction, or worse, death, are a few of the more devastating concerns. However, every day worries such as learning curves, crossing roads, chipped teeth, lost mittens, bullies, failure, self-esteem busters, friends, and many more are enough to sometimes push the limit. Maybe it's because as parents we feel the need to sacrifice whatever it is for the sake of our children and therefore suffer from bouts of self-pity. Or maybe, just maybe, it's because we come to understand that the results of our effort in raising children will be measured by their ability to stand on their own two feet and face the world as the person we helped mold them to be.

They may likely resemble us in their appearance, their hair amazingly parting exactly as ours does, their noses may have the same little crook. We can look at them and be transported back years to see ourselves or our siblings. There may be no denying their ancestry, their heritage; they are of us. But their minds, their souls, their hearts belong to them, and prior to our intervention are fresh and untouched. The greatest lesson a parent can learn is to tread on these untouched regions of our children as gently as possible. The footprints we leave here make lasting impressions on their lives and how they choose to live them. It will be of little consequence that they look like us, but of great consequence that they behave like us. So benefit their worlds by being kind and patient, understanding and empathetic. Provide them with a solid foundation built from values and love. Most importantly, give them the space to develop into their own people and experience life as they see fit with you as their ever-present trusty guide.

When it seems that the job of parenting carries with it little gratitude and you feel hopelessly alone, perhaps even desolate, do what I do, turn on the television. It really doesn't matter which program you tune into, the idea is to watch the commercials. The same advertising companies that play havoc with your children's minds by filling them with wishes for all the new fabulous "must haves" are the companies which also produce commercials aimed straight for the hearts of parents. After all, who can really feel sad after viewing the likes of a baby-faced four-year-old bringing his mom a homemade peanut butter sandwich? Or how can you feel sad when you watch a twenty-second advertisement of a grandfather taking his young grandson skating on a frozen pond in the midst of a snowy meadow? And if these touching moments of media history don't do it for you, then perhaps your heart is in need of a good laugh brought about by the sight of a distorted, muddy five-year-old standing in the middle of an immaculate kitchen floor staring up at the production camera. Take the time to escape and understand the other messages these companies are trying to send. Family is vital, no matter how it is composed, and without it our world would be in danger of obliteration.

Sweet Dreams, My Child

At the end of a difficult day, when as a parent you are feeling both mentally and physically exhausted and you think you have nothing left to give the world because your day has been filled with providing for and worrying about your children, you find yourself wondering, was I successful, did I do right? When your heart feels heavy and your mind continues to race, take this opportunity to go to their room. You will see them wrestling with the will to sleep and the want to stay awake. Even when they become older and full of independence and indifference, it is at this moment that they all become our babes again. Their long, dark eyelashes gently sweep their reddened cheeks. Their skin gleams from their day of ambition. Their hair is ruffled yet seems perfectly placed. At last they are quiet and at peace, and so too will you be after just five minutes of watching them sleep. You can listen to each precious breath they take and watch their chests rise up and down. You can see their eyes flutter back and forth as their day rewinds in their minds. You can trace their faces with your finger, lightly as not to awaken, and yet with the supernatural strength of love known to no other. You can bend over and kiss their foreheads then step back and marvel in the tiny noises they will make in response, watch as they shift in their blankets and notice a crooked smile adorn their faces. Then as you turn to leave their room you will find yourself longing for just one more minute of embrace, with their soft heads pressing against your neck. You will dream of a stolen moment of slow dancing in your kitchen, their feet firmly placed on yours, to a song so explicitly appropriate, "What a wonderful world."

As a parent, your sleeping child becomes a vision of a world at rest, a world at peace, and if you could program their dreams you would — dreams in pastel colours, filled with happiness and goodness, nothing that could harm them — and they would wake up enveloped in a sense of joy and serenity, love and security. There is no better therapy for an overwrought parent than the vision of their babes in blankets.

There Really is No Instruction Manual

Think back if you might to a time when you purchased something that required assembly or specific instructions. The package was labelled "instructions included," and they were. So you fumbled your way through it, you put things on upside down, you cursed a few times, you forgot a few parts, but ultimately you completed the task. Well, I have come to the conclusion that raising children is much the same, except the package does not come bearing the label "instructions attached." Wouldn't that be wonderful? Instead, the package comes out, you are handed it carefully, and you quickly realize that it's entirely in your hands now. Your world is about to change, but in a positive way if you will allow it. If my overtly-sensitive, overly-organized, excessively-analytical, and sometimes annoying self-centered persona can handle it, then anyone can. There will be moments of pure despair where you lay your head on the table and sob, moments of doubt regarding the choices you've made, moments of longing for a life that was much less complicated and much less responsible. But there will also be many more moments of pure exhilaration, moments of triumph for the choices you have made, and moments where you couldn't imagine your life without children.

Our world is filled with parents who have sacrificed that piece of themselves which thrived on fleeting moments of self-indulgence in exchange for being a piece of another person's life and a lifetime of invaluable moments. Once you become a parent, you must realize that you are not alone and your effort to survive this challenge is not unique. Somewhere in the small dimension of our world someone is experiencing the same feelings of uncertainty you are, at the very same moment and with the very same intensity, and may this knowledge help to guide you through the journey you have embarked upon.

Statistically Speaking

No good book would be worth its weight in paper if it didn't include some widely researched, worldly acceptable, profoundly accurate statistics. Sorry to disappoint you, folks, but this book does not deliver those kinds of numbers. Instead, the following information is based on the experiences of a few good, well-intended, over-qualified, practising parents whose only PhD stands for Parent Has Done-it.

The following statistics are based on a sample group of two children. After carefully calculating the numbers, the Sample Median was determined by none other than the not-scientifically-proven method of good old-fashioned usually always accurate guessing — exactly how the experts do it. If you have three children, simply take the calculated number and divide it by two, then add the half to the original. If you have four children take the calculated number and times it by two. If you have more than four children, **BLESS YOU**.

1. Diapers changed (based on 2 years)	8,760
2. Bottles cleaned (based on 2 years)	7,300
3. Loads of laundry (based on 10 years)	2,600
4. Shoelaces tied (based on 7½ years)	4,905
5. Unmatched socks (based on 10 years)	541
6. Bandaids used (based on 10 years)	1,560
7. Picked up clothing (based on 10 years)	25,550
8. Sleepless nights (based on 10 years)	1,240
9. Halloween costumes (based on 10 years)	19
10. Noses wiped (based on 4 years)	1,288
11. Kleenex used (based on 10 years)	2,860
12. Visits to the doctor (based on 10 years)	102
13. Refereed arguments (based on 10 years)	2,591

14. Bedtime stories told (based on 8 years)   5,475

15. Boxes of cereal (based on 10 years)   832

16. Litres of milk (based on 10 years)   1,954

17. Taxiing time in hours (based on 10 years)   2,433.33

18. Booboos kissed (based on 8 years)   2,688

19. Teeth lost/pulled (based on 10 years)   48

20. Money for tooth fairy (based on $2 a tooth) $96

21. Forgotten library books (based on 10 years)   30

22. Days off school (based on 10 years)   875

23. "Stop that" said (based on 10 years)   5,840

24. "No" said (based on 10 years)   23,745

25. Repeated requests (based on 10 years)   8,160

26. Displayed fridge art (based on 10 years)   560

27. Tears wiped (based on 10 years)   9,004

28. Hugs given (based on 10 years)   21,900

29. Hugs received (based on 10 years)   21,899

30. Homemade cards (based on 10 years)   80

31. I LOVE YOUs (based on 10 years)   Infinite

The years are referred to in chronological age measurement.

Afterword

I'll Leave You For Now But Shall Return in the Teens

This part of my parenting journey has come to an end. My children are ten and eleven and in too short of a time will be entering the turbulent years of teenhood. I have already begun writing the next title, *When Pigs Fly, Living With a Teenage Alien*. I am not anticipating that the journey will get any easier, it'll just be different. I figure if I have made it this far I can most likely make it another ten, as long as I keep my wits about me. I am lucky enough to have been part of watching four nephews and one niece grow and spread their wings and consequently turn into wonderful, mature, loving adults. I know their parents struggled, but I am confident that they also reaped enormous benefits. Their hard and sometimes trying work paid off ten-fold, and I join them in saying how proud we all are of their children. These beautiful, young adults are my source of strength for the next ten years. As I look at them I visualize what being a tenacious yet loving parent can produce. Thank you Brent (Lindy), Jeff, Mark, Trish, and Daniel for giving me hope and for letting me be part of your lives.

If you open your heart to your children, they will move in, and in return for a wonderful place to be, they will give you the greatest love you will ever know. There is nothing more formidable than the love of your child.

Thank you Brad and Krysta for enriching my life.

Glossary

Void: Fancy yet often unfamiliar medical term for emptying one's bladder.

The Centre: If you are new at the parenting gig, you may be unfamiliar with the term centres, as referred to at parent helper day. Centres are more commonly known as groups of children, usually four to six, placed into a shared learning experience. The centres are situated around those tiny tables and desks and equipped with different assignments to be completed by the group, but in individual workbooks. Each centre has a set of instructions clearly printed in eighteen point type on a clean white sheet of paper. Unfortunately, the instructions are not always clear. The duty of the helping parent is to explain the objective of the centre and subsequently supervise the children as they complete the assignment. On the surface this task may appear simple, but once you are surrounded by five eager little people who are more interested in telling you the story about how their cat threw up a giant hairball or having a sword fight with their pencils, you will soon learn centres are more of a challenge than imagined. The teacher will walk around and assist you in keeping the socialization to a minimum, but inevitably there will be an announcement, "five minutes to finish up," and you will find yourself panicking. So like any good parent helper, you take all of the children's workbooks and in the sloppiest printing you can do, you finish the assignment for each one of them. If you are really lucky you will get the colouring centre. Not only does this please the little people, but it is one of the easiest to take over at last call.

Juniorete: The editors won't find this one in any dictionary. This is my politically incorrect term for the female version of junior.

Occupieous Misbehavous: Parental Latin for any and all misbehaviour occurring when the parent is otherwise occupied.

Competition Ignoramus: Parental Latin for a variety of non-registered competing events intended to demonstrate the true ignorance of the players, thus awarding them with the less than momentous victory.

Fridge Art: For those of you unfamiliar with the term, it consists of a variety of well-intended works of art created for parents by artistically ambitious children, often by request and sometimes by necessity proudly displayed on the fridge with tiny animal magnets.

About the Author

During her two pregnancies, Lori Larsen also managed to obtain her B.Sc. and M.A., as well as continuing to teach in the Criminal Justice field at Lethbridge Community College. She took five years off from teaching to pursue her passion for writing, and this has led to the publication of her first book, *Why Some Pigs Eat Their Own*. Lori has recently returned to the classroom where she combines her knowledge of business law with her keen ability to see the funnier side of life.

Our payment comes in the form of hugs,
Our rewards come to us in smiles.
Our success is measured best by their love,
Our duty is to raise a happy child.

You cannot scare us, our constitution is strong,
We have the ability to see and know more,
If our world is quiet, then there's something wrong.

Wonder who we are?
We are parents
Hear us roar.

 *LoL Inspirations, 2005*